# FUBAR

## SOLDIER SLANG
## OF WORLD WAR II

# FUBAR

## SOLDIER SLANG
## OF WORLD WAR II

### GORDON L. ROTTMAN

**METRO BOOKS**
New York

**METRO BOOKS**
New York

An Imprint of Sterling Publishing
387 Park Avenue South
New York, NY 10016

Originated by United Graphics, Singapore
Front cover images: istockphoto.com

For information about custom editions, special sales, and premium and corporate
purchases, please contact Sterling Special Sales at 800-805-5489 or
specialsales@sterlingpublishing.com.

ISBN: 978-1-4351-2063-1

Manufactured in China through Bookbuilders

2   4   6   8   10   9   7   5   3

www.sterlingpublishing.com

## DEDICATION

This book is dedicated to the brave members of the armed forces serving round the world today and their forebears who have given us such entertaining additions to the English language.

# CONTENTS

# ACKNOWLEDGMENTS

The author is indebted to many people who contributed entries, information, and insight to this book. Numerous members of on-line World War II and TOE (Tables of Organization and Equipment) discussion groups unselfishly provided valuable information. Especially useful contributions and advice were received from Russell Folsom on German slang, Akira "Taki" Takizawa on Japanese slang, Mikko Härmeinen of Finland, William Paull of the 10th Marines, Ben Frank of the 6th Marine Division, William "Jay" Stone of the 101st Airborne Division, Chuck Baisden of the American Volunteer Group, Clarence F. Gunther of the Fifth Army, Alexei Vasetsky on Soviet slang, Tommy Hichcox, Ray Cresswell, Jim Miller, and Pat Holscher. Thanks also go to John Weal, Dmitry Belanovsky, Ken Brooks, Bruce Gudmundsson and Ken Kotani for their help.

## AUTHOR'S NOTE

The author makes no apologies for the language used in this book – nothing is gained by sugar-coating the language of soldiers. Profanities are fully spelled out, as are numerous words that are racially or sexually derogatory by today's standards. A dictionary such as this, striving to provide an accurate record of how soldiers really talked and thought, is no place for hollow "political correctness." It would paint an unrealistic picture of the realities of the soldier's life.

Since slang is informal, exact pronunciation can vary, as can spelling. In written correspondence it was common for spelling to vary according to an individual's interpretation. There was no dictionary for the soldier to consult. An effort has been made not just to simply translate the term or phrase, but to provide some insight into where it came from and how it was used. No doubt some definitions may differ from expectations or perceptions. The author can only say that meanings and connotations vary and change, and reasonable efforts have been made to verify definitions and meanings. The book specifically covers slang used by soldiers. Naval and air force slang are not addressed.

# INTRODUCTION

Whether he wanted to be in uniform or not, the soldier of World War II was on an adventure – often a tragic one, but an adventure nonetheless. He was in a new world of strange places, meeting different peoples (with possibilities of either killing them or sleeping with them), working with powerful and complicated equipment, and seeing things he had never even imagined. It is easy to understand how such a life demanded its own language.

Military slang is as old as warfare. Of course, there is a formal military "jargon" of tactical and technical terms, as alien to the uninitiated as any foreign language. Official terminology, however, does not fulfill the needs of the soldiers doing the fighting. They develop their own, far earthier, terminology covering all aspects of their lives. Words, nicknames, acronyms, abbreviations, and phrases are bestowed on all manner of things, often with a cynical, humorous, or completely profane twist. Slang can be sarcastic, sober, pessimistic, fatalistic, dirty, and even defeatist at times – if there is anyone who has the right to be cynical it is the soldier. Many terms and phrases underplay the dangers of combat. *Das war prima!* (lit. "that was first-rate!"), for example, was a German shrug-off comment made after being pounded by a heavy artillery barrage. The soldier often possesses a high degree of humor, though experience means the jokes tend to be dark. His country provides him with food, clothing, and salary – much of it poor, late, or inadequate – and declares him its defender even as he is often looked down upon by the civilians he defends. His country also expects him to be dutifully killed if necessary. A certain degree of cynicism can be forgiven.

It is therefore understandable why the soldier of 1939–45 created a broad range of words and phrases to describe his world – his tools, weapons, vehicles, machines, notions, superiors, equals, subordinates, specialist individuals, routine activities, training, where he lived, what he ate and drank, awards and decorations, illnesses, environment, women and related affairs, entertainment, his allies, his enemies, what he inflicted on the enemy and they on him, and much else. The choice of words often reflected the society from which he came. Yet war is usually an international adventure, so the soldier also borrowed words from other cultures, if only by learning to swear in several different languages.

Soldiers' slang evolves as does any slang. Words and phrases from earlier wars or peacetime service may be dug up again for a new conflict, but often their context is changed or they are abandoned as technology progresses and a fresh generation of soldiers emerges. It should never be assumed that a word used in World War I had the same meaning if used again in World War II. New words and phrases were constantly introduced, developed, and dropped from use. Much slang was regionally specific. The war was fought in many theaters including Europe, the Mediterranean, and the Pacific. A US Army European veteran and one from the Pacific might as well have been in two separate armies when it came to slang, which for all practical purposes they were.

Early in the war, and indeed throughout it, there was a rush by radio reporters and correspondents to spice up their reporting with colorful slang. It was not uncommon for the words to be fabricated or overheard in rare and brief use. Contemporary slang dictionaries were filled with numerous terms many servicemen professed never to have heard. Caution must be used in the blind acceptance of such words, nicknames, and phrases, especially the "cutesy" ones.

World War II military slang probably introduced more slang terms, nicknames, and phrases into the civilian world than any other conflict before or since. Probably as many American slang words in use today can be traced to World War II GIs as can be traced back to cowboys and gunslingers. While some terms entered general slang or, in rare instances, have become accepted words, many of the words have become obsolete. For better or worse, this book aims to bring them to life once again.

# PHONETIC ALPHABETS

Phonetic alphabets substitute words for letters so that spelt-out letters are clearly understood over poor connections and static on radios and telephones. The selected words do not sound like any other, as some letters do – B, C, D, E, G, P, and Z, for example. The headings for each letter's section in the slang sections provide the country's phonetic alphabet.

The American phonetic alphabet traces its origin to the International Code of Signals, which was adopted in 1897 as a means of communicating by flag, semaphore, and light. Problems during World War I led to refinements of the system at the 1927 International Radiotelegraph Conference in Washington DC. The new version was adopted in London in 1928. Originally, only certain letters were identified by words to differentiate them from similar sounding ones. It was not until 1938 that all letters were assigned a word. The Flag and International Code Alphabet was slightly modified in early 1941 by the replacement of certain words; the old words are shown in parentheses. In typed message transcription the phonetic words were usually upper case. This system was used until 1 March 1956 when the NATO Phonetic Alphabet was adopted.

The British Commonwealth armed forces initially used a different system from the United States, but in 1943 the US International Code Alphabet was adopted to standardize communications during combined operations. The old British system is used in Part II. When speaking a individual letter over wireless/telephone it would normally be said as "G for George," for example.

The German phonetic alphabet used both male and female first names. The parenthesized words heading the letter sections in Part III are alternatives. Umlauts (ä, ö, ü) are long letters. When written in English they may be expressed as "ae," "oe," and "ue" respectively. They are sometimes shown in English with the "e" in parentheses, for example *Cäsar* may be shown as "Ca(e)sar" although this is an unnecessarily burdensome practice. The German character "ß" (*eszett* – pronounced "ess-zett") signifies a double "s" and is written in English as "ss." In 1996 it was officially declared acceptable to use "ss" in lieu of the *eszett* in most instances. The cases in which the *eszett* is still used are long vowels and diphthongs. Phonetically it was transmitted as *Siegfried-Siegfried*. The Germans designated some units with Roman numbers: battalions organic to regiments, brigades organic to divisions, corps, and some other commands. When transmitting Roman numbers by radio or telephone the numbers were spoken as Arabic numbers, but preceded by the word *römisch* (Roman), for example, *römisch ein zwei Armeekorps* (Roman One-Two Army Corps). Individual guns within artillery batteries were typically designated by the phonetic system Anton, Bertha, Cäsar, and Dora, as four guns were assigned to most types of batteries.

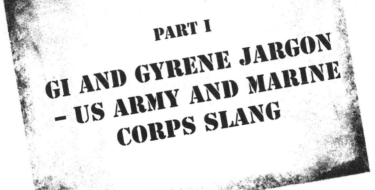

PART I

GI AND GYRENE JARGON
– US ARMY AND MARINE
CORPS SLANG

# BACKGROUND

American soldiers' slang came from a wide variety of sources. Long service in the Philippines and China contributed some terms, as did the Great War. However, many World War I terms, though encountered early in the war, fell by the wayside as the Army grew through mass conscription and modern weapons and equipment were fielded. Other terms can be traced back to the Indian frontier days, the Civil War, and even earlier. The soldiers' backgrounds made their own contributions, be they farming, ranching, trucking, or railroading. The United States possessed two land services, the Army and the much smaller Marine Corps. Both had their unique languages, the latter being especially influenced by the Navy. Being a land service, the Marines also used many Army terms. It was not uncommon for terms and phrases to cross over from one service to another, especially in the Pacific theater where the Marines fought alongside the Army. Little of the colorful British slang of North Africa was picked up by the GIs, as few units fought beside the British there. Even in Northwest Europe little British slang found its way into the US vocabulary.

# A                Able (Affirm)

**acting jack**      The term applied to both acting corporals and acting sergeants. A "Jack" was a corporal, so it may be interpreted as a private first class (pfc) acting as a corporal or a corporal acting as a sergeant, the latter lovingly known as a "jawbone corporal."

**ADC**           Alaskan Defense Command, alternatively known as "all damn confusion" owing to disputes between the Army, Air Force, and Navy commanders, all flexing big personalities.

**air-cooled thirty**   Browning .30-cal. M1919A4 and M1919A6 light machine-guns, also known as the ".30-cal. light."

**all hands**       All Marine unit personnel, as in the expression "All hands fall in."

**all hot and bothered**  Upset and angered, or passionate and lusting. Both were common emotional states for young soldiers encountering both enemy fire and local prostitutes.

**allotment Annies**   Opportunistic girls who married servicemen purely for the allotment check that military wives were entitled to receive.

**all-out**         Maximum effort, full-throttle.

**almost civilians**   Servicemen being processed for discharge.

**ammo**          Ammunition.

**ammo can**       Watertight metal ammunition can for small-arms rounds.

**amtrac**         Amphibian tractor, a term that avoided the labored official description – Landing Craft,

Vehicle (LVT). Those who used them also referred to LVTs as "Large Vulnerable Targets," or sometimes "amphtrac." Amphibian tank versions, however, were not called "amtanks."

**anchor clanker**  Sailor – a classic example of inter-service respect.

**Andy Gump**  This is term refering to someone who was "not too bright, not too rich, not too good-looking" after the cartoon character who had a small chin and prominent nose. Some felt the Army was heavily populated by Andy Gumps.

**Ann**  A sweetheart name for the nasty anopheles mosquito, responsible for transmitting malaria.

**Anzio amble**  A muscle-clenching sprint to cover from incoming artillery, which kept all men fit in the Anzio beachhead.

**Anzio Annie/ Express**  Nickname for two German 28cm K5 railroad guns employed around Anzio, Italy, known to terrify all on the receiving end. See *Robert und Leopold*, Part III.

**apple-knocker**  Hick. Also called "acorn-cracker," "country clod," and "acre-foot," the last of these inexplicably associating country life with disproportionately large feet.

**arm-dropper**  Artillery crew chief who signals with his arm to fire.

**armored cow**  Canned milk. Also "armored heifer" and "canned cow."

**armored diesel**   A personnel refueling mixture of triple whiskey, lemon juice, and sugar on ice.

**army bible**   Army Regulations (AR).

**army dick**   Military policeman. "Dick" was a term for a detective. Also known as a "goon." See "gumshoe."

**artillery punch**   Potent mixture of rum, rye, brandy, champagne, wine, tea, and fruit juices served at dining-ins and receptions, known to kick like a recoiling breechblock.

**asparagus bed**   Post-type antitank obstacles driven into the ground in belts.

**ass–chewing**   A harsh rebuke or reprimand, usually delivered with all the panache of a wound-up pitbull terrier.

**At ease!**   This is a command to assume a modified position of attention, but it is also an informal command to shut up, stop fighting, or to halt any shenanigans going on – basically "knock it off!"

**Aussie**   An Australian.

**aviation beer**   A French beer, also called "P-38 beer" (referring to the P-38 fighter) – you drank one and peed 38 times.

**AWOL**   Absent without leave. Not present for duty. Pronounced "a-wall."

**Axis Sally**   See box overleaf.

**axle grease**   1) Butter.
2) Hair oil, grease, pomade.

## AXIS SALLY

Mildred E. Sisk was born in Portland, Maine, in 1900. Her name was changed to Mildred Gillars when her mother remarried. An aspiring actress, she dropped out of an Ohio acting school and lived in France and the US between 1927 and 1933, before moving to Germany in 1934. First employed by the Berlitz School of Languages, she was later hired as an announcer for *Reichsrundfunk* Overseas Service in Berlin. Introducing herself catchily as "Midge at the mike," her program "Home Sweet Home" ran from 8.00pm to 2.00am. She became known to GIs for her sultry voice when making propaganda broadcasts, backed by popular American music. Soldiers dubbed her "Axis Sally," but she was also known as "Berlin Betty" and "Berlin Bitch." One of her most infamous broadcasts was made less than a month before the June 1944 Normandy landing, when she took on the role of an "American mother" dreaming that her son was killed in the English Channel. She continued her broadcasts until two days before Germany's surrender, then was returned to the States in 1948 and charged with ten counts of treason. Among the charges were accusations that she signed an oath of allegiance to Germany and had posed as an International Red Cross worker to solicit interviews for propaganda purposes from American prisoners of war. Her defense argued that her broadcasts stated an unpopular opinion, but were not actual treason and that she was under the influence of her romantic interest, a German national. In March 1949 she was convicted of only one count of treason and sentenced to 10–30 years' imprisonment. She was paroled in 1961. Gillars remained in the States, taught music in schools, and completed a degree in 1973. She died of natural causes in 1988 in Columbus, Ohio.

# B Baker

**baby carriage**
M4A1 two-wheel, hand-drawn machine-gun cart. Marines used the similar M3A2 Cole cart with larger wheels.

**baka bomb**
*Baka* is Japanese for "foolish." The word was aptly used to described the suicidal Yokosuka MXY-7 *Ohka* (Cherry Blossom) rocket-propelled piloted bombs dropped from Japanese bombers to attack ships.

**baloney**
Nonsense, absurd. Baloney was made from scrap meat and considered low-quality, hence, "That's a bunch of baloney." Also "balony."

**BAM**
Broad Ass Marine. Female Marines had no identifying acronym as with other services' women. The USMC Commandant contended they were simply Marines. A female reporter touchingly coined the term BAM – "Beautiful American Marines." Naturally, it was quickly rephrased by less considerate souls as "Broad Ass Marines," based on the Quartermaster calculation that eight men, but only seven women, could sit on the benches of a 2½-ton truck. The women retaliated by calling the men HAMs – "Hairy Ass Marines," or RAMs – "Raggedy Ass Marines." Poorly conceived terms like "femarines," "jungle Juliets," and "leathernectarines" were little-used newspaper expressions.

**Barracks 13**
Guardhouse, but also bad luck.

**barracks bags**
Bags under the eyes, usually the result of a hangover or lack of sleep.

**barracks lawyer**
A soldier, frequently irritating, who spoke or acted like an authority on military law,

regulations, and the soldier's rights. See also "guardhouse lawyer."

**bars** Single gold bar for 2nd lieutenants ("butter bar"), single silver bar for 1st lieutenants, and double silver bars for captains ("railroad tracks," "ladders," "double-silver-bar Johns"). See cartoon below.

**basic load** Basic load of ammunition, the standardized quantities of ammunition carried for specific weapons.

**bat** *or* **shoot the breeze** To talk, a lively discussion.

**battery acid** K-ration lemonade powder, which was so awful that it was usually discarded or used as a cleaning fluid.

**battle blaze** Marine unit sleeve insignia worn on left shoulder.

**battle pin** Marine brass pin holding the field scarf (necktie) and shirt collar in place.

**bazooka** See box opposite.

bean
: A person's head. To be "beaned," therefore, was to be hit on the head and knocked unconscious.

bean counter
: Logistics and administrative officer concerned more with numbers and efficiently ticked boxes than the realities of the field.

bean king, beans
: Mess officer, mess sergeant, or commissary, individuals obviously concerned with beans.

beans and bullets
: Logistics, supplies, rear services.

## HOW THE BAZOOKA GOT ITS NAME

In 1941 the US Army developed a large, shaped-charge, antitank rifle grenade, the M10. Obviously someone had not thought things through – it was too heavy to fire from a rifle without damaging it and the firer. It could not even be fired from a "rifle" grenade launcher on a .50-cal. machine-gun. That same year the Army purchased a number of British 2in antiaircraft rockets to test under its fledgling rocket development program. In 1942, modified copies of the rocket motors were fabricated and the M10 warhead fitted to them. A 60mm steel tube was fitted with two handgrips, a shoulder stock, a rudimentary sight, and a simple electrical firing system. The result was the 2.36in T1 antitank rocket launcher. Irreverently, Major Zeb Hastings noted the weapon's similarity to an amusing musical instrument called the "bazooka" used by radio comedian and musician Bob Burns, the "Arkansas Traveler." The nickname was applied and stuck to what became the M1 rocket launcher (while under development the bazooka was code-named "The Whip"). The bazooka was also called the "stovepipe," for obvious reasons. Later versions of the bazooka included the M1A1, M9, M9A1, and M18. Examples of the original "bazooka" (instrument) are displayed in Bob Burns' home in Hot Springs, Arkansas.

**beans 'n' weenies**  C-ration beans and franks, a cornerstone of infantry nutrition.

**beating his gums**  A Marine Corps term referring to talking, usually too much. Also known as "gumming," "jawing," and "chin music."

**become a gold star in mom's window**  Gentle, but ominous, way of saying killed in action. A red, white, and blue banner was displayed in service family windows, with a blue star for each son in the service. If a son were lost a gold star replaced a blue.

**bed-check Charlie**  Lone Japanese bombers disturbing US sleep on Guadalcanal's Henderson Field. Also "Washing Machine Charlie" (after the noise made by poor quality Japanese aviation engines) or "Louie the Louse."

**bedpan commando**  Platoon medic (Army) or Corpsman (Marines). Also "Bones," "pill-pusher," pill-roller," "bandaid," and "Doc."

**bellhop**  Soldier or Marine wearing dress blues, and looking as if his destiny could be in the hotel industry.

**bellyache**  To complain, gripe.

**belly out**  For a vehicle to sink partly into mud to its underside or become jammed on rocks or stumps.

**belly robber**  Mess sergeant, cook, obviously not much respected for his qualities as a kitchen professional. Also known as a "hash-burner."

**B-girl**  Bar girl. Bar and club hostesses who encouraged women-starved servicemen to drink more and to buy them drinks.

| | |
|---|---|
| **Big Three** | United States, Great Britain, and the USSR. |
| **bimbo** | Young woman, possibly (for most servicemen, hopefully) eager to please. May refer to one who is not too bright or a prostitute. "Bimbo dust" – face powder. |
| **bingo** | 1) A hit or AA round close enough to an aircraft to damage it.<br>2) Dead on, correct answer. |
| **bird on a ball** | Marine "globe and anchor insignia" worn on headgear and collars. |
| **birds** | Colonel's rank eagles, "chickens," "buzzards." |
| **biscuit bomber/ bombing** | Ration parachute or freefall bundle drops from aircraft. |
| **bitch/bitcher/ bitching** | 1) A gripe or complaint/complainer/grousing or complaining.<br>2) Pejorative for a woman, especially a malicious one. |
| **bite the dust** | Time-honored term for killed or wounded, destroyed or damaged. |
| **Black Dragon** | 240mm M1 howitzer – the Army's largest-caliber mobile artillery piece, although the barrel and carriage were transported as separate loads. |
| **blackstrap coffee** | Thick, strong coffee with the viscosity of blackstrap molasses. |
| **Blancoed** | Used of web gear – spruced up with Blanco, a cleaning substance in powder or cake form. |
| **blank *or* empty file** | Soldier widely recognized as really very dumb. |
| **blanket drill** | Sleep or nap. |
| **blanket party** | Nocturnal visit by platoon mates to a nonconformist, barracks thief, or troublemaker. |

The celebration consisted of a blanket thrown over the transgressor, who was held down as others applied fists.

**blanket wife** Temporary wife, prostitute, a common comfort when deployed an ocean away from home.

**blind** Court-martial sentence forfeiture of two-thirds pay for a specified period of 1–3 months, e.g., "two months blind without confinement."

**blitz** 1) Polish brass with a special impregnated "Blitzcloth®." To blitz something was to clean it with murderous zeal.
2) The term was also a popularization of the German Blitzkrieg (lightning war), hence blitz meant to storm something, to make something happen fast.

**blitz car** Dodge ¾-ton command car; also a jeep.

**blivit/blivet** 1) A flexible container for fuel made out of rubberized fabric.
2) Any item that is awkward to handle or transport.
3) A fat person, who could also be awkward to handle or transport.
4) Adding further disparagement to the previous definition, a serving of any food that is soft and squishy, as in "a blivet of mashed potatoes."

**blob stick** A leather-covered bayonet with a padded point used for soldier-against-soldier bayonet training.

**block** To square and straighten a Marine field scarf.

**Blood and Guts** 1) Lieutenant General George S. Patton, Jr. (1885–1945.) Another GI take on the ultra-tough leader was "His guts, our blood."
2) Anyone flamboyant and boisterous.

| | |
|---|---|
| **blood stripe** | Red stripe on Marine blue trousers. |
| **bluejackets** | In the Navy a "bluejacket" is an enlisted sailor. The Marines refer to all Navy personnel as "bluejackets," including those assigned to the Marines – medical personnel, chaplains, judge adjutant generals (lawyers), and "Seabees." |
| **blue letters** | Personal letters which soldiers did not wish read by their chain-of-command (their immediate officers), which were submitted for censoring in blue envelopes. Soldiers could send two such letters a month, which would instead be censored by the base censorship detachment. They would not be forwarded in blue envelopes to addresses. |
| **blues** | 1) A Marine Corps blue uniform, issue of which ceased in wartime. Only recruiters, Marine Barracks at the Washington Navy Yard, 8th and I Streets (see "8th & Eye"), and the Marine Corps Band were issued blues.<br>2) Army officer's dress blue uniform worn on formal occasions, often when there were well-dressed ladies to impress. Its purchase (officers purchased their uniforms) was not required in wartime. |
| **blue star commando/ranger** | Member of European Theater of Operations Services of Supply, owing to the blue star on his patch. |
| **blue ticket/ discharge** | Conditions other than honorable discharge which were printed on blue paper and were a bar to reenlistment. Refers to both the discharge paper and the act of discharge. |
| **bobtail discharge** | Discharge without honorable character. This heinous condition was indicated by cutting off |

the character section from the bottom of the form, resulting in a shortened document.

| | |
|---|---|
| **body snatcher** | Litter-bearer. |
| **Bogo** | Tanambogo, a small island north of Guadalcanal. |
| **bolo** | Failure to qualify with a rifle. Poor marksman. This term originated during the 1899–1907 Philippine Insurrection, when it was observed that some soldiers would be better off with a bolo machete than a rifle. |
| **bone-up** | To study, prepare for a test. |
| **boondockers** | Marine field boots worn in the "boondocks." |
| **boondocks** | Any remote rugged area, from the Philippine Tagalog word *bundok* (mountain). |
| **boot** | Marine basic trainee attending boot camp. |
| **bootleg coffee** | Weak or low-grade coffee, brewed as a last resort. |
| **booze** | Liquor. Alcohol's status as a favored pastime is indicated by its number of nicknames, including "hooch," "firewater," "moonshine," "joy juice," "tarantula soup (whiskey)," and "Al K. Hall." |
| **Bore War** | American name for the largely eventless October 1939–April 1940 Phony War in Europe. Play on "Boer War." |
| **bouncing Betty** | German Schützenminen 35 and 44 – cylindrical (can-shaped) bounding-type antipersonnel mine. Also "S-mine," "bouncing bitch," or, acknowledging one of the mine's much-feared wound effects, "castrator" (it bounded 3–4ft before detonating). The French called it the *soldat silencieux* (silent soldier). |
| **bowlegs** | Derisive term for cavalrymen, ignoring the fact they rode in tanks rather than on horseback. Also |

"Yellowlegs," derived from branch-of-service colored trousers stripes.

| | |
|---|---|
| **Brad** | General of the Army Omar N. Bradley (1893–1981), "The GI's General." |
| **brass, brass hat** | 1) Officers. Nickname owed to the large US Coat of Arms eagle, gold chin cord, and other brass headgear adornments. 2) A collective term for brass insignia worn on the uniform – cap badge, branch of service insignia, belt buckle, etc. |
| **brass-pounder** | Radiotelegraph operator – telegraph keys were mostly brass. Also "dit-dah artist" and "dit-dah," referring to Morse code dots and dashes. |
| **brave** | Forceman, a member of the combined US–Canadian 1st Special Service Force ("Devil's Brigade"). Its lineage was connected to the Indian Scouts, hence the obvious slang term. |
| **bread sergeant** | Satirical title for the dining room orderly (DRO) or member of the "kitchen police" (see "KP"), who sliced and served bread, cleaned the dining room, and served officers. Also "punk sergeant." |
| **breakout** | 1) Take out or issue, e.g. "breakout the ammo." 2) Fight one's way out of an encirclement or trap. |
| **brig** | The Marine equivalent to stockade. |
| **brig rat** | A Marine confined in the brig. |
| **brownnose/er** | A total ass-kisser. To curry favor, or "bootlick." |
| **BS** | 1) Opinions widely regarded as Bull Shit. "A bunch of hooey." 2) Something evidentally disliked. 3) To nimbly explain one's self out of a difficult situation, usually through a talented mix of |

plausible facts with outrageous lies. A
questionable explanation.

**buck**
1) To bypass or beat something, e.g. "to buck the system," "he bucked the court martial charge."
2) To "buck rank," "pull rank," "pull stripes," i.e. overriding one of lower rank.
3) $1 bill. "Bucks" – money, cash, e.g., ten bucks.

**bucking for...**
Trying for a promotion, an assignment, etc.

**buck private/ sergeant**
Private (grade 7) with no stripes, the lowest rank, as opposed to private first class (grade 6) with one chevron. Also "buck ass private." Sergeant (grade 4) with three chevrons. Higher grade sergeants were prefixed with a title (staff, technical/gunnery, first, master sergeant) and wore 1–3 inverted arches (rockers). A buck ($1) is the lowest denomination bill, the source of the phrase.

**Buck Rogers Men**
Jaunty title for members of Marine rocket detachments/platoons. Named after the popular science fiction character, as the 4.5in rocket launchers were considered futuristic. See "Sandy Andy."

**buck slip**
Correspondence from the adjutant passed to the responsible officer for action or response. To "pass the buck," meant to hence conveniently shift the blame or responsibility.

**buddy**
Pal. "Friend" was considered too formal and suspiciously feminine.

**bug juice**
1) Insect repellent.
2) Home-brewed alcoholic beverage.

**bull**
1) Man in charge.
2) Military policeman or stockade guard.
3) Short, handy version of "bull shit."

**bullet with your name on it**    The bullet whose destiny lay in your insides.

**bum**    Lazy, disliked, or untrustworthy person.

**bum steer**    False or incorrect information, e.g. "I was given a bum steer."

**bunk**    1) Bed, "rack," "sack."
2) Nonsense, exaggeration, a lie.

**bunkie**    A homely term for a person sharing a tent or barracks.

**bunk lizard**    A lazy soldier with a sloth-like attraction for his bed. Also "sack rat."

**burp bag**    Airsick bag, also viscerally described as a "honey bucket."

**burp gun**    1) German 9mm MP38 and MP40 machine pistols (submachine-guns), which, apparently, had rasping full-auto fire like a violent belch. See "Kraut burp gun."
2) Any submachine-gun.

**bust, busted**    Reduced in pay grade, e.g, "two months confinement and a bust."

**butcher**    Barber ("nappy") or surgeon.

**butcher shop**    Hospital – a term to cheer up any war casualty.

**butt**    The remaining un-smoked cigarette stub. See "field strip."

**butt can**    No. 10 (1-gal.) can with water or sand in the bottom used as a barracks ashtray.

**buttoned up**    Tank or bunker with all hatches closed. Prepared for action.

**buy/bought the farm**    Killed in action. Serviceman's Group Life Insurance paid the beneficiary (usually the

|  | parents if unmarried) $10,000, which was said to be enough to pay off a farm mortgage. Shortened to "bought it." |
|---|---|
| **buzzard** | 1) US Coat of Arms eagle.<br>2) Discharge paper. |
| **buzzard meat** | A tasty reference to chicken or turkey. |
| **buzzer** | Signalman. Derived from buzzer signal devices used before WWII. |
| **by-pass, haul ass, send for the infantry** | Tank unit procedure, as seen from the infantryman's embittered perspective – bypass resistance, advance fast, let the infantry mop up. |
| **by the numbers** | To perform tasks by prescribed drill or sequence. The military way of doing things. There are three ways of doing things, the right way, the wrong way, and the Army way. |

# C      Charlie (Cast)

|  |  |
|---|---|
| **cabbage** | Money, cash. Also "dough," "lettuce," "greenbacks," and "moola." |
| **cackle fruit** | Chicken eggs. |
| **Calliope** | Sixty-tube 4.5in T34 rocket launcher mounted atop an M4 tank. So named because of its visual similarity to a steam organ's pipes. |
| **Canal, the** | 1) Guadalcanal Island, "Guadal."<br>2) Panama Canal. |
| **can do** | Handy universal phrase meaning "It can be done," "we will do it," simply switched to the negative by adding "no" – "no can do." From Chinese Pidgin English. |

**canned morale**    Motion picture, movie. Many wartime movies were scripted to improve public morale and promote the armed services, and contained a degree of propaganda.

**canned Willie**    Canned bully beef ("Willie"), or "monkey meat," both descriptions to excite the taste buds. In the Pacific a great deal of tinned beef and mutton was procured from Australia.

**Cannibal Battalion**    Showing a lack of respect, this was a term for Australian–New Zealand Administrative Unit (AZNAU) natives serving as porters, guides, and scouts in the South and Southwest Pacific.

**cannibalization**    Removal of parts from an inoperable or destroyed vehicle to use on another. "The tank was cannibalized for parts."

**cannon cocker**    A boiled-down description of an artilleryman. Also "Redleg," "gun bunny," and "muzzle monkey."

**canteen check/chit**    Credit coupon at the post exchange (PX). See also "jawbone."

**canteen commando**    Rear-area personnel. Also known as a "garritrooper."

**canteen medal**    Food or drink stain on one's uniform.

**Casey cookie**    Improvised and nasty hand grenade made in the Philippines in 1942 by inserting part of a stick of dynamite, along with nails and pebbles, into a section of bamboo, capping the bomb with concrete and fitting a length of time-delay fuse. Named after Brigadier General Hugh J. Casey.

**cat hole**    Small, hastily scrapped hole used as a one-time use latrine.

**cathouse**        House of prostitution, brothel, whore house.

**CBI**        China–Burma–India Theater of Operations. Alternatively said to mean "corned beef indefinitely" owing to the generous issue of Australian bully beef in the theater.

**chair-borne**        Administration officers and clerks experienced in desk-bound combat operations, or "chair-borne commandos." A play on the term "airborne."

**chamber pot**        Drastic reuse of a helmet as a "night soil" pot when occupying a foxhole. Soldiers could not leave their foxholes at night for fear of being shot as infiltrators.

**chaser**        Guard who escorted prisoners in the guardhouse/stockade, during work details, to a court martial, hospital, etc.

**chewed out**        Reprimanded, harshly rebuked, given an ass-chewing.

**chicken shit**        Seemingly endless make-work tasks, mind-numbingly restrictive regulations, senseless requirements, unnecessary harassment, and pettiness on the part of pretentious leaders. A leader who followed the rules too closely, no exceptions.

**chief**        1) Senior NCO in charge of a subunit.
2) General term from a Wild West movie generation for a unit member who was of Native American origin.

**chink**        Derisive term for the Chinese. Also used were "gook," "slope," "slant-eye." Apart from "slant-eye," these terms were seldom used to refer to the Japanese.

| | |
|---|---|
| **chink berries** | Rice. |
| **chippie wagon** | Trailer house used by enterprising prostitutes to provide mobile pleasure. If police pressure increased it could be moved. Also "whore house/cathouse on wheels." |
| **chow** | Food, a meal, from the West Coast Chinese term. "Chow down" – to eat. |
| **chow hall** | Mess hall, including kitchen and dining room. |
| **chow hound** | Someone always hungry, salivating, and overly fond of food. |
| **chump** | Stupid person, sucker, as in "all-American chump." |
| **cigarette and city camps** | Units deploying to France in 1944 were passed through staging and assembly camps around Le Havre on their way to the front. Staging camps were named after American cigarette brands; the assembly camps after American cities. These names were given for security reasons, as they identified no geographic location and any enemy radio intercept would assume cigarettes or cities were being discussed. There was also a subtle psychological reason for the system as it was thought troops heading into battle would not mind staying in places with familiar back-home names. |
| **cigs** | Cigarettes, "smokes," "scag," "scrag." Also "fags" (see Part II, adopted British term). |
| **civvies** | Civilian clothes. |
| **clap, the** | Gonorrhea, venereal disease, or, more vividly, "the drip." |
| **cloverleaf** | Container consisting of three tubes in which artillery or mortar rounds were shipped. The |

cross-section appeared as a three-leaf clover. In bulk the containers required less shipping space than a rectangular box.

**cocksucker bread** French bread. The term fused a schoolboy appreciation of shape with a general suspicion of the French.

**coffee cooling** Loafing, taking a break. A "coffee cooler" was one who sought a softer job.

**cold feet** Fearful or having second thoughts, surprisingly common among soldiers regularly facing death. "To have cold feet."

**cold steel** Bayonet. "Go in with cold steel" means to use the bayonet.

**collision mats** Pancakes, "flapjacks." Marine/Navy term.

**combat loading** Loading an assault transport with equipment, supplies, and materials in layers in the order that they would be needed ashore.

**Come and get it!** Enthusiastic call announcing that chow was served. "Chow bunks" was the relevant bugle call.

**commo** "Communications." "The commo platoon can't make commo." A "commo man" was a signalman, radioman.

**commo wire** Field telephone line, "land-line."

**company/battery monkey** A clerk, obviously not always appreciated by combatants.

**Concrete Battleship** Fort Drum, El Fraile Island, Manila Bay, Philippines. The tiny island was leveled and a concrete fortress built that looked like a battleship.

**concussion grenade** Mk III series offensive hand grenade – "demolition or demo grenade." It contained

½lb of TNT but produced little fragmentation and was used to attack pillboxes.

| | |
|---|---|
| **Condition Red** | Anything important or critical. From the air-raid alert warning, red alert. Condition Black was also considered serious. There were four conditions of alert:<br>Green – Normal, all clear.<br>Yellow – Cautionary warning.<br>Red – Air attack.<br>Black – Enemy landing. |
| **cooking-off** | US hand grenades were activated by pulling a safety pin while the arming lever was held in place. When thrown the lever flew off, allowing the "mousetrap" to ignite the 4–5-second delay fuse. To prevent the enemy from having time to throw the grenade back, the thrower might release the lever and hold the grenade for 2–3 "cooking off" seconds before throwing. |
| **cooking with gas** | Making progress, doing something right, on the go. "Now we're cooking with gas!" Also "on the front burner." |
| **cork off** | Going to sleep. "Corking off," "knocking off." |
| **corner pocket** | Guardhouse, where a soldier was out of circulation, like a pool ball in a corner pocket. |
| **Corps, the** | The US Marine Corps, a component of the Navy Department, not a component of the Navy. |
| **cosmolines** | Artillerymen. So called owing to the thick cosmoline grease weapon preservative. |
| **cover** | Marine term for headgear. |
| **crack like that, a** | Smart-alecky comment, snide remark. |

| | |
|---|---|
| **crapper** | Latrine or commode. Also "crap house" and "shitter." |
| **creeping crud** | Formerly a malaise, or ominous feeling of discomfort at the beginning of an illness, but came to be another term for "jungle rot" and "crotch rot." |
| **crossbar hotel** | Stockade or guardhouse, "bull pen." |
| **crotch rot** | *Tinea cruris.* A fungal infection of the groin that could spread to the anus area, producing rashes, and severe itching. Caused by heat, trapped moisture, and the inability to bathe, hence it was especially prevalent in the tropics. Also "jungle rot," "jock itch," or "creeping crud." |
| **crumb hunt** | Minutely executed mess hall/kitchen inspection for cleanliness. |
| **Cullin cutter** | Pointed steel beams made from German hedgehog obstacles from the Normandy beaches and mounted to the bows of tanks to ram through hedgerows. |
| **cumshaw** | 1) Marine term from the Chinese *kam sia*, meaning grateful thanks, a kickback. The term was used at the start of WWII to describe payoffs, of one kind or another, by Honolulu's Hotel Street prostitutes to local police officials.<br><br>2) The covert military skill of one unit stealing government property from another to make up for shortages. "Because Sergeant Brown was a master of cumshaw, his unit never lacked for anything." |

# D  Dog

| | |
|---|---|
| **Dago Red** | 1) Cheap wine produced in the San Diego, California, area and sold to local servicemen. |

2) Any homemade cheap red wine. From "Dago," referring to Italians.

**daisy cutter**  Pretty name for quite ghastly antipersonnel bombs. Their fragmentation effect sheared off ground vegetation. Derived from a baseball that skims along the ground. Also "grass cutter."

**Daisy Mae hat**  Denim fatigue uniform hat with a floppy all-round brim.

**Dan**  Dynamite, "dino." Used in construction demolition tasks, but not in combat, as it can be detonated by gunfire.

**Darby's Rangers**  1st, 3d, and 4th Ranger Infantry Battalions under Lieutenant Colonel William O. Darby.

**dead battery**  A pessimist. A boring, dull person.

**deadeye**  Sharpshooter, marksman, crack-shot.

**dead-lined**  Broken down vehicle, undergoing repair.

**dead soldier**  Empty beer bottle, or "dead dog." "He killed the bottle."

**deep-sea chicken**  Canned salmon or other fish.

**demo**  Demolitions, explosive charges, or the act of detonating them.

**detail**  Small body of troops assigned a task, such as a fatigue (work) detail, guard detail, etc.

**detcord**  Detonating cord, primacord. Instantaneous detonating explosive cord similar in appearance to a safety fuse. Used to link demolition charges together for simultaneous detonation.

**deuce**  Two or second. Used in unit designations, e.g. Five-Oh-Deuce – 502d Parachute Infantry Regiment.

**deuce-and-a-half**　General Motors Corporation 2½-ton 6x6*
cargo truck, also called a "six-by" from "six-by-
six." Its off-road cargo capacity was 2½ tons.
On improved roads it could carry twice its rated
load (this applied to all other truck and trailer
capacities). Declared by General of the Army
George C. Marshall, Chief of Staff of the Army,
to be one of the weapons that won the war.

**Devil Dogs**　1) Marines. Reported as a German WWI
nickname, *Teufelshunde*.
2) The Japanese called Marine war dogs "devil
dogs." Scout dogs were considered "weapons" as
their powers of scent and hearing enhanced a
unit's capabilities.

**DI**　The truly feared Marine drill instructor. The
term was not used by the Army, which used
"drill sergeant."

**Digger**　Australian. See "Digger," Part II.

**dispensary**　Troop medical clinic.

**ditty bag**　Small cloth bag in which personal items were
carried in the backpack.

**dog biscuit**　K-ration crackers and other hardtack-like crackers.

**dogface**　1) Soldier, specifically an infantryman who led
an outdoor life little different from a dog's.
2) Dog-tired, haggard expression. Marines
referred to soldiers derisively as "doggies."

**dog food**　Canned corned beef hash in C- and K-rations.

**dog robber**　Aide (usually a lieutenant or captain) to general
officers whose duties were extremely varied. The

---

* *Three-axle truck with power to all wheels. A 4x4 such as a jeep had power
to all four wheels; an automobile was 2x4 with power to only the rear wheels.*

nickname implied an aide would do whatever was necessary for his boss, legal or illegal.

**dogs**　　Feet. "My dogs are worn out."

**dog tags**　　Two oval or rectangular (with rounded ends) tags worn by servicemen on a chain. Stamped data varied between services and period, but typically included name, serial number, blood type, and religion. Examples of other entries were tetanus inoculation dates and home address. If a soldier were killed one tag was left with the body and the other turned in. One tag had a notch in one end and it was rumored that this was to be inserted between the teeth of the dead man. This is a myth; it was a positioning notch for a stamping machine.

**doll woman**　　Attractive woman, as opposed to a far less complimentarily named "dog woman."

**Donald Duck**　　Duplex Drive (DD) propulsion and floatation system fitted to an M4 tank, allowing it to became amphibious.

**donut girl**　　Red Cross volunteer passing out coffee and donuts.

**Doodlebug**　　1) German remote-controlled light demolitions carrier vehicle, incorrectly "robot tank." See "Goliath," Appendix 3.
2) German V-1 rocket bomb, "buzz bomb."

**dope**　　1) Information, also "poop," or "skinny."
2) Dumb person.
3) To dope-off, act stupid, or fall asleep.

**double-dose**　　1) Double-issue of ammunition or grenades. Infantrymen typically carried two hand grenades, so a double-dose would be four.

Derived from a "double-dose of medicine."
2) A "double-dose" of anything was double the trouble, so the unfortunate individual with "a double-dose of the clap" should be pitied.

**double time**   Running. Derived from double-quick time, twice the speed of the standard quick-time march rate of 76 paces a minute.

**double ugly**   Lowest gear on a truck with all drive wheels engaged. Also "double-clutching."

**douche bag**   Low-life person.

**doughboy**   A solider, specifically an infantryman. This term was widely used in WWI and saw some use in WWII, but by 1943 it had been largely replaced by "GI" and the gritty "dogface." "Old soldiers" with prewar experience still used it. While

## ON THE MENU...

| | |
|---|---|
| armored diesel | fisheyes |
| artillery punch | goozlum |
| battery acid | grappa |
| beans 'n' weenies | graveyard stew |
| blackstrap coffee | Greasy Dick |
| bug juice | jungle juice |
| buzzard meat | kennel ration |
| cackle fruit | monkey balls |
| canned Willie | pig's swill |
| chink berries | poggy bait |
| cocksucker bread | scum |
| Dago Red | seagull |
| deep-sea chicken | SOS |
| dog biscuit | Wimpy special |

connected to WWI, doughboy originated during the 1846–47 Mexican–American War and was used in the Civil War. Its origins are uncertain, but have been attributed to white dust collected on the uniforms of marching infantry, fried dough dumplings that soldiers ate, white pipe clay used to whiten belts, and the rounded shape of uniform buttons.

**doughboy helmet**  M1917A1 steel helmet, so named to differentiate it from the M1 helmet. It was used in WWI and was replaced by the M1 in 1942/43. Also "dishpan helmet," "tin hat," and "tin pan hat."

**dough-puncher**  A baker.

**dozer**  Caterpillar ("Cat") bulldozer. Also used as artillery prime-mover.

**dozer-tank**  Medium tank mounting a dozer blade to clear obstacles.

**dragon's teeth**  German angular reinforced concrete blocks set in medieval-looking belts as antitank obstacles.

**dressed down**  Reprimanded, chewed out. "He received a harsh dressing down."

**drill and be damned**  Drill and command. Repetitious cadence system of drill. Also "Prussian drill," "eight-man squad drill."

**dry run**  Originally "dry firing" or "snapping in." Marksmanship practice without ammunition, to familiarize the shooter with firing positions, sighting, breath-control, and trigger squeeze. In time the term referred to any practice run or rehearsal.

**dry socks and hot chow**  Considered the basic necessities of what was needed to maintain the morale of frontline troops.

| | |
|---|---|
| **duck** | Water-repellent heavy cotton canvas fabric. |
| **Duck** | DUKW-353 2½-ton amphibian truck. (General Motors model designation: D – 1942, U – amphibian, K – all-wheel drive, W – dual axles.) |
| **duckbills** | Steel extension flanges fitted to the ends of track links on tanks to provide a wider track for use in mud. |
| **duck day** | When a serviceman receives his discharge. Derived from the "ruptured duck" discharge badge. |
| **dud** | 1) Malfunctioned projectile or other munition, e.g., one that did not detonate on impact. 2) A malfunctioned or incompetent person. |
| **duffle bag** | Army canvas bag for carrying clothing, a "barracks bag." See "sea bag." |
| **Dugout Doug** | General Douglas MacArthur (1880–1964), the term neatly overlooked any achievements and picked on his reported "hiding" in the Corregidor tunnels. Also "Mac," or "Emperor MacArthur" during the occupation of Japan. |
| **dump** | Supplies, ammunition, rations, field depot, etc. An open-air field storage site. |
| **dungarees** | Work uniform; "fatigues" in the Army, "utilities" in the Marines. |
| **duration plus six** | Servicemen were conscripted for the war's duration plus six months if necessary, rather than for a specific time period. |

# E — Easy

| | |
|---|---|
| **8th & Eye** | 8th and I Streets, the address of Marine Barracks, Navy Yard, Washington, DC. |

| | |
|---|---|
| **ear-banger** | Overly talkative person. "He'll talk your ear off." "Ear-banging" – talking. |
| **egg grenade** | German egg-shaped hand grenade – the Eigranate 39. |
| **eight ball** | Chronically unfortunate and ineffective person. The eight ball is the only black ball in a billiard set, the odd ball, hence "black-balled." "Behind the eight ball" is a difficult position from which one is unlikely to escape. |
| **eight-incher** | 8in M1 howitzer and M1 gun; most accurate field pieces in the US artillery inventory. |
| **eighty-eight** | German 88mm antiaircraft gun. While sometimes employed as an antitank gun, it was not the standard field artillery piece and was not used as indirect-fire artillery as often stated in movies, novels, and memoirs. The Germans used 105mm and 150mm howitzers as divisional artillery. See *Acht-Acht*, Part III. |
| **eighty-one** | 81mm M1 mortar, the standard battalion mortar. |
| **elephant gun** | Ridiculously powerful British-designed, Canadian-made .55-cal. Boys Mk 1 antitank rifle, which saw limited use by Marine Raiders and Army Rangers. |
| **Elsie** | Landing Craft, Infantry (Large) – LCI(L), the nickname derived from the pronunciation of LCI. The largest type of landing craft. |
| **e-tool** | Entrenching tool. Short spade carried by combat troops, an "army banjo." *Never* called a shovel. |
| **Eureka boat** | Landing Craft, Personnel (Large) – LCP(L). Early landing craft without bow ramp, hence the occupants had to experience a water immersion "Eureka" moment. |

| | |
|---|---|
| eyewash | Making something look better than it actually is. Also "hogwash" – one can wash a pig, but it still looks like a pig. |

# F      Fox

| | |
|---|---|
| 40 & 8 | French railroad boxcar carrying 40 cramped men or eight horses (*Hommes 40, Chevaux 8*), "forty and eights." |
| fair-leather belt | Marine cordovan belt with brass buckle worn with blues. |
| fair wear and tear | Unserviceable military property worn out by normal use. |
| fart sack | 1) Sleeping bag. <br> 2) Cotton mattress cover (Marines). |
| fatigue duty | Work detail. |
| fatigues | Loose-fitting work uniform. In 1942 fatigues became the combat uniform. Marines did not use the term fatigues, but "utilities." |
| FBI | 1) Forgotten Bastards (Boys) in India. <br> 2) Forgotten Boys in Iceland. |
| feather merchant | 1) Snide term for civilians, especially dishonest salesmen who preyed on servicemen. <br> 2) Lightly built or lightweight person. <br> 3) Person avoiding responsibility; a loafer. |
| feeding his face | Eating heartily, a "chowhound." |
| field scarf | Marine necktie. |
| field strip | 1) Degree to which a weapon can be disassembled for cleaning by a soldier as opposed to more complete disassembly by an armorer. |

2) Soldiers "field stripped" cigarette butts before discarding; i.e., tore the paper into small pieces and scattered the tobacco.

**fifth column**     Sabotage, espionage, and other subversive activities. The term was coined during the Spanish Civil War (1936–39) by rebel General Emilio Mola who stated that four columns were advancing on Madrid, but a fifth column of rebel sympathizers was inside the city waiting to aid the attackers.

**fifty-seven**     57mm M1 antitank gun. Copied from the British 6-pdr gun to replace the obsolete 37mm M3A1 antitank gun.

**fighting-hole foot**     Immersion foot, a disability caused by prolonged exposure of the feet to cold and wet conditions, like the "trench foot" of WWI.

**fin**     A $5 bill is a "fiver," "fin," or "finnif." From *finf*, Yiddish for five.

**fire guard**     Individual assigned guard duty inside a barracks or tent to keep the stove going and sound the alarm if fire broke out.

**Fire in the hole!**     1) Shouted warning just prior to detonating demolitions. It was to be shouted three times, but in combat it was often only shouted once. 2) Description of a woman with venereal disease.

**first shirt**     First sergeant, the senior NCO in a company/battery/troop. Also "top," "top kick," "top sergeant," "top sarge," "top soldier," "top knocker," and "top cutter."

**fisheyes**     Tapioca pudding.

**five-incher**     5in Mk 15 seacoast defense gun used by Marine defense battalions early in the war.

**flame tank**
Tank mounting a flamethrower, "Zippo tank." See "Zippo."

**flaming piss-pot**
Ordnance Corps branch of service insignia, a flaming old-style spherical grenade. Also "flaming onion."

**flash-bang ranging**
Estimating the range to enemy artillery by timing the interval between sighting the muzzle flash and the sound of the report arriving.

**flasher**
Not a person indulging in an antisocial practice as one might assume, but rather a Signalman. Derived from signal lamps flashing Morse Code. Previously referred to heliograph signals.

**flyboy**
Aviator, airman, "buzzard." Members of the Army Air Forces or other services' air arms.

**flying coffin**
1) C-47 transport, so called by nervous paratroopers.
2) Other aircraft in general.

**flying saucer cap**
Service cap.

**footslogger**
Infantryman. His lowly status was expressed by his many other nicknames, including "ground pounder/rat," "gravel crusher/cruncher," and "mud cruncher/eater."

**forty**
40mm M1 Bofors antiaircraft gun, a Swedish-designed weapon.

**forty-eight**
Forty-eight hour pass, two days' liberty. Also a "weekend pass."

**forty-five**
Colt .45-cal. M1911 and M1911A1 pistols.

**forty winks**
Short nap, "I'll grab forty winks." Forty represents an indefinite number, meaning a few.

**four-eyes**
Individual wearing eyeglasses. The joke goes: a draftee told the examining doctor he was

short-sighted. The doctor rated him as "Suited for close combat."

**foxhole**
Officially a "one-man or two-man fighting position." Foxholes allowed soldiers to kneel or stand to fight. They offered cover and were deep enough to protect from tank-overrun, if the occupants had the cast-iron toughness to stay.

**frag**
1) Fragmentation hand grenade.
2) Small fragmentation bomb.

**freeloader**
A hanger on, a moocher, someone expecting a free ride.

**French seventy-five**
75mm M1897 series field gun. Standard divisional artillery until replaced by the 105mm howitzer in 1940–42. The "seventy-five" served on as a halftrack-mounted tank destroyer.

**Frog**
Frenchman, "Frenchy."

**frog suit**
Four-color camouflage uniform, or "frog skin," that was too heavy and hot for wear in the Pacific. It was also withdrawn from European wear as it was mistaken for Waffen-SS camouflage uniforms.

**front and center**
Present one's self in the front of the unit formation, usually for an award or promotion.

**fruit salad**
Ribbon bars worn on the left breast bearing decorations for valor and service. So called owing to the multi-colored ribbons. Also used by the British.

**FUBAR**
Fucked (Fouled) Up Beyond All Recognition – a typical situation appraisal.

**FUBB**
Fucked (Fouled) Up Beyond Belief.

**full bird**  Colonel, a "full" colonel as opposed to a lower-ranking lieutenant colonel. Also "bird colonel" "chicken colonel," and "full bull."

**full field layout**  Inspection on the parade ground in which all field equipment is laid out in a prescribed manner.

**full pack**  All field equipment carried on an individual. "Fall out in full pack" meant a bad day for the soldier.

**fuselage**  Description of a woman's body, which obviously resembles a particularly shapely aircraft fuselage.

# G  **George**

**G-2**  Sneaking, snooping, analyzing. "He's G-2ing the situation." G-2 was the official name for the Intelligence Branch of the US Army.

**Gammon grenade**  British No. 82 hand grenade, consisting of an impact fuse attached to a cloth bag filled with plastic explosives. Used by US paratroopers.

**garbage catcher**  Six-compartment stainless-steel or rust-brown plastic mess tray.

**garrison belt**  Wide leather belt with brass buckle worn with olive-drab uniforms. Wrapped around the fist the buckle made a good knuckle-duster.

**gas house**  Saloon, bar.

**'gators**  Contraction of "alligators." Navy Amphibious Forces.

**gazoonie**  A dumb person.

**gear**  1) Individual equipment, including belt and the equipment attached to it, backpack, etc. "Put on your gear." "Gear up."

2) Communications equipment.

3) Specific types of items, e.g., "mess gear," or "shaving gear."

**gedunk**    Refers to ice cream stands on larger warships. Came to mean any snacks and candy. See also "poggy bait."

**gedunk shop**    Marine PX or canteen.

**General Mud**    General Mud controlled the battlefield, and was an enemy to both sides. When new Army posts were established, with troops housed in tents on dirt company streets, heavy motor vehicle traffic churned the ground into dust. When the rains subsequently came General Mud took command, bringing with him a thick "gumbo."

**Geronimo!**    Supposedly shouted with spirit when paratroopers jumped. Probably seldom practiced, as jumpers were taught to count off 6 seconds and pull their reserve if the main 'chute failed to open. Said to be proposed in August 1940 by Private Aubrey Eberhardt to prove to his buddies that he retained the presence of mind to shout a distinctive word when he made his first jump. The term became the motto of the 501st Parachute Infantry Regiment.

**get off the ground**    Originated with the feat of an aircraft getting off the ground. Came to mean getting something started or accomplished. "That idea won't get off the ground."

**GI**    1) Government Issue. The term became synonymous with the Army. It can mean the soldier himself, or any government or military property, or can be tagged to just about anything relating to the Army or the soldier's life. It was not until late 1943 that GI came into general use for identifying soldiers.

2) Gastrointestinal illness – diarrhea, dysentery. See "shits."

3) Galvanized Iron, with particular reference to the "GI can," a galvanized iron trash can that was used for a wide variety of purposes (trash, laundry, cleaning weapons, cooling beverages).

4) "To GI" means to clean up.

| | |
|---|---|
| **GI ashcan** | Artillery projectile. |
| **GI brush** | All-purpose scrub brush of infinite uses. |
| **GI cocktail** | A laxative beverage designed to get things moving. A dose of Epsom salt (magnesium sulfate). |
| **gig, to gig** | Demerit to cite the violation of a uniform or conduct rule. "He received two uniform gigs." |
| **gig-line** | Imaginary line on which the trousers' fly, left end of the belt buckle, and shirt front-closure had to be aligned. If they were out of alignment, the soldier received a gig. |
| **GI haircut** | Short on the sides, 1–3 inches high on top. Recruits bore the shorter style. |
| **GI hop** | Dance on an Army post, to which local girls were optimistically invited. Also "GI struggle," a clear reference to what happened when combat soldiers attempted to dance. |
| **GI jacket** | A waist-length, wind-repellent, water-repellent M1941 field jacket, "Parsons jacket." |
| **GI Jane** | Member of the Woman's Army Corps (WAC – pronounced "wack"). |
| **GI Joe** | The average soldier, influenced by the civilian term, "the average Joe." Cartoonist Dave Breger |

coined the term in his *GI Joe Trooper* cartoon in June 1942. Also "Joe Blow," and "John Doe."

**GI party**      Traditional way to spend a Friday night – barracks clean-up to get ready for the Saturday-morning inspection.

**GI shoes**      Low-topped marching shoes, "GI gunboats." Replaced by high-topped combat boots.

**Give an inch of steel**      Marine phrase for giving the bayonet. "Give cold steel" – a bayonet thrust.

**Give it the gas**      Step on the gas, speed up.

**GI war**      Peacetime maneuvers.

**gizmo**      Substitute word for an unremembered technical word or mechanical part. Other precision terms included "thingamajig," and "whatchamacallit."

**glider-rider**      Glider troops. Paratroopers were volunteers, they received special insignia, uniform distinctions and "jump pay." Glider troops were assigned the duty and received no hazardous duty pay or special insignia until June 5, 1944.

**gobbledygook**      Unintelligible radio transmissions owing to static and transmission break-up. Sometimes referred to unintelligible foreign speech. Coined in March 1944 by Maury Maverick, Chairman of the US Smaller War Plants Corporation, in a memo banning "gobbledygook," i.e., obscure language in documents.

**God box**      A rather irreverent description of a chapel on a Marine base.

**go juice**      Gasoline or diesel fuel.

**gold bird**      Brass US coat of arms spread-winged eagle insignia worn on the front of hats. Also "gold buzzard."

**gold brick**    A lazy individual avoiding work. An individual detached for a special duty assignment. "Gold bricking" – goofing off. This phrase evolved from the "gold brick swindle" that occurred in Colorado in 1879, a fraud involving gold-plated bricks. Somehow the term came to be used by soldiers in the late 1800s for a girl who was unattractive or a poor dancer or conversationalist. During WWI it came to mean a soldier who could not "pull his load," a shirker.

**goldfish**    Canned salmon.

**goofball**    Fouled-up person, with a strange and amusing personality. Goofy.

**goof off**    Make mistakes, shirk or relax when there is work to be done.

**goon**    A low category of soldier, not too bright, and big and ungainly. A thug.

**Gooney Bird**    Douglas C-47 Skytrain/Skytrooper transport, called an R4D by the Navy/Marines, and Dakota or "Dak" by the British.

**Goon gun**    4.2in M1, M1A1, and M2 chemical mortars. Also "four-point-two-inch," or "four-deuce."

**goozlum**    Thick gravy or syrup. Also "hydraulic fluid," or "machine oil."

**gorilla**    A large, strong man.

**GP**    General-purpose. Anything that could be used for routine purposes.

**grab ass**    Cutting up, horse-play, skylarking. "Cut out the grab ass!"

**grapevine**    Unspecified "source" of information or rumors. "I heard it on the grapevine."

| | |
|---|---|
| **grapevine sling** | Method of wrapping the rifle sling around the left arm to steady the aim. Also "hasty sling." |
| **grappa** | Italian brandy … of sorts, cheaply brewed from whatever was available and sold to Allied troops. |
| **Grasshopper** | Piper L-4 and L-5 liaison/observation aircraft. Also "Cub," "puddle-jumper," "Maytag Messerschmitt," "Piperschmitt," or "Messercub." |
| **graveyard stew** | Weak stew with little or no meat, mostly bones. |
| **gravy** | Money or valuables beyond what one would normally earn. Something extra. "We're in the gravy." |
| **graybacks** | 1) Lice, "leatherhides." <br> 2) German soldiers. |
| **grease gun** | The .45-cal. M3 and M3A1 submachine-gun; low-cost weapon made from stampings appearing similar to, and with the quality of, a lubricating grease gun. |
| **grease monkey** | Mechanic, a "grease ape or hound." |
| **greaser** | One of a large collection of demeaning names for Hispanics. Also "spick," "Mex," and "Poncho." |
| **Greasy Dick** | Griesedieck Brothers beer. |
| **green** | Inexperienced, e.g., "green soldier," "green unit." |
| **green eggs** | Powdered eggs. "Green" implied they were GI-issue. Cooks would actually add a couple of broken eggshells so that the bits would lead troops to believe they were eating fresh scrambled eggs. |
| **green light** | Permission to go ahead with an action or project. |
| **green-light hotel** | Prophylactic station where one was issued with condoms before getting the green light to go on pass, and all that entailed. |

**greens**     Marine forest-green uniform.

**green-/brown-side** Marines wore reversible camouflage helmet
  **out**     covers and the side out would be specified
              for an operation. In monotone photos the
              "brown-side" appears lighter than the
              "green-side." The camouflage cover became
              a Marine distinction, as the Army used bare
              helmets or camouflage nets.

**grinder**    Marine drill field.

**Guard, the** National Guard. A component of the Army
              under state control in peacetime. In time of war
              or national emergency the Guard is mobilized
              into Federal service (Federalized) and becomes
              indistinguishable from the Regular Army. The
              National Guard was organized from the state
              militias in 1903.

**guardhouse lawyer** Soldier who assumes knowledge of regulations
              or challenges authority, a know it all.

**guarding the flag** Light punishment. In a temporary camp without
  **pole**    defined boundaries a soldier was restricted to
              within sight of the flagpole.

**gu-gu**     Derisive term for Filipinos, "goo-goo." The term
              originated during the Philippine Insurrection
              and gave rise to "gook."

**Gumshoe**    Military policeman owing to thick rubber shoe
              soles worn by civilian police. See also "Dick."

**gun**       1) Long-barreled artillery piece as opposed to a
              short-barreled howitzer.
              2) General term for an artillery piece, whether a
              gun or howitzer. Small arms such as rifles,
              carbines, or pistols were never called "guns,"
              hence the popular verse "This is my rifle, this is

my gun [grabbing crotch]. This is for fighting and this is for fun."

**gung-ho**  Supposedly Chinese for "All together" – *gōnghé*. Motto adopted by the Marine 2d Raider Battalion encouraging unity of effort and later widely used by the Marines. It became a word for anything exemplifying military spirit. The reality is different. *Gōnghé* is the abbreviation for *gōngyè hézuòshè* – Industrial Workers' Cooperative. *Gōng* does mean work and *hé* means together, but by itself *gōnghé* is not a Chinese term, but an abbreviation. Even during the war it came to mean overzealousness.

**gunner's tap**  Technique of tapping a machine-gun's grip repeatedly with the heel of the hand to traverse the gun 3 mils with each tap. There are 6,400 mils in a circle, one degree is 17.777 mils. A "mil tap" traverses the gun approximately 10 inches at every 100 yards of range.

**gunney**  Marine gunnery sergeant, equivalent to Army technical sergeant (grade 2).

**gyrene**  Marine. Derived from the Chinese pronunciation of marine.

# H  How (Hypo)

**hack it**  The ability to deal with situations and difficulties. One could "hack it" or not.

**Hagensen pack**  Demolition charge developed by Navy lieutenant (jg) Carl Hagensen for destroying Normandy beach obstacles. Consisted of 2½lb of C2 plastic explosives in a sock, providing a flexible tube-like pack. Any number could be fastened together to wrap around obstacles. Later, factory-made Mk 20 charges were produced and retained the name.

**handcuffed volunteer**
In January 1943 voluntary enlistment in the armed forces was halted and all personnel were conscripted. Up to this point the Marines had accepted only volunteers. Drafted personnel could request the service they desired. Those selecting the Marines were known as "handcuffed volunteers" or "draftee volunteers."

**handie-talkie**
SCR-536 handheld platoon radio, today commonly called a "walkie-talkie." Also "Spam can radio" owing to its similarity to a can of Spam.

**handmade**
Hand-rolled cigarettes. Also "twist a daisy," "hand-rolled," and "roll-your-own." Hand-rolled cigarettes were nimbly put together from "makings," i.e., tobacco in a bag and paper in a thin cardboard package – "blanket and freckles."

**hash mark**
Diagonal Service Stripes worn on the left cuff of coats, a "hitch mark." Each stripe represented three glorious years of eating Army hash. Marine hash marks represented four years, and were called "bean stripes."

**haul ass**
Move out, quickly. "We hauled ass outa there."

**hay-burner**
Horse or mule.

**hayseed**
Hick, country boy.

**haywire**
Used to describe a piece of equipment that was not behaving itself, or events that took a bad turn. Derived from the use of haywire (baling wire) to make farm repairs.

**head**
Latrine in the Marine barracks and aboard ship.

**headspace** A not too bright person or one who is behaving oddly. When machine-gun barrels were replaced the headspacing, the spacing between the cartridge's head (base with extractor groove) and the bolt face, had to be readjusted. Too much headspace prevented the weapon from firing or affected the rate of fire.

**hell box** Ten-cap blasting machine. Traditional demolitioneer's name for the electric blasting machine.

**hell to pay** Suffer the consequences. "There'll be hell to pay for that little stunt."

**herringbone** 1) Pattern of vehicles in a march column when they pulled off the alternating sides of a road at angles for dispersal to protect against air attack. 2) Hard-wearing cotton twill fabric in fatigues/utilities, named owing to its angled weave.

**Hershey bar** Overseas Service Bar or Overseas Bar/Stripe. Short horizontal gold stripe on an olive-drab backing worn on the right cuff of coats signifying six months in a combat zone. Named after Lewis B. Hershey, Selective Service director, and its similarity to a Hershey chocolate bar in a gold and dark-brown wrapper.

**hex tent** Six-sided, center-peaked, hexagon-shaped, six-man tent.

**Hide and Hope** Unofficial motto of Tank Destroyer forces, especially less mobile towed antitank units. It refers to hiding to ambush tanks and hoping to survive. The official motto was the more orthodox "Seek, Strike, Destroy."

**higher ups** Those higher up the chain-of-command; higher echelon commanders and staff.

**highpockets**   A tall, lanky person with, by consequence, long trouser legs.

**Hindy ho!**   Flippant version of *Hände Hoch!* (lit. "Hands up!") shouted to surrendering Germans.

**hitch**   1) Hitch of service, an enlistment – three years for the Army, four for the Marines – as in hitched to a team of horses.
2) Hitched – married.

**Hitlerland**   Germany. Also "Krautland," and "Jerryland."

**hit the beach**   1) Amphibious assault landing on a hostile shore.
2) To enthusiastically embrace shore leave.

**hit the deck**   1) To lie on the ground when under fire.
2) To do something fast, immediately, "Hit the deck running."

**hit the silk**   To jump from an aircraft with a parachute, although from 1942/43 parachutes were made of nylon.

**hog-caller**   Portable loudspeaker.

**Hollywood Marines**   1) Marines trained at San Diego, California, owing to their liberty destinations of San Diego, Los Angeles, and sinful Tijuana, Mexico. Marines trained on the East Coast at Camp Perry, South Carolina, despised the assumed "easy life" of the West Coast Marines at "Dago," which had a pleasant climate and nearby big cities, and was free of sand fleas. East Coast marines even claimed that their slimy West Coast counterparts were issued sunglasses and got dates with movie starlets.
2) 2d Marine Division raised in San Diego and called Hollywood Marines for the same reason and "accused" of serving as extras in prewar motion pictures.

3) The "real" Hollywood Marines were the Marine Corps Reserve 22d Battalion (artillery), who actually did serve as movie extras.

**Hollywood private** Acting corporal (see "acting jack") or a pfc awaiting promotion to corporal.

**Holy Joe** Chaplain. Also, and reflecting a widespread military appreciation for the church, "sky-pilot," "Holly Joe," "padre," and "GI Jesus."

**hooker** Prostitute. Also "street walker," "lady of the night," and "chippie."

**horse blanket** Marine wool overcoat.

**horse cock** Baloney, "donkey dick." GI baloney lacked the red dye that gave it its characteristic reddish tint, resulting in pale flesh-colored baloney and an unfortunate analogy.

**hot stuff**
1) Important information.
2) Exclamation of approval.
3) Warning of actual hot stuff (such as food), or important or fragile items being carried through a crowd, "Hot stuff! Comin' through!"

**hubba-hubba** Exclamation of excitement or approval, especially at the sight of an attractive woman.

**Hungry Hill** Married NCOs' quarters. Also "soap suds row," as NCOs' wives would do officers' laundry for extra money.

**Hurry up and wait** Routine Army deployment maneuver involving rushing to be in place on time, and then waiting around. Typically when a report time was specified it was moved up at each echelon to ensure the troops were on time.

| | |
|---|---|
| **hutment** | Small wood-frame and tarpaper shack housing a squad. |

# I — Item (Int)

| | |
|---|---|
| **IC** | Inspected and Condemned. Letters stamped on articles of equipment deemed unusable for military service and to be disposed of. Sometimes undesirable individuals were also "declared" IC. The Insular Constabulary was organized in the Philippines in 1901 and bore "IC" on its collar insignia. It was poorly disciplined and ragtag in appearance, which led to open derision. They were reorganized as the professional Philippine Constabulary two months later, demonstrating the strength of the "IC" stigma. |
| **Ike** | General of the Army Dwight D. Eisenhower (1890–1969). |
| **in everybody's mess and nobody's watch** | An irksome individual who interferes in others' business, but is not around when work is to be done. |
| **iron crab** | German portable steel pillbox. See *gepanzerte Krabbe*, Part III. |
| **Iron Man divisions** | Five divisions that fought in most of Lieutenant General George Patton's Third Army's actions and saw 250–280 days of action: 4th and 6th Armored and 5th, 80th, and 90th Infantry Divisions. |
| **Island X** *or* **Xray** | Name for an island objective during rehearsals prior to releasing the actual name to assault troops. |
| **IT** | ITEM TARE in radio and telephone transmissions. In 1943 war correspondent Ernie Pyle related an incident in North Africa in which |

a hilltop US observation post reported that "two Italians" were coming up their hill. Through a poor telephone connection the message center heard "two battalions." The hill's forward slope erupted in an artillery barrage. It was soon directed that the code ITEM TARE be used in radio and telephone traffic for Italians. "IT" or "Itey" ("Itie") was commonly used in conversation.

**Iwo**　　Iwo Jima (Sulfur Island), in the Kazan Retto (Volcano Archipelago), within the Nanpo Shoto (Three Groups of Islands).

# J　Jig

**jack**　　Corporal (grade 5) identified by two chevrons. Also "two-striper," "corp," and "corpuscle." The lowest NCO rank.

**Jane**　　A generic woman, as in "Jane Doe."

*The Allied view of the Japanese was far from complimentary. Propaganda portrayed them as less than human.*

| | |
|---|---|
| **JANFU** | Joint Army–Navy Fuck-Up (Foul-Up). Refers to the harmony of joint service exercises. |
| **Jap** | Japanese. Also "Nip" (from Nippon), "son of Nippon," "slant-eye," "slope," "monkey," "Jape" (contraction of Japanese and ape), "ringtail," "rice-belly," and "Yap-pan" (Pidgin English). |
| **jarhead** | 1) Marine. Origin theories abound. Most likely it was the early pillbox cap and high stiff collar making a marine appear similar to a Mason jar. 2) Mule, its head empty like a jar. Also "hardhead." |
| **Java** | Coffee, aka "Joe." "A cup of J" or "cuppa Joe." "Java/Joe with sidearms" – coffee with sugar and cream. The island of Java was a main source of coffee. |
| **jawbone** | Credit at the PX to be paid on payday. Also a record of who owed what to whom between poker and blackjack players. |
| **jeep** | See box opposite. |
| **jerk** | Unpopular or mean person. |
| **jerrycan** | A 5-gal. gas or water can. Also "jeep can" and "blitz can." The water-can version could carry stew or soup to the front line. Both versions were copied from German fuel/water cans. |
| **jewelry** | Metal fittings used to fasten pontoon causeways and barges together. |
| **Jewish infantry/ cavalry** | Finance or Quartermaster Corps. These were jealously said to have been a haven for Jewish personnel. |
| **John** | Recruit, rookie, from "John Doe." "Johnny Raw" meant a raw-ass recruit. |

# THE JEEP

The "jeep" was standardized as the "truck, 4x4, ¼ ton" in July 1941, and provided a lightweight, all-terrain utility vehicle. The requirement for the jeep goes back to 1936 when the infantry stated a need for a compact four-wheel-drive reconnaissance car to replace the motorcycle. Development of what would become the jeep ran from 1939 to 1941, with three firms submitting candidates: American Bantam Car Company's Mk I and II; Willys-Overland's Quad, MA and MB; and Ford Motor's Pygmy and GP. After modifications gleaned from testing, the Willys (sometimes misspelled "Willis") was standardized, but these were also built by Ford to total 640,000 vehicles.

The origin of the jeep's name has been much debated. "Jeep" is said to have been a nickname for mechanics in WWI, but fell from use in the 1930s. In March 1936 an unusual character was introduced in the Popeye cartoons, Eugene the jeep, whose only words were, "jeep, jeep." The strange little creature could walk through walls or on ceilings, and go any place, and may well have been the source of the jeep's name. Other vehicles named "jeep," also believed to be derived from Eugene, included ½-ton Ford trucks modified by FWD Corporation as oil exploration/survey vehicles in 1936, and the Minneapolis Moline Company's tractor-like UTX artillery prime-mover offering to the Army in 1940. It is also suggested that "jeep" may have been derived from the Ford GP – "gee-pee" (general-purpose). The name Jeep was not actually trademarked until 1950. Regardless, it stuck to the nimble little vehicle, also known as the "blitz wagon" or "blitz buggy," "bantam car," "peep," or a "No. 14 roller skate with motor, windshield, mud-guards." Ford also produced an amphibious version, the "seep." War correspondent Ernie Pyle described the jeep as being "as faithful as a dog, as strong as a mule, and agile as a goat."

| | |
|---|---|
| **John Ls** | Long underwear, "long Johns." |
| **Johnnie** | Soldier, as in the song "When Johnnie Comes Marching Home." |
| **Johnnie gun** | The .30-cal. Johnson M1941 light machine-gun used by Marine paratroopers and the 1st Special Service Force. |
| **joker** | Wise guy, smart mouth, smart aleck, smart ass. |
| **jughead** | An affectionate term for a mule, and less affectionate term for a stubborn man. |
| **juice** | Electricity. "It's not gettin' any juice." |
| **juicy** | Excellent, exciting, first-rate. "I've got some juicy dope." |
| **Jumbo** | M4A3E2 Sherman tank with up-armored turret as an assault tank. |
| **jump pay** | Officially Hazardous Duty Pay paid to paratroopers, $50 per month for enlisted men and $100 for officers. |
| **Jump School** | Officially the Parachute Course. Contrary to popular perception, paratroopers were not trained to pack their own parachutes from 1942. This was accomplished by parachute riggers. |
| **jumpwings** | Parachutist Badge awarded to paratroopers after completing five jumps. Also presented to non-jumpers who volunteered for a combat jump, although in order to remain on jump status they would later have to complete the Parachutist Course. Known simply as "wings." |
| **jungleer** | Lightly equipped infantryman trained in jungle warfare. A motivational term rather than doctrinal. |
| **jungle happy** | Someone who had been in the jungle too long and demonstrated eccentric characteristics. |

Other "happy" combinations existed, e.g., "rock happy" – on an island too long, "girl happy" – speaks for itself, and "bomb happy" – stressed because of frequent bombardment.

**jungle juice**
Illegal homebrewed liquor made from K-ration dried fruit, canned fruit, and sugar. Coconut milk and Kava tree roots were also used to concoct alcoholic libations.

# K
# King

**K-9 Corps**
Military dogs employed as scout, guard, and messenger dogs. A publicity term and not officially used. The Marines collectively called them "war dogs." K-9 derived from "ca-nine."

## KA-BAR FIGHTING KNIFE

This Marine 7in-blade fighting knife was a virtual symbol of the Corps. The Union Cutlery Company offered its heavy-duty Model 1217 fighting knife to the Marines in 1942, based on a proven design. The Marines adopted it and other companies manufactured it as well, but it became known as the KA-Bar. According to the company's own history (the company changed its name to KA-BAR Cutlery Inc. in 1952), the name was derived from the pre-WWII testimonial of a satisfied trapper who crudely wrote that his rifle had jammed and he had used their knife to kill a wounded bear attacking him. In thanking the company for their quality product, the trapper described using his knife to "kill a bear." The way his writing was scrawled across the paper it looked like "ka bar." The company adopted it as their trademark, KA-BAR. It did *not* mean "knife, assistant Browning automatic rifleman" as is rumored – they carried bayonets.

| | |
|---|---|
| **KA-Bar** | See box on previous page. |
| **Kangaroo John** | An Australian. |
| **Keep your powder dry** | A comradely warning to take care of oneself, just like "Keep your head down." It originated in the old days of muzzle-loading weapons, when damp powder could cause a disastrous misfire. |
| **kennel ration** | Meat loaf or hash, common garrison fare that became chronically monotonous. The term is derived from the "Kennel Ration" brand of dog food. |
| **khaki fever** | Some women, in a naïve form of patriotism, freely offered sex to servicemen. |
| **khakis** | Army and Marine summer uniform of khaki (light tan) cotton. |
| **khaki-whacky** | Woman overly enthusiastic for men in uniform. |
| **kick** | 1) Dishonorable discharge – "kicked out." <br> 2) Weapon recoil. <br> 3) To kick something upstairs – forward a request or recommendation up the chain-of-command. <br> 4) Kick downstairs – to be demoted. |
| **kike** | Jew. A degree of anti-Semitism existed in the armed forces, especially in the officer corps, and society in general. Jewish personnel were exempted from the requirement to eat kosher food. |
| **Kilroy** | See box opposite. |
| **Kiwi** | 1) New Zealander. <br> 2) Kiwi® was the popular Marine Corps boot polish. |
| **knee mortar** | Japanese 5cm Type 89 (1929) grenade discharger (*jutekidanto*). It was popularly called the "knee mortar" by the Allies because of a string of |

# KILROY WAS HERE

The bald cartoon character peeking over and gripping a wall, who, widely appearing as wartime graffiti, had his origins with British cartoonist George "Chat" E. Chatterton in 1938. During the war, Chatterton's half-hidden character called Chad complained of ration shortages through inscriptions such as "Wot, no bread?" or "Wot, no fags?" In the case of a British glider he was seen on its fuselage exclaiming, "Wot, no engines?"

His American cousin is believed to have been created in 1940 by James J. Kilroy, a shipyard riveter who marked his work "Kilroy was here." Troops sailing on the ships found the graffiti in out of the way spaces and around 1942 it was merged with the Chad figure. Kilroy began to appear wherever US troops were stationed. It was not so much the mere appearance of the figure, but where it appeared that made it so humorously outrageous.

While a soldier's and sailor's prank, Kilroy sometimes found his way to the highest echelons. It is reported that German intelligence found him on captured American equipment, leading Hitler to believe Kilroy was a high-level Allied spy. At the Potsdam Conference Stalin found him in the VIPs' latrine, prompting him to ask who this Kilroy was. Neither story has been confirmed, but he did appear on Paris' Arc de Triomphe, on countless *Westwall* bunkers, inside 40x8 boxcars, and on other structures throughout Europe.

misinformation. It was rumored that the mortar's curved base plate was to be braced on the thigh for firing, with the knee on the ground. In reality, this technique would result in injuries. Another theory for its nickname was that it was carried in a bag strapped to the thigh – again this is not true, as it was carried in a canvas case slung over the shoulder.

| | |
|---|---|
| **Knock it off!** | Cease what you're doing … now! |
| **knucklehead** | Dumb person, "bonehead," "knot-head." As in "The knucklehead don't get it." |
| **KO** | Knock out or knocked out. To destroy something. From the boxing term. |
| **KP** | Kitchen Police, kitchen duty, often involving emotionally sapping quantities of potatoes, hence KP could mean "Kept Peeling potatoes." Also "Spud duty." |
| **KP pusher** | The soldier assigned to head the KP detail and keep them busy. |
| **Kraut** | Name for the Germans used by the United States, Canada, Australia, and Britain. Long in use and derived from *Sauerkraut* (fermented preserved cabbage). The term "kraut-head" saw limited but no doubt forceful use. |
| **Kraut burp gun** | German 9mm MP38 and MP40 machine pistol, incorrectly called "Schmeisser." This was because its design was often attributed to Hugo Schmeisser who, while an arms designer, did not design these weapons. |
| **Kwaj** | Kwajalein Island, Marshall Islands (pronounced "Kwa-dja-linn"). |

# L          Love

| | |
|---|---|
| **ladies' fever** | A delicate way of phrasing syphilis, or "Old Joe." |
| **Land of the Rising Sun** | Japan, Nippon. |
| **Large Slow Target** | Alternative name for Landing Ship, Tank (LST), the largest beaching landing ship. Also "Long Slow Target," "Love-Sugar-Tare" (phonetic alphabet), "green dragoon," "green snapper" (owing to green tropical camouflage schemes), and "whale." |
| **latrine lawyer** | Argumentative soldier, a complainer with nothing more than a toilet audience. Also "smoke-blower." |
| **latrine rumor** | News from the grapevine, an unofficial, unfounded report. Also "latrine telegram." |
| **lead penny** | Zinc-plated steel pennies minted in 1943 to conserve copper. When corroded they appeared to be made of lead. Also known as "steelies," they were sometimes mistaken for dimes. From 1944 to 1946 pennies were made from recovered cartridge cases with the addition of more copper and tin, and were known as "shell case pennies." |
| **leatherneck** | A Marine. The name is derived from the 19th-century stiff leather collar that gave neck protection from cutlass slashes. |
| **let daylight into** | Shoot holes through something. |
| **Let 'em have it!** | Informal order to open fire. |
| **liberate** | A euphemistic interpretation of looting, scrounging stealing. |
| **library** | The latrine, where much serious study was done. Also "other office," and "reading room." |
| **lights out** | Extinguish lights in quarters. Bedtime, time to turn in, Taps (the final bugle call). |

**lingo**
Language, jargon, foreign language, local language, or dialect. "He speaks the lingo."

**lip burner**
Cigarette butt smoked down to the point it burnt one's lips.

**Lister bag**
Officially "bag, canvas, water, sterilizing, complete with cover and hanger." The 36-gal. bag was hung from a tree limb or pole tripod. It had six spigots for filling canteens.

**Little Joe**
Auxiliary power generator on Sherman tanks.

**little poison**
37mm M3A1 antitank gun. The standard AT gun copied from the German 3.7cm Pak 36/37. The name was given because of the unpleasant effects of its accuracy and high velocity. However, the nickname was dropped once it proved ineffective against newer tanks and it became known as the "thirty-seven."

**Long Tom**
155mm M1A1 gun.

**looie** *or* **looey**
Lieutenant. Also "loto," "2nd or 1st John," and "shavetail."

**Loose lips sink ships**
Slogan warning that speaking of pending military operations, troop movements, etc. could be overheard by spies, and the information passed on to the enemy naval forces.

**Lost Battalion, the**
There were several incidents when battalions were cut off or isolated, but a unit was never actually "lost." Correspondents concocted the term based on a well-known WWI incident, actually involving nine companies from three different 77th Division battalions in Belgium's Argonne Forest in October 1918. The two most noted WWII Lost Battalions were of the Texas National Guard. The 2d Battalion, 131st Field Artillery, was en route to the Philippines

at the time of the Pearl Harbor attack and diverted to Java, where it fought with the Dutch and British from February to March 1942 when it surrendered. The 1st Battalion, 141st Infantry, 36th Infantry Division was surrounded in France's Vosges Mountains in October 1944 and was rescued by the Japanese-American 442d Infantry, which suffered over 800 casualties rescuing 200 men.

**lousy**    Terrible, used of a place, person, or thing. Derived from "lousey" – lice-infested.

**lowdown**    News, information. "Give me the lowdown."

# M    # Mike

**M1 pencil**    When a soldier was said to have "qualified with an M1 pencil" he either had not actually fired his weapon but his score had been penciled in anyway or, as another worrying shortcut, holes were punched through the target to give a poor shooter a passing score.

**M1 thumb**    On being given the command "Inspection … Arms!" an M1 rifle-armed soldier brought the piece to port arms diagonally across the chest, muzzle to the left (port), opened the bolt by slapping the operating lever to the rear with the right hand's heel, and quickly glanced into the chamber confirming it was empty. On the command, "Order … Arms!" the heel of the right hand pushed the operating lever slightly to the rear, disengaging the bolt, which was held open by the magazine follower. With the right hand's thumb the follower was depressed and the operating handle released, allowing the bolt to slam forward. A high degree of coordination and practice was required to ensure the thumb cleared the bolt or, as a fleshy and painful round, it might be chambered resulting in a bruised or broken thumb – the "M1 thumb."

**Mac**      General nickname for a Marine or sailor.

**mackerel-snapper**      A creativity-stretching term for a Roman Catholic. Roman Catholics serving in the US Armed Forces were given dispensation from the obligation to abstain from meat on Fridays. Nonetheless, whenever it was possible to do so military mess halls continued the tradition of serving fish on Fridays if available.

**Ma Duce**      Browning .50-cal. M2 machine-gun, principally an antiaircraft weapon, but also used on some armored vehicles.

**Mae West**      1) Life vest or life jacket, as it made the wearer appear formidably big-chested.
2) Parachute malfunction in which one or more suspension lines were strung over the canopy, causing two large mammary-like "bubbles" to appear. Also "line-over."
3) Prewar M2A2 light tank, owing to its twin side-by-side turrets.
All definitions are derived from Mae West's buxom figure.

**Maggie's drawers**      Red flag used on rifle ranges and waved from the butts (trenches from which targets are raised and lowered for scoring) to signal misses.

**magpie**      Hit on the inner black ring (3 ring) on a target during range firing.

**mainside**      The main portion of a Marine base where the headquarters and other permanent facilities were located. Many units were located in outlying camps. On an Army base these were known as the "cantonment area."

**Make every bullet count**  Roughly and worryingly interpreted, "We're low on ammo."

**Maken**  Makin Island is the main island in Butartitari Atoll, Gilbert Islands. Makin and Butartitari were used interchangeably for the island and atoll. Makin was pronounced "Muc-kin," but Americans pronounced it "Maken."

**Marauder**  Member of the 5307th Composite Unit, Provisional, a long-range penetration unit operating behind Japanese lines in Burma. Also "Merrill's Marauders," and "Galahad Force."

**Marfak**  Butter. Texaco brand lubricating oil, "skid grease."

**marge**  Margarine, butter substitute. Wartime margarine was white and came in a can with a packet of yellow dye powder to be mixed into the margarine, but cooks often discarded the dye.

**Marsmen**  Members of the 5332d Brigade, Provisional or Mars Task Force. This was a long-range penetration unit continuing the mission of the disbanded Merrill's Marauders.

**Marston matting**  Pierced steel plates (PSP) used to surface forward airfields. Field tested during exercises at Marston, Georgia.

**Mary**  Pidgin English for a native woman. Mainly used in New Guinea.

**master guns**  Marine master gunnery sergeant (grade 1).

**McCoy**  Something authentic or a person with good qualities. "He's the real McCoy."

**meat ball** — Japanese red disc rising sun national symbol (*hinomaru* – disk of the sun) on aircraft and flags.

**meat chopper** — Any machine-gun, but specifically the halftrack-mounted twin and quad .50-cal. machine-guns. See "quad-fifty."

**meathead** — Thick-headed person with no appreciable brain.

**meat wagon** — Ambulance. More terms that were no doubt equally reassuring to casualties were "crackerbox" and "agony wagon/buggy."

**Mermite can** — Insulated 5¾-gal. container for carrying hot food to forward positions.

**mess gear** — Mess kit, eating utensils (knife, fork, spoon), and canteen cup.

**mess kit** — Officially "meat can," a deep oval pan with a folding handle and a shallow two-compartment lid serving as a plate.

**MG** — machine-gun. "Em-gee" became the universal term for any machine-gun. Also "typewriter."

**Mickey Mouse money** — Japanese occupation money in the Philippines. Also used for other military payment script and foreign money.

**midnight/moonlight requisition** — Illegal acquisition of items and material, often conducted with stealth under the cover of darkness. It was common to "permanently borrow" spare parts, materials, and whatever else from other units. While technically theft of government property, this action was tolerated to some decree as such

---

\* *Traditionally there is no Company/Battery/Troop J. In the 1800s, "I" and "J" were handwritten the same and "J" was not used to prevent confusion. A myth asserts that in some unspecified conflict a "Company J" lost its guidon to the enemy. This is unfounded.*

requisitions were for the benefit of the unit and not sold on the black market for personal gain.

| | |
|---|---|
| **Mike boat** | Landing Craft, Mechanized (LCM). |
| **MILK Battalion** | 3d Battalion of an infantry regiment, as its companies were lettered I, K, L, and M. Dates from WWI and fell from use early in WWII.* |
| **mill** | Typewriter. "Beat (or pound) the mill." |
| **million-dollar wound** | A wound that gets one sent home, worth a million bucks. |
| **minuteman** | People selling War Bonds and Stamps. A poster depicting a Revolutionary War Minuteman promoted the effort. |
| **Mister** | Title for addressing Marine (but not Army) lieutenants and Army warrant officers. |
| **mitt-flapper** | 1) Person currying favor from superiors, obviously with gesticulatory fervor. 2) A yes-man, raising his mitts to volunteer. |
| **mitts** | Hands, derived from mittens. "Keep your mitts off my chow!" Also "gloms" (Marine). |
| **mobile pillbox** | Tank or assault gun dug into a pit. |
| **Molotov cocktail** | Bottle filled with gasoline or other flammable substances and fitted with a rag wick in its opening. Used to attack armored vehicles and fortifications. Developed during the Spanish Civil War and named after Vyacheslav M. Molotov (1890–1986), People's Commissar for Foreign Affairs. There is little doubt that the "incendiary bottle" predates that conflict. |
| **Mona and Clara** | Air raid siren due to its apparently feminine moaning sound and the subsequent all-clear signal. |

**monkey balls**    Canned kadota figs, which were detested but seemed to be the only fruit issued.

**monkey dicks**    Vienna sausages, described with a nickname that no doubt whetted the appetite.

**monkey suit**    1) Mechanic's overalls.
2) Military uniform in general.

**Montezuma red**    Bright red lipstick worn by female Marines. Derived from "The Halls of Montezuma …" line in the Marine Corps Hymn.

**Montford Point Marines**    African-American Marines named after Montford Point Camp at Camp Lejeune, North Carolina, where they were trained.

**mooch**    To "borrow" money or items with little intent to repay. A "moocher." "He's mooching smokes."

**moo juice**    Milk.

**moonlight cavalry**    Antiaircraft searchlight units.

**moo oil**    1) Butter, "grease."
2) Smooth talking, exaggerations.

**Moro**    Morotai Island, Netherlands East Indies.

**Motor T**    Marine term for "motor transportation."

**Mount Sonofabitchi**    *Suribati-yama* (Mount Suribachi), a bitterly defended 546ft extinct volcano on the southwest end of Iwo Jima. Also Mount Plasma or HOTROCKS (codename). Site of the legendary Marine flag-raising.

**mousetrap fuse**    Spring-loaded firing device that ignited hand-grenade delay fuses when the arming lever was released.

**mud**    1) Strong coffee. Also "ink" or "battery acid."
2) Chocolate pudding.
3) Indistinct radio-telegraph signals.

| | |
|---|---|
| **mule skinner** | Mule-handler, "packer" – referring to those who rigged and loaded pack mules, apparently so mean and hard they could skin a mule alive. |
| **Mulligan battery** | Mobile field kitchen (from Mulligan stew). |
| **mummy bag/sack** | Close-fitting sleeping bag making the occupant appear similar to a mummy. |
| **musette bag** | M1936 field bag, a haversack carried by officers, paratroopers, and armored infantry rather than a backpack. |
| **mustang** | Marine officer who came up through the ranks. A mustang is a stray or half-wild horse usually found on its own. |
| **mystery hash** | Meat hash of unidentifiable or questionable content. |

# N          Nan (Negat)

| | |
|---|---|
| **90-day wonder** | New 2nd lieutenant, owing to the 90-day Officer Candidate School (OCS). |
| **NAFF** | Not Available For Fornication. A discriminating woman. Term originated in Britain and is derived from Naafi (Navy, Army, and Air Force Institutes). See "Naafi," Part II. |
| **name, rank, and cigarettes** | This is a reference to being taken prisoner by the Germans. Prisoners of war were only required to give their "name, rank, and serial number" to their captors. Date of birth was also required, but left out of the POW's mantra. The "cigarettes" referred to the common, tortuous practice of captors taking the POW's smokes. |
| **nervous in the service** | One uncomfortable with or experiencing difficulties with service life, often while under heavy fire. |

| | |
|---|---|
| **nest** | Small crew-served weapon position, e.g., machine-gun nest. |
| **New Guinea salute** | The jumpy practice of constantly waving one's hand over the mess kit, chasing off flies. |
| **new wrinkle** | New tactic, technique, or equipment. |
| **Nicaraguan onion/ pineapple** | Tear-gas hand grenade, the term derived from their use by the Marines in Nicaragua and other 1920–30s Banana Wars. |
| **nighthawk** | Night patrol or guard duty, "owl." |
| **night maneuvers** | Date with a WAC, hopefully leading to "undercover operations." |
| **ninety** | 90mm M1, M1A1, and M2 antiaircraft guns, which replaced 3in AA guns. |
| **No-clap Medal** | Army Good Conduct Medal awarded for maintaining a clean record during a three-year enlistment. Contracting VD, never a good career move, denied its award. |
| **noncom** | Noncommissioned officer (NCO) – corporal through master sergeant. |
| **nookie** *or* **nookey** | Sex/intercourse. Also "poontang," and "poon." |

# O     Oboe

| | |
|---|---|
| **oak leaves** | Gold-colored oak leaf insignia of a major, silver-colored for a lieutenant colonel. Also "leaves." |
| **off-limits** | 1) Civilian business establishment from which servicemen were barred owing to illegal, immoral, or unfair practices carried out inside. 2) Any restricted-access place or information. |
| **OHIO** | The draft began in October 1940, and in the early summer of 1941 President Roosevelt asked |

Congress to extend the term of service beyond 12 months. Many soldiers drafted in October 1940 threatened to desert once their original 12 months had expired. OHIO was sometimes painted on barracks in protest – "Over the Hill in October" meant they intended to desert in October. Few actual desertions occurred when enlistment was extended six months.

**OK**
Okay. Affirmative. "Everything is OK." "He's an OK guy." OK quickly became a universal acknowledgment in US-occupied areas.

**Okie *or* Oki**
Okinawa Island. "Okies" – island inhabitants.

**Old Army/ Old Corps**
Prewar Army or Marine Corps, before conscription was introduced resulting in their massive expansion.

**Old China hand**
Soldier or Marine with a long tour of duty in prewar China. An experienced "old salt."

**old file**
Officer or NCO with long service owing to the worn and well-thumbed appearance of their personal record file folders.

**Old Man**
Commanding officer, "Ol' Man," "CO." The unit commander at any echelon, but most commonly referring to company and battalion commanders. Most were far from old. Rifle company commanders were in their mid-20s and battalion COs in their late 20s to early 30s.

**one a-shootin', ten a-lootin'**
Referred to the ratio of combat troops to rear support troops.

**one-five-five**
155mm M1 and M1A1 howitzers, the standard divisional medium artillery, and the 155mm gun.

| | |
|---|---|
| **one-oh-five** | 105mm M2A1 howitzer, standard divisional light artillery piece. Also the "snub-nosed 105mm." |
| **one-percent loan** | Loan from one soldier to another – loan a dollar, get two back on payday. |
| **one-star general** | Brigadier general. Also "shavetail general," "gigadier breneral," and "jigadier brindle." |
| **on the blink** | Defective, malfunctioning. Derived from electronic equipment with blinking lights. |
| **on the carpet** | Ordered to appear before the commanding officer. "He's in big trouble, been called on the carpet by the Ol' Man." |
| **organized grab ass** | Calisthenics (pull-ups, sit-ups, jumping jacks, etc.) by the numbers. |
| **Oscar** | Dummies dropped by parachute as a deception for actual airborne operations. |
| **outfit** | Military unit, a term with cowboy origins. |
| **out of uniform** | Wearing the uniform improperly, with missing or mixed components, improper wear of insignia or decorations, etc. |
| **overseas cap** | Garrison cap. Less restrained terms included "go-to-hell cap" and "cunt cap." For Marines, "piss-cutter" and "fore-and-aft cap." |
| **overseas pay** | Sea or Foreign Shore Pay given to Marines, 20 percent over their base pay. |
| **over the hill** | A soldier no longer "AWOL," but one who has made the lifestyle decision not to come back. An AWOL soldier absent for over 30 days was declared a deserter. |
| **over the hump** | Completing half of one's enlistment or some assignment, and so past the hard part. |

# P       Peter

**P-38**      Not the Lockheed Lighting fighter or the German Walther pistol, but a small can-opener with a folding cutter issued with C- and K-rations, officially (and hilariously) "opener, can, hand, folding, Type I." The origin of P-38 is unknown. It was said that 38 punctures were required to open a can, but the author knows this is not true. Some say it operated as fast as a P-38 fighter.

**Panama mount**      Semi-circular, pit-type, concrete emplacement for the 155mm M1918 M1 gun when employed in the coast defense role.

**Papa boat**      Landing Craft, Vehicle and Personnel (LCVP). Also "P-boat" and "Landing Craft, Very Pregnant" (when stuffed full of troops). The most widely used landing craft.

**paper-pusher/ shuffler**      Officer with a tough administrative assignment, "chair-borne."

**paperwork**      Administrative work, the correct documents, always in at least triplicate.

**Paramarines**      Unofficial name for Marine paratroopers. The term was officially discouraged as it implied that they were "half-marines."

**pass the buck**      To pass blame or shift responsibility. See "buck slip."

**Pearl**      Navy Operating Base, Pearl Harbor, Oahu, Territory of Hawaii.

**pearl divers**      Kitchen Police (KP) washing dishes.

**pee/piss break/halt**      Welcome 10-minute bladder-emptying sessions were taken every 50 minutes during marches. Hence "Take ten."

| | |
|---|---|
| **pencil pusher** | Administrative personnel, clerk. |
| **permanent KP** | 1) Not literal, but referred to badly behaved soldiers who were frequently in trouble and constantly given additional duties.<br>2) An incompetent soldier who might as well have been placed on permanent KP duty, as he was of little use at anything else. |
| **PI, the** | Philippine islands, the Commonwealth of the Philippines. |
| **Pick 'em and put 'em down** | The instruction to march or run. It alluded to the foot action of the unfortunate soldier being forced to participate. |
| **piece** | 1) Generic artillery piece, whether a gun or howitzer ("hows").<br>2) Rifle or carbine. Other small arms were not called pieces. |
| **pig's snout** | Gas mask, term owing to the porcine profile it gave the wearer |
| **pig's swill** | Poor food, "dog food," "garbage." Usually stated in response to all the hard efforts of the mess staff. |
| **pig-sticker** | Bayonet, "frog-sticker." |
| **pineapple** | Tagged on to anything having to do with Hawaii. |
| **pineapple grenade** | Mk II series fragmentation hand grenade, "frag." |
| **pinks and greens** | Army officer's uniform with dark olive-drab (greenish tinted) and light olive-drab (dark tan) trousers. In sunlight the coat appeared dark green and the trousers beige (pinkish tinted). |
| **pinup** | Photograph of a provocatively dressed, attractive woman, usually an actress, pinned up in quarters to provide stimulation of one kind or another. |

**pip**    Something easy. The seizure of Roi-Namur island in 1944 was a pip owing to light resistance.

**piss**    Beer, "brew" (see "3.2 beer"). Excessive consumption reminded the consumer that one merely borrowed "horse piss."

**pissed off**    Irritated, angry.

**Pistol Pete**    Japanese 10cm (actually 105mm) Type 92 (1932) guns on Guadalcanal that kept up a sporadic and annoying long-range fire on Henderson Field.

**pits, the**    Bad place or situation. Derived from working the "pit detail" in the butts on rifle ranges. It was hot, dusty, and boring work.

**pneumonia hole**    Any poorly unheated, drafty quarters (barracks, tent, hut, barn).

**pocketbooks *or* paperbacks**    Small-format Armed Services Editions of novels provided to servicemen.

**Podunk**    Condescending nickname for a small, out of the way, hick town.

**poggy bait**    Marine term for candy and snacks. "Poggy" is said to derive from a Chinese word for bartering. Marines in China bartered with prostitutes using candy bars. The 6th Marines while sailing to China are said to have bought out the ship's store candy, but purchased barely any bath soap. Hence, "I'm a poggy bait Sixth Marine. I can't keep my rifle clean, I don't want a BAR, I just want a candy bar."

**poggy rope**    French *fourragère* (woven shoulder cord) of the *Croix de Guerre* awarded in WWI to the 5th and 6th Marines and worn on the left shoulder.

**pogled**    Dazed, confused, slap-happy. Referred to German prisoners still bewildered from combat.

**pogo stick radio**  SCR-511 company radio replaced by the SCR-330 (see "walkie-talkie"). A short pole protruded from the bottom allowing it to be carried on horseback in a guidon carrier.

**pogue**  Sissy individual or platoon. A name bestowed by Marine DIs on those failing to meet standards, not working hard enough, or failing to display sufficient *esprit de corps*. Unfit to wear the globe and anchor insignia.

**pointie talkie**  Phrasebook containing basic words and phrases in English and foreign languages. Rather than attempting to pronounce the words, and hence sound ludicrous, an American serviceman would point to the words and phrases, showing the native what he meant. The 4x5in books included several languages found in specific regions; e.g., the CBI Theater Pointie Talkie No. 4 contained Chinese, Burmese, French, Annamese, Thai, Shan, Lolo, and Lao phrases. There were also "phrase books" covering a single foreign language and including a pronunciation guide.

**point system**  After the war in 1945 a point system was instituted to rotate long-serving men home. It was based on one point for each month of service up to September 1945, an additional point for each month overseas, five points for each battle star and combat decoration, and up to 12 points for dependents. The number of required points kept changing as the needs of the service changed.

**police**  To police up, i.e., clear up. When on a "police call" personnel swept through an area to police up refugees and anything that didn't grow there.

**poodle palace**    Base commander's quarters.

**poop sheet**    1) Unit newsletter.
2) List of work details, class assignments, work or class schedule.

**popcorn bomb**    German antipersonnel cluster bomb – Sprengbombe Dickwandig 2kg (SD.2), which sprayed out bomblets like popcorn. Lone harassing bombers dropping the bombs were called "Popcorn Petes." See also "butterfly bomb," Part II.

**post**    1) Military installation, garrison. Usually designated a "fort" or "camp."
2) Place of duty, e.g., a guard post.

**pot**    M1 steel helmet, "piss pot," "steel pot," "tin pot," "tin hat," "bucket." Doubled as a wash basin and cook pot.

**pots and pans man**    KP responsible for cleaning cooking utensils, a job no one in their right mind would want.

**pouring it on**    1) Directing a high volume of fire on a target.
2) Applying speed.

**powder monkey**    Romantic term for an artilleryman's girlfriend. It comes from the old days when powder monkeys carried propellant changes from the magazine to cannons.

**Praise the Lord and pass the ammunition!**    Popular battle cry attributed to Chaplain Lieutenant (jg) Howell Forgy on the USS *New Orleans* (CA-32) during the Pearl Harbor attack. Early in the war rumors were spread attributing the quickly famous battle cry to different chaplains aboard other ships. A popular song titled by the cry written by Frank Loesser was released in 1942 and made Number 1 by Kay Kyser and His Orchestra in 1943. While his shipmates urged him to set the record straight, Chaplain Forgy responded with, "The episode should remain a legend rather than be associated with any particular person." Events overcame him when the cruiser's officers held a press conference to set the record straight and crew witnesses verified that it was Chaplain Forgy who moved down the ammunition line, patting the men on the back and making that remark to cheer them and keep them going.

| | |
|---|---|
| **prang** | Bomb a target heavily, pour on the heat. |
| **praying for corporal** | Another name for a private first class (pfc) (grade 6). |
| **Priest** | The 105mm M7 self-propelled howitzer, so named for its pulpit-like forward .50-cal. machine-gun mount. |
| **pro-kit** | Individual chemical prophylactic packet for those inevitable post-sex worries. It contained a soap-impregnated cloth, cleansing tissue, and a tube of calomel-sulfathiazole ointment. |
| **pro-station** | Prophylactic station, a medical office on or near military posts where servicemen, in testimony to their single-minded leisure activities, were required to report for VD preventive treatment when returning from pass. |
| **punk** | Bread. "Punk and plaster" was bread and butter. |
| **punk and piss** | Bread and water served to Marines in the brig. They could, however, ask for all they wished and every third day received regular meals. |
| **pup tent** | Two-man tent comprising two shelter-halves buttoned together, one half being carried by each soldier. |

**Purple Heart battalion** — A unit repeatedly suffering high casualty rates. The Purple Heart was presented to those killed or wounded in action.

**Purple Heart box** — Troubling term for a halftrack armored vehicle. So called because its light armor could be penetrated by armor-piercing machine-gun rounds and its open top exposed the crew to grenades and artillery airbursts. Halftrack "personnel carriers" transported armored infantrymen while "motor gun carriages" mounted antitank or antiaircraft weapons.

**put the bug on** — Turn on a flashlight. Derived from a firefly.

**pyramid tent** — Square, center-peaked eight-man tent. Also "squad tent," and "boudoir."

# Q          Queen

**Q Company** — 1) The "awkward squad," in which clumsy troops received additional drill instruction. The "Q" stands for "queer" as in oddballs and goof offs.
2) Reception station where new recruits reported for processing and assignment to a training unit.

**quad-fifty** — Four-gun mounting for .50-cal. M2 machine-guns on halftrack M16 and M17 motor gun carriages or two-wheel M51 or M55 trailers. There were also "twin-fifty" versions, the M13 and M14 motor gun carriages. Intended as antiaircraft weapons, they were frequently employed against ground targets, which was completely legal regardless of rumors it was not.

**quarters and rations** — "Room and board" provided to soldiers attached to another unit for support.

| | |
|---|---|
| **queer** | Homosexual. "Gay" meant only happy or lighthearted in the 1940s. |

# R — Roger

| | |
|---|---|
| **ration box commandos** | Self-imposed name for Marine depot companies or colored stevedore units. |
| **rations** | See box opposite. |
| **Ratzy** | American name for the Germans. Composite of rat and Nazi. |
| **raunchy** | Miles away from its modern usage, "raunchy" indicated someone dirty, sloppy, and unacceptable. |
| **raw recruit** | Newly enlisted soldier who had not yet or had just commenced basic training; "'cruit," "'croot." |
| **ready-mades** | Factory-made cigarettes, "tailor-made" or "hard-rolled," as opposed to "handmade." |
| **rear, the** | Rear area behind the frontline in which headquarters and support and service units operated. |
| **recon** | Reconnaissance or reconnoiter. |
| **red ass** | Extremely angry. "The Ol' Man's got the red ass." Derived from the baboon's combination of an angry personality and a fiery red rump. |
| **Red Ball Express** | Transportation organization that rushed munitions, fuel, and supplies to the front from the Normandy beachhead to keep pace with the advancing forces. Trucks were marked with a red disc identifying their priority. They were not to be halted or rerouted and their routes were kept clear of other traffic. The term comes from the |

# RATIONS

An army travels on its stomach, as attested by Napoleon. Food was still a widespread concern for US troops in WWII. In combat there never seemed to be enough food nor time to eat it, and its quality, whether in prepackaged field rations or served out by cooks in a mess hall, was a subject of much discussion and derision. Regardless, the US Army made great strides in the packing and distribution of rations. It divided field and garrison rations into several lettered categories. The letters had no meaning in themselves, except for the R-ration.

A-rations – Regular fresh and frozen foods served in garrison mess halls and aboard ships.

B-rations – Canned, dried, and preserved foods prepared in field kitchens.

C-rations – Individual one-day ration of six cans, three with meat/vegetables, three with crackers, plus candy and coffee. The complaint was that C-rations were heavy and greasy.

D-rations – Enriched hard chocolate bar as an emergency ration, to be consumed only on order. Specifications said it was to "taste little better than boiled potato" to prevent it from being eaten as a snack.

K-rations – Three individual meals used in combat, containing canned meat/vegetables, crackers, and spreads. The complaint was that they were not filling.

R-rations – Based on the Chinese march ration, these consisted of rice and fresh bacon and were tested by the Marine 2d Raider Battalion. They were a failure as they required prolonged cooking, not just heating, the bacon went rancid, and they were not to American tastes.

10-in-1 rations – Rations containing B- and K-ration components to feed ten men three meals for one day. They required little preparation. There was also a less used 5-in-1 ration.

| | |
|---|---|
| | name of the railroad practice of marking priority railcars with a red disc. |
| **Red Book** | *The Marine's Handbook* by Major Luther A Brown, which "boots" were required to purchase for $1. |
| **Redleg** | Artilleryman, owing to the old practice of wearing branch-of-service strips on trouser legs. |
| **red paint** | Catsup, ketchup. Also "redeye," "red ink," and "red lead." |
| **red tape** | Bureaucratic delay and complications. |
| **reefer** | Refrigerator. Reefer trucks transported fresh foods. |
| **repple depple** | Replacement depot, "repo depot," where troops were processed and acclimatized before assignment. |
| **retread** | WWI veteran recalled to active duty. |
| **re-up** | Reenlist, an option that disappeared with the declaration of war as service was for the duration. |
| **revival tent** | Any of the large general-purpose tents used when large floor spaces were needed for mess halls, chapels, theaters, briefing rooms, supply rooms, etc. Reminiscent of large tents used at religious revivals. |
| **Rhino ferry** | Self-propelled ferries constructed of Navy box-like pontoons and provided with large outboard motors. Used to transport lighter vehicles and supplies ashore and for utility craft. |
| **RHIP** | Rank Has Its Privileges. A lighthearted explanation for the privileges and benefits of those with higher rank. |
| **ride** | 1) To take advantage. A free ride. "He's been riding the sick list." |

2) To harass, needle, make fun of a person, to "ride his back."

**Rock, the**     Corregidor Island, Manila Bay, Philippines.

**Rocks and Shoals**     Articles of the Government of the Navy. The Navy's rules and regulations for discipline, which applied to the Marines.

**rock the boat**     Make trouble.

**Roger**     Radio/telephone proword for "Your message received and understood." Roger was the phonetic alphabet word for "R." It dates back to the earliest days of wireless when transmissions were made only by Morse code and "R" meant "Received." It came into everyday spoken use for "understood" and sometimes used as "yes" or "affirmative."

**Rommel's asparagus**     Vertical poles erected in fields in France as anti-paratrooper and anti-glider obstacles. Sometimes wire was strung between the poles.

**rubber**     Condom, officially and not so romantically described as "individual mechanical prophylactic."

**rubber boat**     Any model of inflatable or pneumatic boat used for landing troops, river-crossings, reconnaissance, or as a life raft.

**Rudolf**     Man-weighted parachute dummy for testing parachutes. Named after Nazi official Rudolf Hess, who parachuted into Britain in 1941 in an effort to effect a peace treaty.

**runaround**     1) Skirting the issue, misleading someone. "He's givin' me the runaround."
2) A new unit member could be given a runaround, a prank errand looking for some fictitious item.

**ruptured duck**  Honorable Discharge Emblem and Honorable Discharge Pin worn over the right breast pocket signifying a serviceman had been discharged. Also "Discharge Button/Pin," "Screaming Eagle Button," "bird of paradise," "the Duck," and "homing pigeon" (heads for home). The soldier was authorized to wear his uniform for up to 30 days after discharge.

**Russki**  Russian, "Russ."

**rusting gun**  Marine Reising .45-cal. M50 and M55 submachine-gun, issued until replaced by Thompsons. Also referred to as "Buck Rogers gun" owing to its somewhat streamlined futuristic appearance. Its low-grade metal rusted, it jammed in the sand, and Marines declared, "It's not even a good club."

# S  Sugar (Sail)

**782 gear**  Marine individual equipment, web gear, derived from the title of the form for which Marines signed for the gear.

**sack time**  Sleeping. "Hit the sack."

**Sad Sack**  Sad Sack was created by Sergeant George Baker and debuted in May 1942 in *Yank Magazine*, an Army weekly. Private Sad Sack was a hopelessly inept and clumsy soldier. The name was applied to anyone similarly cursed.

**salt and batter**  Assault and battery, a chargeable offense.

**salty**  1) Someone experienced, an "old salt."
2) Something well used, "broken in," like "salty-assed utilities" that had been washed until they were almost white.

| | |
|---|---|
| Sandy Andy | Pair of 4.5in Mk 7 barrage rocket racks (each gravity-fed rack held 12 rockets) mounted on a 1-ton truck and used by the Marines. A Sandy Andy was a type of turn-of-the-century sandbox toy. |
| satchel change | Haversack or other fabric container packed with 8–20lb of demolitions and fitted with a friction igniter, short length of time delay fuse, and detonator. They were hand-thrown into pillboxes, defended buildings, caves, etc. Also used to destroy obstacles. |
| saucer cap | Service cap with visor. |
| sawbuck | $10 bill, from the crossed legs of a sawhorse and an X – the Roman number 10. Also "saw," and "ten-spot." A "double-sawbuck" was $20. |
| scattergun | Shotgun. Two types of 12-ga. pump shotguns with 20in barrels were used: "trench guns" with barrel protector and bayonet lug, and "riot guns," which lacked these fittings and were used for guard duty. |
| score, the | Accurate information. "What's the score?" meant "what's going on?" |
| screaming mimis | 1) German multiple-tube/rail rocket launchers of various calibers known as the *Nebelwerfer*. The name was owed to the rocket's shriek. 2) Japanese 320mm spigot mortar firing a 675lb projectile. 3) Screaming mimis was also slang for *delirium tremens*, the "shakes" of alcohol withdrawal. |
| screwball | Unstable or odd person. |
| scum *or* slum | Mulligan stew, a meat stew of chopped beef, potatoes, onions, and gravy. It was quick to |

prepare and easy to keep hot, though its "scum" nickname indicates that it was less than tasty. The "slum" is derived from Slumgullion or SOB stew/slum made of similar ingredients. A West Point football song was *Sons of Scum and Gravy*.

**scum-burner**
1) One who eats Army chow.
2) A cook.

**scum-wagon**
Mobile field kitchen, "scum/slum cannon."

**scuttlebutt**
1) Shipboard water fountain.
2) Rumors, gossip as told around the scuttlebutt.

**sea bag**
Marine canvas bag for carrying clothing. See "duffle bag."

**Seabees**
Naval Construction Battalions. "Seabee" is derived from the abbreviation "CB," also interpreted as Confused Bastards.

**sea daddy**
Veteran Marine taking a recruit in hand and teaching him.

**sea-going soldier/ bellhop**
Marine. Specifically those assigned to ship's detachments.

**seagull**
1) Chicken served on Sunday in Marine mess halls.
2) Prostitute specializing in the unique requirements of Marines and sailors.

**sealed in a blanket**
Dead and buried on the battlefield. This term comes from the fact that the body was simply wrapped in a blanket for burial. Also "sealed in a poncho."

**sea stories**
Exaggerated stories related by Marines and sailors.

**Section Eight**
A "crazy person." This term comes from the Army Regulation 615-360, Section 8

(paragraph 148 1/2 in the old regulation) regarding mental instability or insanity. A discharge under this section was known as a "Section Eight Discharge".

**seventy-five**    Any of the 75mm field guns, tank guns, and pack howitzers.

**seventy-five pack**    75mm M1A1 pack howitzer. Lightweight howitzer that could be broken down into components to be loaded on pack mules ("jackass gun") or dropped by parachute.

**seventy-six**    76mm gun mounted on later M4 tanks and M18 tank destroyers.

**shanghaied**    Transferred to another unit without request or against the soldier's desire. The term originated in the Chinese port of Shanghai where masters of American tea-clippers were delayed for want of crews. They would pay the Chinese owners of bars to drug the drunken seamen's drinks and hustle unconscious sailors aboard waiting ships.

**shavetail**    Uncomplimentary term for a newly commissioned 2nd lieutenant, "half-lieutenant," "twink." The old-style rectangular shoulder tabs for a 2nd lieutenant did not have gold bars, but were bare. Newly broken Army mules had their tails shaved bare for identification. The similarities were obvious.

**shell shock**    Physical and metal exhaustion, extreme stress, neuroses. Also "battle fatigue," "combat exhaustion," "combat fatigue," and "cracked up." The Army listed such casualities as exhaustion cases. It was not until 1943 that combat fatigue began to be accepted as a psychiatric problem and an anxiety-related disorder.

**shingles**
Toast. The term originated from the rather uninspiring fact that it was square and brown like a roof shingle.

**shit–can**
1) Abort, cancel.
2) To throw away something, to trash–can it.

**shit–paper**
Toilet paper or "TP" (pronounced "tee-pee"), a hugely valuable frontline material.

**shits**
Gastrointestinal illness, diarrhea, dysentery. Also "runs," "trot," or "mess gear shits" (if contracted from poorly cleaned gear).

**shit, shower, and shave**
Rushed morning ritual, but one that covered all major bases, performed when reveille was sounded and before falling out for formation.

**shoebox mine**
Small German antipersonnel mine in a wooden box, the Schützenmine 42 and 43. It could not be detected by magnetic mine detectors.

**short–arm inspection**
A venereal disease inspection, conducted by medical personnel ("pecker-checkers") and initiated with the command "Fall out in raincoats and jock straps." Also "pecker parade," or "pecker check."

**short round**
1) Artillery or mortar round falling short of the target, especially if it fell among friendly troops.
2) Something fouled up.

**short–snorter**
US dollar bill or enemy occupation currency notes on which one would have buddies, commanders, and VIPs sign their names as a keepsake. When one was filled with signatures additional bills would be pasted end-to-end similar to a scroll.

**short–timer**
Individual with only a short time remaining on his enlistment or overseas duty tour.

| | |
|---|---|
| **shove off** | Depart, scram. "Why don't you shove off?" "I'm shovin' off." |
| **sick, lame, and lazy** | The troops reporting for sick call or the injured and ill troops left in the rear. |
| **sidearm** | Handgun, pistol, or revolver. |
| **Siegfried Line** | German western frontier defenses. The German name was the *Westwall*. |
| **since Christ was a corporal** | A long time. "He's been top kick since Christ was a corporal." |
| **sixty** | 60mm M2 mortar, the standard company mortar. |
| **Ski** | Standard nickname for anyone whose last name ended with "ski." |
| **skinny** | Information, news. "What's the skinny?" |
| **Skipper** | Commander of a Marine company/battery. |
| **skirt** | A touching word for girl. Also "apron." |
| **skirt-chaser** | Woman-chaser, ladies' man, Jane-crazy. |
| **skivvies** | Underwear, "undergear." |
| **Skivvies house** | House of ill-repute. |
| **slacker** | Lazy, unmotivated person who does not carry his load, or who tries to beat fatigue details. |
| **slit trench** | Short trench used for shelter and not usually intended as a fighting position. |
| **slob** | An uncouth, grubby, and generally unpleasant person. Not someone good to share long hours in a foxhole with. |
| **slop chute** | Canteen on a Marine base (from ship's garbage chute). A "wet canteen" sold beer. |
| **Slot, The** | New Georgia Sound, a channel between the two chains of islands comprising the Solomon |

|   |   |
|---|---|
| | Islands. Japanese ships ("Tokyo Express") heading for Bougainville to attack American positions on Guadalcanal made their run down The Slot. |
| **Smiling Al** | Field Marshal Albert Kesselring (1885–1960), Senior Commander, South (Italy). GIs bestowed this nickname because of his invitingly happy smile seen in the one published photograph. |
| **smokescreen** | 1) Smoke laid by artillery, mortars, grenades, pots, or aircraft to screen friendly movements or blind the enemy.<br>2) Cover up or mislead. |
| **smoking lamp is lit/out** | Permission to smoke is granted/extinguish smokes. Marine term. |
| **SNAFU** | Situation Normal, All Fucked Up. The most common of several similar acronyms for venting frustration with the military way of doing things – the right way, the wrong way, and the Army way. |
| **sneaking and peeping** | A more accurate description of scouting and patrolling. |
| **snow job** | To hoodwink or fool someone. Pulling the wool over someone's eyes. The term comes from not being able to see when caught in a blinding snow storm. |
| **snow suit** | Any white coverall for snow camouflage. |
| **Snow White** | Army nurse, owing to the white duty uniform. |
| **snub-nosed one-oh-five** | 105mm M3 howitzer, a shorter-barreled, lighter-weight piece than the standard M2A1. Also "sawed-off one-oh-five," or "infantryman's cannon." |

| | |
|---|---|
| SOL | Shit Out of Luck. Cleaned up for polite conversation to mean "Sure Out of Luck." |
| sore | Angry. "The Top's sore at ya." |
| SOS | Shit on a shingle. Also "stuff on a shingle," "mud on a shingle." The ever-popular creamed, chipped, or ground beef on toast. |
| sound off | 1) To identify oneself in formation when one's name is called.<br>2) To gripe, complain, state a grievance. |
| sound-powered phone | TS-10 field telephone. It did not require batteries. |
| sour | Something turned bad. "The patrol's gone sour." |
| southpaw | Nickname for left-handed person. Also known as a "leftie." |
| Spam-basher | An amateur prostitute or promiscuous girl soliciting food rather than money. See also "victory girl." |
| Spam Ribbon | European–African–Middle Eastern Campaign Medal, named on account of the wearying excess of Spam served to troops in these theaters. The term originated during the North Africa Campaign. |
| sparks, sparky | Radio operator. |
| spinning wheels | Wasting time or effort, just as a vehicle stuck in mud spins its wheels to no avail. |
| spit-shine | Method of polishing leather footwear to a high gloss. A can of polish was opened, lit with a match, and the flame blown out after a few seconds. The melted polish was dabbed on a rag then, with either water or spit, was worked into |

# WHAT *NOT* TO CALL YOUR CO...

| | |
|---|---|
| apple-knocker | goon |
| army dick | hayseed |
| blank | jerk |
| bowlegs | joker |
| brownnoser | knucklehead |
| bum | latrine lawyer |
| bunk lizard | meathead |
| chump | pogue |
| dead battery | screwball |
| eight ball | slacker |
| freeloader | slob |
| gazoonie | tough guy |
| gold brick | whiskey warrior |
| goofball | zero |

the boot. The process would be repeated, building up layers of polish. It would require several sessions to develop a deep shine and many more to maintain it and buff out scratches and blemishes. The phrase "spit-and-polish," clean to excessiveness, was derived from the term.

**spokane**  Pork and beans.

**spud**  Potato.

**spreading it thick**  Being overly, and irritatingly, complimentary. Also "laying it on thick," "spreading applesauce," "baloney," "bull," "bunk," and "crap."

**squad bay**  Room within a barracks; ostensibly for a squad (8–12 men), but in reality most were for a platoon (30–40 men).

| | |
|---|---|
| **squared away** | Everything in order, shipshape. "Get your gear squared away." |
| **squawk box** | Intercom loudspeaker or radio, "bitch box." |
| **stack arms** | 1) To stack rifles in a tripod-like arrangement when they were not needed for training or fatigues.<br>2) An individual who, fed up with his lot, gives up, becomes unmotivated. |
| **stacking swivel, by the** | 1) A stacking swivel was a double-hook on the forearm of rifles allowing them to be fastened together in a tripod when stacked. See "stack arms."<br>2) To "grab someone by the stacking swivel and shake him by the neck," meant to launch a surprise attack on someone and grab him by the throat. |
| **stars and bars** | Officers in general, referring to their rank insignia. |
| **Stateside** | Continental United States – Home, Zone of Interior (ZI) in impenetrable military parlance. |
| **steak 'n eggs breakfast** | Called a "battle breakfast" in the Navy, a traditional hearty breakfast served to troops aboard transports on the morning of an amphibious assault (interestingly saving the best food for serving to men sick with worry). |
| **stiff** | A dead body. |
| **stockade** | A military post's confinement facility or jail. |
| **stow it** | 1) To store something, to pack it up.<br>2) An order to stop, to keep one's opinion to oneself. "Stow it buddy, I don't wanta hear it." |
| **straddle trench** | Narrow latrine trench over which one precariously squatted. Also "shit hole." |

| | |
|---|---|
| **straight leg** | A non-parachutist. Often said to refer to the way paratroopers landed with bent knees, while other soldiers had straight legs. It actually referred to the paratrooper practice of blousing trousers in jump boots, while non-parachutists had straight trousers. |
| **streamer** | Parachute malfunction in which the canopy failed to open and streamed above the falling jumper – not a good situation. |
| **striker** | Officer's enlisted aide, "personal orderly." An unofficial duty for which an officer paid a volunteering enlisted man for minor personal services. The practice quickly fell from use early in the war. |
| **stripes** | Point-up chevrons (inverted "V") and inverted arches (rockers) identifying enlisted rank. Also "crow tracks," "hooks," and "doglegs." |
| **stovepipe** | "Bazooka," and also a mortar. |
| **sugar report** | Love letter. |
| **SUGAR-SUGAR** | The SS. In message traffic abbreviations were spelled out using the phonetic alphabet. Therefore, the SS was identified as Sugar-Sugar. |
| **sulfa powder/ tablets** | In 1941 the drug sulfanilamide was introduced to prevent wound infections. A packet of sulfanilamide powder was enclosed with Carlisle bandages to be sprinkled on wounds. Six or eight sulfa tablets were also taken by mouth with half a canteen of water. They could not be taken without water or wine, unless it would be available within a couple of hours as without ample water sulfa crystallized in the kidneys and was not absorbed properly. |

| | |
|---|---|
| suntans | Army tan wool "tropical worsted" uniform, "TWs," "trops" (Marines). |
| SUSFU | An expression of continuing military efficiency – Situation Unchanged, Still Fucked (Fouled) Up. |
| sweating it out | To wait with obvious anxiety. To endure anticipation of an upcoming event such as action. |
| swell | Good, great. With the right delivery it could mean exactly the opposite. |
| Swing cap | Billed field cap promoted by Major General Joseph M. Swing, 11th Airborne Division. |

# T                          Tare

| | |
|---|---|
| 3.2 *or* three-two beer | Annoyingly weak 3.2-percent alcohol content beer, "Army brew." Sold on military posts as opposed to civilian 4.7-percent beer. |
| take off | To leave, to tell someone to leave. |

*The emphasis on the importance of sulfa tablets resulted in a lack of reluctance in taking them when wounded.*

| | |
|---|---|
| **tank-buster, tank-killer** | Any effective antitank weapon. |
| **taps** | Dead. The bugle call Taps was heard on two occasions, it signaled the end of the duty day and it was sounded at military funerals. |
| **TARFU** | Things Are Really Fucked (Fouled) Up. |
| **target paste** | White gravy. This watery gravy had the consistency of the paste used for sticking paper patches over bullet holes in targets. Both were made of flour and water, although the gravy also included bacon grease. |
| **tarpaper shack/hut** | Temporary quarters of wood-frame construction, walled with tarpaper (felt) and roofed with corrugated steel on wooden decks or concrete slabs. Sometimes plywood-sided. They could be squad-size huts or large H-shaped barracks. |
| **tear gas** | Chloracetophenone is not really a gas, but a micro-fine powder that when burned induced tears in the eyes and a burning sensation in the nose, mouth, throat, lungs, and on moist body surfaces such as under the arms and the groin. It was used as a riot-control agent, flushing the enemy from enclosed structures (though it was seldom used in combat), and to simulate chemical agents in training. Officially "irritant" or "riot-control agent." |
| **tear off a strip** | To rebuke or reprimand. The term was figurative as it seldom resulted in a reduction in grade. Also "tear off a piece of ass." |
| **tent city** | Temporary encampment, less than luxuriously composed of tents erected in blocks gridded by dirt streets. Apart from quarters, all facilities, |

including headquarters, supply rooms, kitchens, mess halls, chapels, theaters, etc., were housed in tents.

**tent peg**        Short, light bayonet for Johnson M1941 rifle.

**terps**        Quick-fire term for interpreters.

**thirty-cal**        Any .30-cal. weapon, but most commonly .30-cal. machine-guns. "Get that thirty into position!"

# THOUSAND-MILE *OR* -YARD STARE

The sightless stare of the combat-exhausted infantrymen gazing vacantly, not only into the distance, but also at an indefinite future. Also "gooney bird stare" – a detached, vacant gaze that gave the impression that the soldier was looking right through anyone in his field of vision. The shock of prolonged combat was an assault on all the senses, aggravated by fear, apprehension, physical and mental exhaustion, sleep deprivation, irregular and poor food, dehydration, and exposure to climate extremes. Confusion, detachment, disorientation, and sensitivity to sound were among the symptoms. With the immune system battered the soldier became susceptible to illness and infections. The psychological and physiological impact affected each individual differently and there was no predicting who would suffer, or to what extent. Tom Lea, a Marine combat artist, captured the haunting representation in the eyes of a Marine on Peleliu in 1944, in his artwork *The Two-thousand Yard Stare*. Of his unnamed and perhaps composite subject Lea said, "He left the States 31 months ago. He was wounded in his first campaign. He has had tropical diseases. He half-sleeps at night and gouges Japs out of holes all day. Two-thirds of his company has been killed or wounded. He will return to attack this morning. How much can a human being endure?"

| | |
|---|---|
| **thirty–eight** | Smith & Wesson .38–cal. special revolvers. |
| **thousand–mile shirt** | Olive-drab wool shirt. It might have to last a "thousand miles" before replaced. |
| **thousand–mile** *or* **–yard stare** | See box on previous page. |
| **three–incher** | Any 3in antiaircraft, antitank, or tank destroyer gun. Weapons designated 3in and 76mm were the same caliber and used the same projectiles, but different cartridge cases. |
| **three up and three down** | Master sergeant (grade 1) owing to three chevrons and three rockers. Also "six-striper." |
| **three volleys** | Three seven-rifle volleys are fired at military funerals by a "firing party" (*not* a "firing squad," which was employed for executions). It is not a "21-gun salute," in which each shot is fired individually for heads of state. |
| **throw the book** | Punishment meted out at a court martial. The book was the Manual of Courts Martial. A court might be lenient if it chose, but if really fired up it could also impose the maximum sentence or charge the individual with all applicable crimes – "throw the book at him." |
| **thumbs up** | Giving/given approval. "The CO's given a thumbs up." A positive response, green light, everything is okay. A gesture with the same meanings. "Thumbs down" is a negative. |
| **tie-tie** | Soldier's name for a length of cord with two clips every 10in. It was cut in lengths between each clip. The clips held laundry and the cords were tied to a cloth line. |
| **T-mine** | German *Tellermine* (plate mine), an antitank mine. |

| | |
|---|---|
| **toe parade** | Foot inspection. Care of the feet was absolutely essential to maintain efficiency. Such inspections were the responsibility of NCOs, and must have been rather unpleasant. |
| **Toilet Seat** | Meritorious Service Unit Insignia. A circular embroidered gold wreath open at the top, reminiscent of a toilet seat and worn on the right coat cuff. |
| **Tokyo Rose** | See box below. |
| **tombstone promotion** | Practice of promoting retiring combat-decorated officers one grade for distinguished service. They received only the rank, though, and not the pay, unless they came on active |

# TOKYO ROSE

"Tokyo Rose" is usually thought to be Iva Ikuko Toguri, a California-born Japanese-American who was stranded in Japan when the war began. She was coerced into broadcasting an entertainment and propaganda show on Radio Tokyo called "The Zero Hour" (340 broadcasts). Her radio name was "Orphan Ann" and she was never introduced as "Tokyo Rose." "Tokyo Rose" was a fabrication of American servicemen and was in limited use by late 1942 and general use in mid-1943. It was the collective name for 14 English-speaking female announcers. Many of the others broadcast more adverse propaganda such as "Madame Tojo" (Foumy Saisho) and "Little Margie" (Myrtle Lipton). After the war the search for "Tokyo Rose" began. Iva Toguri was the only one arrested and charged with treason. She served six years, many think unfairly. She was ordered deported, but successfully fought the order. She was pardoned by President Gerald R. Ford in 1977 and died in 2006 in Chicago as Iva Toguri D'Aquino.

duty for at least one year in the tombstone rank, after which they would receive that rank's retirement pay. The practice was halted in 1957.

| | |
|---|---|
| **Tommy gun** | 1) Thompson .45-cal. M1928A1, M1, and M1A1 submachine-guns.<br>2) Any submachine-gun, "chopper." |
| **TNT** | 1) Today, Not Tomorrow – do it now.<br>2) Trinitrotoluene, one of the most widely used US high-explosives. |
| **toothpick village** | Wooden barracks, usually two-story. |
| **top off** | Filling up a vehicle's fuel tank before continuing a mission. A tank might "top off" its ammunition load. |
| **tough guy** | Self-styled hard individual, hard-nose, hard-ass. "So you're a tough guy?" |
| **trench knife** | Fighting knife fitted with "brass knuckles" dating from WWI – the M1917 and M1918 Mk 1 were reissued in WWII. |
| **trigger happy** | Lack of fire discipline. What happens when green or overanxious troops are unavoidably given enormous personal firepower. |
| **tropical chocolate** | Special blend of chocolate developed by Hershey, which was resistant to melting in high temperatures. |
| **triple-A** | 1) Antiaircraft Artillery.<br>2) AA units of the Coast Artillery. |
| **triple-nickel** | Any unit designated "555th," e.g. 555th Parachute Infantry Battalion. |
| **TS** | Tough shit – that's too bad, that's the breaks. An equally sensitive response was "Tough titty!" |

**TS card**     Tough shit card. Gag cards issued by some chaplains listing complaints for which nothing could be done, such as girlfriend problems back at home, a superior who had it in for the soldier, pay problems, no promotion, etc. Once the card was fully punched the bearer was authorized to cry on the chaplain's shoulder.

**tug**     Transport aircraft, usually a C-47, that towed one or two gliders. See "Waco."

**turnkey**     Stockade or guardhouse jailer.

**twenty**     The 20mm Mk 2 and Mk 4 antiaircraft guns made by Oerlikon. These Swiss-designed AA guns were found on warships, but also used by the Marines as a land-based weapon. Also "twin twenty."

*Veterans tended to view green troops with justified skepticism.*

| | |
|---|---|
| **two-bits** | A quarter, 25 cents. In the old West during the gold rush small "bits" of gold nuggets were used as tender and valued at 12 cents, thus two bits was worth a quarter of a dollar. In early America Spanish-milled dollars were cut into eight equal pieces – bits. One bit equaled ⅛ of a dollar and 2 bits equaled ⅜ or ¼ of a dollar. |
| **two up, one back** | Basic tactical concept of units organized into three subunits, two subunits forward, one in reserve. |

# U     Uncle (Unit)

| | |
|---|---|
| **U2** | Gavutu Island north of Guadalcanal. |
| **umbrella** | Parachute. Paratroopers used two parachutes, the back-mounted main parachute, and the chest-mounted reserve. |
| **unbloused** | Refers to shirt skirt or trouser cuffs that are not tucked into trousers or boots/leggings. |
| **Uncle Sam** | Recruiting poster personality ("Uncle Sam wants you!"), also came to mean the US Government. |
| **Uncle Sam's party** | Payday. |
| **Uncle Sugar** | US Government or the United States of America, derived from the phonetic alphabet, UNCLE SUGAR for US. |
| **USO card** | Gag card that supposedly granted one the privilege of having sex with United Services Organizations (USO) hostesses. Established by request of the President, the USO was a private, nonprofit organization providing morale and |

recreational services to forces personnel and sponsored by the National Catholic Community Service, National Jewish Welfare Board, National Travelers Aid Association, Salvation Army, Young Men's Christian Association, and Young Women's Christian Association.

**utilities**   Marine field and work uniform, "dungarees."

# V   Victor

**Vella**   Vella Lavella Island, New Georgia Group.

**Very pistol**   Flare or signal pistol or gun. Sometimes misspelled "Verey."

**victory girl**   An ever-popular amateur prostitute or promiscuous girl, often a teenager. Also "V-girl," "good-time girl," "pick-up girl," "cuddle bunny," "patriotute," "chippy," and "round-heel." Some did not solicit money, but were compassionate for young men going overseas to possible death. They were caught up in the excitement and patriotic fervor of the times. See also "Spam-basher." and "khacki-whacky."

**vitamin pill**   M7 grenade-launcher auxiliary cartridge fitted in the muzzle end of a rifle grenade launcher, boosting the grenade's range by 60–100 yards.

**V-mail**   Airgraph letters. From May 1942 servicemen wrote letters on special forms, which were microfilmed, flown to Washington, DC, enlarged, photo-printed, and mailed to the address to save weight and space.

# W          William

**Waco**             CG-4A cargo glider, the most widely used US
                     glider. Waco means Weaver Aircraft Company,
                     but they were built by 12 companies. The British
                     called it the "Hadrian."

**wagon train**      Truck convoy.

**walkie-talkie**    SCR-300 backpack company radio. Compare to
                     "handie-talkie."

**war baby/child**   A child of a serviceman born during the war
                     years. Some couples decided to have a child in
                     case the serviceman did not return. Many more
                     chose to wait until after the war, resulting in a
                     postwar "baby boom."

**war bride**        Soldier's foreign bride. Special permission had to
                     be granted to marry a foreigner, and it was
                     officially discouraged, but frequently to no avail.

**war nerves**       The jittery effects of war on the minds of
                     military and civilian populations.

**war time**         Daylight saving time or "summer time," which
                     was one hour ahead of standard time; an effort to
                     conserve power by using less electricity and
                     heating. In effect from February 2, 1942 to
                     September 30, 1945.

**washout/washed out** Soldier terminated from a training course, failed.

**water-cooled fifty** Browning .50-cal. M1921A1 and M2 AA
                     machine-guns. Most Browning .50-cal. M2s
                     were air-cooled.

**water-cooled thirty** Browning .30-cal. M1917A1 heavy machine-
                     gun, ".30-cal heavy machine-gun."

**weapons carrier**  ¾-ton 4x4 cargo truck used to tow or transport
                     weapons as well as for other general uses.

**web gear**          Cartridge and pistol belts, ammunition pouches, first aid pouches, canteen and entrenching tool carriers, belt suspenders, and other individual equipment made of woven cotton webbing and canvas.

**wheelbarrow**       Sedan used to transport officers, "staff car." These were slightly modified civilian automobiles.

*"Th' krauts ain't followin' ya so good on 'Lili Marlene' tonight, Joe. Ya think maybe somethin' happened to their tenor?" (Bill Mauldin © Stars and Stripes)*

FUBAR: F***ed Up Beyond All Recognition

**Where am I room?** Phrase neatly encapsulating the experience of waking in a hotel room with a strange girl, or an empty room and an empty wallet.

**whiskey warrior** A soldier powered by liquid courage. A "lush" or "boozer."

**White scout car** Truck-like M3A1 scout car that saw limited early-war use. Also "tub" because of its open-topped fighting compartment.

**white ticket/ discharge** Honorable discharge which was printed on white paper.

**whitewashing rocks** Performing some useless, terminally dull chore. From the practice of whitewashing the rocks lining sidewalks to headquarters.

**whole nine yards, the** Give it or commit everything, totally. Many explanations have been proposed, one being that it referred to fighter planes, said to carry 9 yards of machine-gun belts, expending their ammunition in one pass. More than likely it originated from an old British term "up to the nines," meaning perfectly or thoroughly.

**whore's bath** Sponge or rag bath from a helmet or bucket.

**Wilco** Radio/telephone proword for "will comply."

**Willie and Joe** Two bedraggled, cynical, dry-humored infantrymen, the quintessential "dogfaces." Sergeant Bill Mauldin rendered these characters in cartoons between 1940 and 1945, first for the *45th Division News* and then, from 1943, in *Stars and Stripes*. See cartoon on previous page.

**Willie Peter** Phonetic alphabet for "WP" – white phosphorus, a bursting-type casualty-producing smoke projectile or grenade. Also "Willie Pete."

## ZOOT SUIT

An exorbitantly exaggerated apparel worn by Mexican-American, Filipino-American, and black youths (sometimes with a criminal element), predominately in Los Angeles and Harlem as well as other areas. It consisted of overly long suit coats with wide lapels and padded shoulders; high-waisted, wide-legged trousers pegged at the ankles; watch chain hanging to the knees; broad-brimmed felt fedoras; and pointed-toe shoes. Zoot suit came to mean any flashy or extreme clothing. Zoot suit production was halted by the War Production Board as being wasteful of fabric. In June 1943 Mexican-American zoot-suiters, known as *pachocos*, in Los Angeles were accused of assaulting servicemen. Servicemen had long resented the unconventional, draft-dodging zoot-suiters roaming streets while they served the country. In the racially charged situation soldiers, Marines, and sailors turned out to find and attack zoot-suiters, ripping off and burning their suits. Hundreds of zoot-suiters were arrested over a ten-day period, but only nine sailors.

*The contrasts between the zoot-suiters and servicemen were readily apparent and went far beyond dress.*

**Wimpy special**     Hamburgers served in Austria and named after the Popeye cartoon character J. Wellington Wimpy.

**wind dummy**     Lone, and lonely, paratrooper who jumped over a drop zone prior to other jumpers. He would not steer so as to allow jumpmasters in the aircraft to determine wind drift and adjust the parachute release point. This practice was done only in training.

**windjammer**     Bugler.

**woodpecker**     Japanese 6.5mm and 7.7mm light machine guns, so called owing to their sharp, slow, firing sound.

**Woofus**     Landing Craft, Medium (Rocket) – LCM(R). A barrage rocket-firing ship. So named as soldiers asked, "Woofus ya' call that thing?"

**woof woof**     A noisy battalion sergeant major, a master sergeant. An older NCO who woofed at the troops over infractions and their many non-regulation faults.

**wop**     An Italian, "Dago," "guinea," "Itey." See "IT."

**working over**     Beat up, place fire on a target, "We gave it a good workin' over."

# X     Xray

**Xmas Island**     Christmas Island, Line Islands. Official shorthand name. There are two Xmas Islands, the US possession southwest of Hawaii and an Australian possession in the Indian Ocean south of Java.

# Y     Yoke

**yardbird** — Recruit quarantined to the reception center, "yearling."

**Yellowlegs** — Cavalryman. Also "trooper."

**yellow ticket/ discharge** — Dishonorable discharge which was printed on yellow paper.

**You don't hear the one that gets you** — A reminder that if you hear an incoming artillery or mortar round then you may be safe, as the round has already passed over. The round you do not hear is the one that may kill or wound you.

**You'll be sorreeee!** — Shouted by recruits undergoing boot camp to newly arrived raw recruits. Shouted to anyone about to undertake something they might regret.

# Z     Zebra (Zed)

**zebra** — An authoritative, long-service NCO with sleeves covered by chevrons, service stripes, and overseas bars.

**Zero** — Nickname for just about any Japanese fighter. The Imperial Navy's "Zero" was the Mitsubishi A6M Type 0 (1940) assigned the Allied codename "Zeke." The Imperial Army's Nakajima Ki43-I Type 1 (1941) was codenamed "Oscar" and often mistaken for the "Zero," as were some other fighters.

**zero** — Loser, an unfortunate person.

**zero-zero** — 1) Point-blank range.
2) Zero visibility.

**Zippo**
1) Flamethrower, portable or tank-mounted, "blowtorch."
2) M4 tank and its alarming propensity for catching fire when struck by a shell. The term Ronson was also used. Both Zippo and Ronson were popular cigarette lighter brands.*

**zombie**
Soldier rated in the lowest classification test category.

**Zoot suit**
See box on page 117.

---

* *"Zippo" and "Ronson" have been attributed to the Germans because of the M4's tendency to catch fire. Neither brand of lighter was produced in Germany, so this origin is doubtful.*

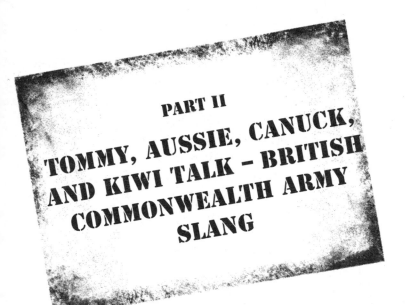

# PART II

# TOMMY, AUSSIE, CANUCK, AND KIWI TALK – BRITISH COMMONWEALTH ARMY SLANG

# BACKGROUND

Soldiers' slang of the British Commonwealth was extremely colorful, with much tracing its etymology to the far corners of the Empire and dating back into the 1800s and before. Many words were derived from Hindustani and other Indian dialects, while others came from Africa and traced their origins back to the Boer Wars or earlier. Many new words were also born in the mud, blood, and absurdity of World War I and were carried over to World War II, although a large number fell from use in the very different age of modern mechanized warfare. Another source that made rich contributions to the soldier's language was the Pidgin English officially spoken in the Northwest Territory of New Guinea. While all members of the Commonwealth contributed to the soldier's vocabulary, the Australians in particular supplied some of the most colorful, ribald, and humorous terms and phrases. A significant amount of slang, to include some of Arabic origin, emerged in the Western Desert and the seesaw battles of North Africa and migrated from there to the Italian theater. A source might state that a particular word was of New Zealand origin, but in the multinational army of the desert it is impossible to say from whom it originated. The same occurred in other theaters, with words and phrases being borrowed from the "Yanks" and others.

# A     Ack

| | |
|---|---|
| **ack** | Assistant in the Royal Artillery, e.g. "GPO Ack" is the assistant gun position officer. |
| **ack–ack** | Anti-aircraft (AA). Said to be the sound of AA guns firing, but it was only the British phonetic alphabet letters for "AA." |
| **ack and quack** | Shorthand for adjutant and quartermaster, the rear elements of a command post. |
| **Ack-I-Foot** | Corruption of the phonetic letters for "AIF," Australian Imperial Force – volunteer expeditionary forces deployable overseas.* See "chocko" and "weekend warriors." |
| **ack-willy** | From the phonetic letters for "AWOL" – Absent Without Leave. |
| **active track** | Active service. |
| **adjie** | Adjutant, a unit's administrative officer. |
| **aeroplane shoot** | Artillery fire directed by a spotter aircraft. |
| **airships and clouds** | Dreamy phrase for sausages and mashed potatoes. Along with "bangers and mash," the term has an Australian origin. |
| **aiwa** | Yes. Used in North Africa and from the Arabic. |
| **Aldershot Cement Company** | Army Catering Corps (ACC) in reference to British Army cooks, which says something of the quality of their food. |
| **all-ways fuse** | No. 247 impact-detonated fuse used on antitank and some other types of hand grenades. |

---

\* *The 1st AIF served in WWI and the 2nd in WWII. Designations of 2nd AIF units were prefixed by "2/," e.g. 2/4th Field Regiment (battalion-size artillery unit).*

| | |
|---|---|
| **ameri–can** | American-made 5-gal. (US) "jerricans." |
| **ammunition number** | Crew-served weapons crewmen who carried, prepared, and passed ammunition to the weapon. |
| **animal** | A contemptuous name for unpopular officers and NCOs. (Australian) |
| **anti–wank** | A schoolboy-crude, but strangely effective substitute for antitank. |
| **aqua** | Water. Used in North Africa and Italy. Adopted from Italian. |
| **Archie** | Field-Marshal Earl Archibald Percival Wavell (1883–1950), commander-in-chief of the Allied Forces in the Middle East until 1940. He was also known as "the Chief." |
| **Archies** | Antiaircraft guns. Derived from a line in the popular song *Archibald, Certainly Not!* When an RAF pilot was asked if German AA fire had given him any trouble, a pilot would give the chipper response: "Archibald? Certainly Not!" It came to mean any AA gun. |
| **armchair commando** | Desk-bound officer or clerk. |
| **Army form blank** | Toilet paper. This form at least had a practical use. |
| **Army right/left!** | Drill instructor's shout when a recruit mixed up his right and left. "Your Army left!" the same as "Your other left!" |
| **arse** | Butt, bum, blot, ass. |
| **arse about face** | Confusion, mix up. "Everything's arse about face in the HQ." |
| **arse crawl** | To curry favor. |
| **arse-hole bored** *or* **punched** | Someone confused or at a loss. |

| | |
|---|---|
| arty | Artillery. A friendly name for a rather unfriendly weapon. |
| "A" Staff | Adjutant-general staff officers responsible for personnel administration. |
| atta-boys | Atebrin anti-malarial tablets taken daily. They gave a yellow cast to the whites of the eyes and the skin. |
| Auk, the | General Sir Claude Auchinleck (1885–1981), commander-in-chief of the Allied Forces in the Middle East. |
| Austen gun | Australian 9mm Mk 1 machine carbine similar in design to the British Sten gun. It saw limited use. |

# B      Beer

| | |
|---|---|
| babbler | A cook, "bab" for short. From "babbling brook," rhyming slang for "cook." Also "greasy." (Australian) |
| back-up | Second helping of food. Also used for left-overs. (Australian) |
| Baedeker invasion | Invasion of Sicily, owing to the Baedeker travel guides issued to the troops. |
| baffle | Royal Corps of Signals security and deception measures. |
| bag, it's in the | Easily accomplished, all but done. |
| bagged | Web anklets (also known as "gaiters") were strapped around the ankles of ankle boots and battle-dress trousers. To allow the trouser to hang smartly over the tops of the anklets, soldiers stamped their feet to "bag" the trousers. |
| bagonet | An old term for bayonet. |

**bailout kit**  Haversack with rations, water bottles, map, compass, etc. used by the Long Range Desert Group (LRDG) and similar units. If they had to abandon their vehicles, they took the kit with them as a survival aid.

**bakelite grenade**  No. 69 offensive blast hand grenade, which created little fragmentation.

**baksheech/ buckshee/bakshish**  Something free of charge. Believed to be derived from Arabic, Urdu, and Hindustani terms.

**banana boat**  Landing craft.

**bandit**  An ack-ack gunner's name for enemy aircraft.

**bandook**  Rifle, "bundook." (Hindustani)

**bang bag**  Simply described cloth-bagged cordite propellant charge for artillery.

**banger**  Sausages had the "honor" of being tagged with more nicknames than any other food item: "bangers," "snags," "snorjers," "bags of mystery" (owing to their questionable contents), "slinger," "barkers," and "dog" (the alleged contents).

**bang-water**  Petrol. (Canadian)

**banjo**  Entrenching tool or shovel. Originally a round-bladed shovel for mining coal. (Australian)

**bantam**  Short-statured individual. Rifles were provided with "bantam" shoulder stocks for shorter troops, especially certain native contingents.

**Bardia Bill**  Nickname for the large-caliber German artillery pieces shelling Tobruk in 1942. Sources are unclear, but they may have been three 21cm Mrs.18 mortars. The term was also applied to any heavy artillery.

| | |
|---|---|
| **bar mine** | German Riegelmine 43, owing to its elongated box shape. |
| **base wallah** | One whose duties kept him in the rear. |
| **bash** | To give or receive a heavy bashing, to suffer high casualties. |
| **basha** | Bamboo hut with thatch or atap roof. Came to mean any small temporary sleeping shelter or billet, including a groundsheet rigged as a "tent." (Indian/Burmese) |
| **bash artist** | Japanese guards notorious for beating up prisoners of war. (Australian) |
| **basher** | 1) Fellow, chap; added as a suffix to a job, e.g. "spud basher" (one peeling potatoes), "sigs basher" (signaller). See "wallah."<br>2) Physical training instructor. |
| **bashing** | Any form of violent effort, such as an assault course, forced march or "square bashing." |
| **bash on** | Carry on, continue doggedly. |
| **BD** | Bomb Disposal Service, Royal Engineers. According to the BD Service handbook, "A member of a BD squad had to be strong, unmarried, and a fast runner. He should be of excellent character and prepared for the afterlife." |
| **beat up** | To attack or to be attacked. "The lorry was beat up." |
| **Beaverette** | Standard 4x2 car with sheet metal armor. An emergency light armored car fielded after Dunkirk, fitted for the Bren light machine-gun or an alternative weapon. The nickname comes from the fact that their production was instigated by Lord Beaverbrook, Minister of Aircraft Production. |

**beehive charge**   A small hand-emplaced shaped charge used to attack pillboxes.

**Belinda**   Barrage balloon, "sausage balloon."

**belly cousin**   A man who slept with a woman whom a pal had also slept with.

**Benghazi cooker/ burner**   A ration tin, often cut down in height, partly filled with sand or soil soaked with petrol on which to brew up tea or heat soup. The term also designated small one-burner field stoves. Also "duke's stove."

**Benghazi stakes**   Punning on horse racing, this refers to the series of advances toward Benghazi, Libya. The subsequent retreats were called the "Benghazi handicaps."

**berker**   A brothel. From the notorious *Sharia el Berker* street in Cairo.

**Betty**   Specifically the Allied codename for the Japanese Imperial Navy Mitsubishi G4M Type 1 bomber. This was one of the most common bombers and consequently "Betty" became a colloquialism for any Japanese two-engine bomber.

**biddy**   A woman, derived from Bridget.

**biff up**   To give oneself a good smartening up for parade.

**big eats**   A stomach-expanding, filling meal.

**Billjims**   Australian soldiers. After the seemingly two most common Australian first names.

**bin**   Poor living quarters.

**bint**   A girl or woman. Arabic word, commonly used in India – usually in a derogatory sense.

**biscuit burgoo**   Porridge made from crumbled up biscuits rather than the usual oatmeal.

| | |
|---|---|
| biscuits | Mattresses comprised of three square sections of the color, shape, and hardness of Army biscuits. |
| bivvy | One- or two-man tent or shelter. Derived from bivouac. |
| black bourse | Black market. Bourse is borrowed from the French for a market or sale. |
| Black Button Mob | The Rifle Brigade (Prince Consort's Own), derived from their black dress uniform buttons. |
| black-out tea | Strong dark tea. |
| Blighty | England. Derived from a Hindustani word meaning "far country." |
| Blimp | Pompous officer. Derived from the *Colonel Blimp* cartoon by David Low, which depicted a typical hidebound, conservative, obese, but heroic regular officer. An officer demonstrating such characteristics was described as being "Blimpery" or "Blimpish." |
| blind | Dud, malfunctioned grenade, mortar bomb or artillery shell. |
| Blitz, the | The incessant air raids on London between September 7, 1940 and May 10, 1941. |
| blitz baby | Child conceived and/or born during the German bombing of London. |
| blitz buggy | Fun-sounding truck with an open troop compartment. Also used for an ambulance. |
| blockbuster | A large high-explosive aerial bomb. It wasn't capable of destroying a city block – the term is actually derived from the British "block of flats," an apartment building. |
| blockhouse | Large reinforced fortification or pillbox. |
| bloke | A man, a fellow. Prior to the turn of the century it meant a low individual as opposed to a "chap" |

and was still considered to mean a man of a lower class than a "chap."

**blood's worth bottling**    Said of a soldier worthy of admiration. (Australian)

**blood wagon**    Ambulance, "blitz wagon."

**bloody**    Extremely. A robust and endlessly used adjective dependent on subsequent adjectives. One can be "bloody good" or "bloody bad." "Bloody hell!" worked as an exclamation of surprise, shock, or anger. "Bloody" was considered a swear word, as it meant "by the blood of God." Also said to be a variation of "by Our Lady."

**bloody balls up**    A no-nonsense way of saying "a total mess."

**blow**    Blow through, leave.

**blower**    Wireless or telephone communications.

**bludge/bludger**    To be idle, usually at another's expense. (Australian)

**blue**    1) Serious mistake.
2) Contradictory nickname for a man with red hair. (Australian)

**blue, the**    The desert. Under certain lighting conditions the distant desert terrain appears blue and merges into the sky.

**Blue Caps** *or* **bluecaps**    Corps of Military Police Vulnerability Points (CMP [VP]) personnel owing to their blue service cap covers. While part of the Military Police, they were actually anti-sabotage security guards for critical facilities.

**blue light**    Exaggerated rumor, mainly in North Africa.

**blue pencil**    An ever-so-polite substitute for a swear word.

"Where is that blue-pencil of a corporal?" Refers to the blue pencil used by censors to line out inappropriate words in letters.

**bluey**

The Middle East, possibly derived for the desert being referred to as "the blue" or the blue of the Mediterranean Sea.

**board**

Medical Board. Wounded soldiers would be "boarded" to determine their continued fitness for active duty and invalided out if unfit. Those sufficiently fit would be found employment in war industries, for which there was a dire manpower shortage, and hence they could unfortunately go from the frontline to the front face of a coal mine.

**bob**

To dither or hesitate before an officer, or on parade.

**bobbery**

Unnecessary noise and fuss. This term was used in India to describe a badly trained pack of hounds.

**bobbing**

1) Fearful of incurring the displeasure of superiors.
2) Currying favor in an obsequious fashion. From "bobbing," to bow or curtsy.

**bod**

Body, a person. "I need three bods for a patrol."

**bodger**

Faker, pretender, a truly worthless person. (Australian)

**bog man**

One whose favorite pastime is abusing troops.

**bog-up**

Make a mess, foul up something. "

**bolo**

Incompetent, eccentric, crazy. It is the imperative of the Urdu verb *bolna* meaning to speak.

**bolshie**

Complainer, a contrary person, and therefore an irritating comrade.

**bomb**                1) Hand grenade.
                        2) Mortar shell.

**Bombay bloomers**     Rather saucy name for a type of khaki drill shorts
                        issued in the Middle East. These had turn-up
                        cuffs, which could be rolled down to ankle length
                        as trousers. They were uncomfortable and short-
                        lived. It also referred to regular shorts of the
                        British-style with widely flaring legs.

**Bombay bowler**       Khaki solar pith helmet with a flattened crown
                        rather than rounded, and a thick brim. It was less
                        popular than the standard "universal foreign service
                        khaki helmet" (Wolseley pattern). See "topi."

**bomb happy**          The curious mental state people enter after
                        being bombed a lot. Also "shell happy," "shell
                        shock," mental stress.

**bombo**               Cheap wine, but no doubt drunk by the gallon.
                        (Australian)

**bone**                Boning boots meant to use the handle of a
                        toothbrush for rubbing spit and leather
                        blacking (polish) into leather ammunition
                        boots. The result was a patent-leather-like finish
                        on the capped toes and heel back. At one time
                        actual smooth bones were used. While it did
                        provide an astounding sheen, the practice
                        eventually ruined the leather, causing it to
                        separate into layers.

**bone sack**           Windproof camouflage jacket worn by
                        paratroopers over web equipment when
                        parachuting. Also "Denison smock."

**bonza**               Very good, all right. (Australian)

**boob**                To make a mistake, blunder. "He boobed that
                        one." Derived from boob, a fool, itself from

booby. The term "booby trap" came from the same word.

**boong**   New Guinea/Papua natives. (See "fuzzy wuzzy"). This was originally a derogatory term for Australian Aboriginals, though by imperial standards it was not considered too derisive when transplanted to New Guinea/Papua natives.

**boong line**   New Guinea/Papua natives operating a line carrying wounded to the rear. Also known, with that curious mix of racism and religiosity common to the empire, as "fuzzy wuzzy angels," hence:
"May the Mothers of Australia
When they offer up a prayer
Mention these impromptu Angels
With the fuzzy wuzzy hair."
(From *The Fuzzy Wuzzy Angels* by Australian sapper H. E. Berous)

**borrow**   Permanently acquire, or, more accurately, steal. Usually refers to items and matériel "borrowed" from other units for the gaining unit's use.

**bought it**   Killed. "He bought it."

**bowler hat**   To be given a bowler hat meant one was sacked and returned to civilian life, or simply discharged upon completion of one's service. No actual bowler hats were involved.

**box**   1) A large fortified complex of trenches, pillboxes, fighting positions, artillery, supply dumps, etc. constructed in North Africa (the Knightsbridge Box, for example). The desert lacked defendable terrain features, so the Allies created well dug-in complexes protected by

minefields, barbed-wire entanglements, and interlocking fields of fire.
2) Positions of all-round defense in Burma.

**box of birds**
Fighting fit, and full of flutterly energy. "He feels like a box of birds today." (Australian)

**box up**
Blotch up, to make a mess of it. "He made a box up of that patrol."

**Boys rifle**
The .55in Mk 1 antitank rifle. Also "Charlie the bastard" on account of its weight, bulk, and ineffectiveness against newer tanks. It did make a nerve-jangling roar, however.

**brass**
Officers, derived from their insignia.

**brassed up/off**
Discouraged, fed up.

**brass hats**
Generals and staff officers.

**brew up**
1) See box on page 136.
2) To brew up a tank or other vehicle was for it to be hit by gunfire and subsequently catch fire, burning vigorously or exploding.

**brick**
Artillery projectile, shell.

**brig**
Brigadier. While often considered equivalent to a US brigadier general, a "brig" in Commonwealth service was not a general officer, but more of a senior colonel. Brigadiers were often promoted directly from lieutenant-colonel (commanding battalions or regiments), bypassing colonel, to go on and command brigades.

**British warm**
Snuggly knee-length, heavy, thick wool double-breasted coat. Worn by colonels and above.

**Broomstick Army**
Local Defence Volunteers and later the Home Guard, known for drilling despondently with broomsticks because of a lack of rifles.

| | |
|---|---|
| **Brothels** | Brussels, Belgium. The city had a predominance of such establishments after liberation. |
| **browned off** | Bored, fed up, angered. Also "brassed off," "cheesed off," and "jarred off." Also, reprimanded by someone. |
| **brown food** | Beery liquid sustenance. Also "wallop," no doubt from its impact on the brain. |
| **brown job** | Service in the Army. A "brown type" was a soldier. Derived from the khaki uniform. |
| **brown nose** | To curry favor, sticking one's nose up a superior's backside. Also "bootlick." |
| **bubble dancing** | Kitchen fatigue, especially when performing the soapy duty of washing pots. |
| **Buck Guard** | Brigade of Guards. "Buck" refers to Buckingham Palace. The Brigade of Guards comprised |

*Even during war soldiers made time for a brew up.*

# BREW UP

Tea is considered to be the quintessential British drink and a great tradition. It was introduced to Britain from China in the 1600s and later imported from India and Ceylon. Britain consequently became the world's largest importer of tea. The tradition of afternoon tea was begun in 1850 by Anna, the Seventh Duchess of Bedford. She ordered that a tray of tea, bread, butter, sandwiches, and cakes be served at 4:00pm – since dinner was at 8:00pm she became hungry in the afternoon. Through invited friends the practice spread and by the 1880s afternoon tea was an established social event. For the Tommy soldier, tea or "brew up" was a far more practical matter, and involved no fine china cups and doilies. At every opportunity, during rest halts, lulls in fighting, or in a bivouac or camp, tea was brewed with a heavy helping of sugar and milk (or, more usually, one of the many milk substitutes). Tea was considered an energy beverage essential to morale and reinvigorating exhausted troops.

Infantry sections and vehicle crews carried an essential "brew up kit" or "brew kit," typically: packets of soluble tea or compressed compo "tea blocks"; sugar; powdered, evaporated, or condensed tinned milk; a book or box of matches; and biscuits, all carried in a 24-hour ration cellophane bag, grenade packing tube, Bren gun magazine pouch, or rifle bandoleer. The "char" was brewed up in a "Dixie" or former ration tin (called a "billy" by Australians) on a "Benghazi cooker," a "Tommy cooker," or a looted German *Esbit* cooker. Often a pair of men was assigned the duty to quickly brew up tea in a well-rehearsed drill during rest halts.

the five Guards regiments, each of which raised a number of battalions to serve in other formations. The Brigade itself was not a tactical formation. The Guards regiments, in order of seniority were: The Grenadier Guards, The Coldstream Guards, The Scots Guards, The Irish Guards, and The Welsh Guards.

| | |
|---|---|
| **bugger** | 1) Ruined, spoiled, "That buggered it." <br> 2) Buggered – wounded. <br> 3) Buggery – sodomy, hence the exclamation "Well, I be buggered!" |
| **Bull, the** | The commanding officer. (Australian) |
| **bull and baloney** | Nonsense, absurd. "Bull" was also used alone and had the same meaning as "bullshit." |
| **bullo** | Nonsense – bull with the common Australian "o" suffix. |
| **Bullocks** | Royal Marines. Also "jollies," "leathernecks," "bootnecks," "the Royals," and "turkeys" (owing to the red on their blue uniforms). |
| **bullshit baffles brains** | A catchy phrase meaning that persistence and a show of knowledge, whether actually possessed or not, is what gets something accomplished rather than actual hard knowledge and experience. |
| **bully beef** | Tinned corned beef, a staple of the Commonwealth soldier. Also "desert chicken" and "bullamakow" (combination of bull and cow in Fijian Pidgin). "Bully" is derived from the French *boeuf bouilli* (boiled beef). |
| **bully beef bomber** | Ration parachute or freefall bundle-drops from aircraft, "biscuit bomber." |

**bumper**     Cigarette butt. "Bumper sniping" was the act of policing (cleaning up) the company area. (Australian)

**bung**     Cheese.

**bunk**     1) Bed, billet.
2) Small room inside the barracks adjacent to troops' barracks room for the platoon's three corporals (section leaders).

**burgoo**     Oat porridge, from the Hindustani *burghul* for porridge.

**bush, the**     Wildness, backcountry. (South African)

**bush artillery**     Australian clerks, cooks, mechanics, and other rear-area personnel manning captured artillery pieces during the defense of Tobruk.

**bush hat**     Slouch hat issued for jungle wear.

**bush shirt**     Lightweight khaki or green drill shirt issued in hot climates.

*The infamous bully beef tin.*

**butterfly bomb**   Small German anti-personnel fragmentation bomb (Sprengbombe Dickwandig 2kg or SD.2). The name is owed to the way the ends of the bomb opened as it descended, the device appearing to flutter to the ground. It was painted green (some all yellow), sometimes with yellow and red stripes, making it appear even more like a large, exploding butterfly. The French called it the *bombe papillon*. The US copied it as the M83 anti-personnel bomb after the war and retained the nickname.

**buzz bomb**   German V1 (Vergeltungswaffe-1). The name "buzz bomb" came about because of the distinctive crackling sound of the V1's pulse jet motor. Also known as the "flying bomb." See also "doodlebug."

**By the centre!**   Mild oath of disbelief. "Wot, you don't know where the maps are! By the centre!" Derived from the drill command for an individual to present and centre himself in front of the formation.

# C   Charlie

**Camel to Consumer**   Gift cigarettes sent from South Africa to troops in North Africa and later Italy. The packages were inscribed with "C to C," which actually stood for "Cape to Cairo." "Camel" implied the draggingly slow mode of delivery.

**came up with the rations**   Said of easily won medals, especially campaign medals – "they just sent them up with the rations."

**Camp Comedian**   Camp Commandant.

**cannon fodder**  Troops who were quite unreasonably expected to follow orders and as Tennyson's poem says, '… not to reason why, … just to do and die.' It specifically referred to infantry and other combat troops.

**Canuck**  A Canadian.

**cap badge**  1) Bone in a soup or stew. "Someone dropped their cap badge in me burgoo."
2) A 3.7in antiaircraft gun, we don't know why.

**cap off**  A soldier ordered to report to the commanding officer on charges. Derived from meekly carrying his cap in hand, as required when reporting indoors.

**caravan**  Clumsy unarmored truck-like command-vehicle described as a caravan-office lorry.

**carry the can**  To take responsibility for one's own or another's actions. To do the job assigned to someone else shirking the duty. See "Joe Soap," and "pass the can."

**castor**  Good, okay. (Australian)

**catch a packet/dose**  To contract the dreaded VD.

**category man**  Soldier who has been assessed by a medical officer (MO), judged unfit for combat duty, and reassigned to services.

**cat stabber**  Issue clasp knife, with a knife blade, marlin spike, screwdriver, and tin- and bottle-openers. Also "jack knife."

**Chad**  A graffiti character complaining of shortages. Originally "Mr. Chad." See "Kilroy was here," Part I.

**chagal**  Canvas water bag used to carry water supplies in the Far East. It was shaped like a goat-skin and the contents were evaporation cooled. (Australian/Indian Army)

**chap**

A fellow, friend. Often considered a higher class than a "bloke." A practice influenced by Public Schools usage, but not limited to that class; a fellow who is "one of us," "of our class." Generally more applicable to officers than humbler soldiers.

**chapplies**

Comfortable leather studded sandals worn by Indian Regiments. One pair was issued in lieu of boots. They allowed sand to fall out and feet to dry. To make sure all toes were retained, extra socks were worn in snowy conditions.

**char**

Tea. Indian units pronounced it "chai." From the Chinese *te chi*, from which both "tea" and "char" are derived. Char is also the numeral "4" in Urdu/Hindustani.

**charpoy-bashing**

Siesta, a favorite leisure activity of the British troops in the Middle and Far East. Charpoy is an Indian word for a bed made from a wooden frame and string cord or bamboo poles and slats.

*Chad complained of ration shortages throughout the war.*

**chatsby**
Substitute word for an unremembered technical word or mechanical part. Also "thingamajig," or "doo-hickey."

**Chelo!**
"Move out!" "Get a move on!"

**cheval de frise**
Portable wooden framework entwined with barbed wire. Also "knife rest," or "Spanish rider."

**chew the rag/fat**
Excessive talking.

**Chicago piano**
Multi-barrel antiaircraft guns.

**chi chi**
Red tape, fuss and bother, from the French slang. Also used to denote the sing-song voice of a person of mixed race in India.

**china**
Mate, companion. So named because of the Cockney rhyming slang for "mate" – "china plate."

**Chindits**
Deep-penetration brigades under Major-General Orde C. Wingate (1903–44) operating behind Japanese lines in Burma. The Chindit was a mythical Burmese beast (*Chinthê*) that guarded temples, half-lion, half-eagle. Also "The Chief's Private Army," the "Chief" being Field-Marshal Lord Wavell (see "Archie"), Supreme Commander of Allied Forces in Burma until August 1943.

**Chinese attack**
Deception operation with a great deal of noise and activity, misleading the enemy into believing an attack was underway and to distract his attention from preparations for the actual attack.

**chocko** *or* **choco**
Australian Conscripted soldiers and militiamen who could not serve outside of Australia or its territories before 1943. The term is derived from "Chocolate soldiers" the name given to them

because of their dark khaki brown uniforms. See also "koalas" and "weekend warriors."

| | |
|---|---|
| chook | Powdered eggs, "chuff." |
| chopped | Dramatically and gruesomely killed, especially if by machine-gun fire. |
| Christmas tree order | Full equipment. An infantryman decked out like an elaborate Christmas tree. |
| chum | Friend. Often used to greet strangers and new arrivals to a unit, hence "new chum." |
| chump | A block-head, a silly fool. "Off his chump" – out of his mind, stupid. |
| Civvy Street | Civilian life. Refers to an individual's pre-military service life. |
| clean fatigue | Work dress. |
| clewing up | Making contact, linking up, conducting liaison (coordinating), giving a briefing. Derived from "clue." |
| clifty | To steal. (New Zealand) |
| clifty wallah | Clever, shrewd fellow. |
| clink | Guard-room, "hutch." Prison, "jug." |
| clockwork mouse or mice | An obviously powerful James ML lightweight motorcycle used by airborne troops. |
| coal box | Black smoke detonations of high-explosive shells. Looked like a coal box had been dropped. |
| coal scuttle helmet | German steel helmet, owing to its similarity to a coal scuttle. |
| cobber | Mate, pal, close companion. (Australian) |

| | |
|---|---|
| **cock** | Nonsense, bull. |
| **cock it up** | Elevate an artillery piece. |
| **cock up** | Complete mess, blunder, as in "He's made a cock-up of it." Not to be confused with "crock up," a nervous breakdown, although one might lead to the other. Derived from beer making – if the batch went bad they turned the cock (tap) up to drain the barrel. |
| **column snake** | Single-file formation in dense jungle or on broken ground. |
| **combined operations** | A military slant on a love affair or marriage which stems from the term for operations involving all three services. |
| **Come up!** | Meaning to "come up" on the promotion list by putting in some service time to gain seniority. |
| **compassionate** | Compassionate leave granted on death of a next of kin or for other serious reasons. |
| **compo ration** | The composition ration fed 14 men three meals for one day. There was also a Pacific compo ration for six men. (The term was also used by US troops, as compos were issued to them in North Africa). |
| **conchie** | Conscientious objector, "Cuthbert." One objecting to military service on religious grounds. |
| **con depot** | Convalescent depot where wounded and ill troops recovered. |
| **cookhouse** | Kitchen. |
| **cookhouse fatigue** | Kitchen duty. |
| **cookie** | Section or crew member who was adept at cooking, and was punished with the task of preparing meals. |

| | |
|---|---|
| cooler | Guard-room, cell, "moosh," "mush." |
| cordex | Detonating cord, primacord. Instantaneous detonating explosive cord similar in appearance to safety fuse. Used to link demolition charges together for simultaneous detonation. |
| corkscrew | Steel barbed-wire picket post with a corkscrew-like end, allowing it to be quietly twisted into the ground rather than hammered in. |
| corp | Corporal, "two striper." |
| crack | Move out fast. "Get cracking!" "Get moving!" |
| crash action | An emergency technique for rapidly getting artillery into action, taking shortcuts around the regular action stations drill. |
| creepers | Lightweight, and very stealthy, suede leather shoes with crepe rubber soles worn on desert night patrols. Also "brothel creepers," or "desert boots." Officers had them custom-made in Cairo. |
| crib | Complain. "To crib." |
| crime | Misdemeanor offence against regulations. To be put on a "fizzer" (charge) was be "crimed." |
| crime sheet | A record of an individual's charges and punishments. |
| croaker | Medical officer, the term having a casualty-troubling connection with "croak" – die. Also, and far more reassuring, "Doc," or "medico." |
| Cross Cocktail | A 40mm cartridge case filled with explosives and fitted with a Mills bomb fuse. Developed by Sergeant A. Cross to attack pillboxes in Italy. |
| cushy | Soft, easy assignment. From the Hindustani *kjush* (pleasure). |

# D Don

| | |
|---|---|
| **dag** | Electric battery, as known by signallers. |
| **dah** | Burmese heavy cutting knife used by some British troops for jungle clearance and as a close-quarters weapon. |
| **Dak** | US-made C-47 Skytrain transport, known as a Dakota to the British. |
| **Dannert wire** | Oil-tempered, barbed, spring-steel coiled concertina wire introduced by the Germans in WWI and invented by a Herr Dannert. The Germans dropped the term, but the British retained it. |
| **Deacon** | AEC Mk 1 6-pdr antitank gun carrier. |
| **dead loss** | Useless person or a waste of time and effort. |
| **dead man's effects** | An appealing name for false teeth, or dentures. |
| **dead meat ticket** | See box opposite. |
| **delousing** | 1) Baking clothing in a special oven to kill lice and their eggs.<br>2) Removing mines and booby traps, a far more dangerous irritant. |
| **demmick** | Soldier on the sick list. |
| **demo** | Demonstration. An exercise to show soldiers how to properly execute tactics, drills, and other actions. |
| **demob** | Demobilization, to be "demobbed," discharged from the service. |
| **demon vino** | Cheap Italian wine. |
| **Desert Rats** | The 7th Armoured Division. Mussolini in a speech referred to the division as the "desert rats." The division quickly and defiantly adopted the name and the jerboa (desert rat) as its |

insignia. Lord Haw-Haw is also said to have referred to the Australian defenders of Tobruk as the "desert rats."

**desert rose**    Large tin with top removed, the bottom perforated with holes, and set in the sand as the crudest of urinals.

**desert-worthy**    Men or equipment conditioned or suited for desert warfare.

## DEAD MEAT TICKET

An identity disc. The Australians first issued a tag in 1906 and the two-tag system became a Commonwealth standard in WWI. Identity discs were issued in sets of two, the green circular No. 1 and the red octagonal (eight-sided) No. 2. They were worn on a cotton tape or cord, leather thong, or metal chain, the latter being provided by the soldier. The No. 1 disc had two holes and the No. 2 disc was attached to it by a short length of cord. A second No. 2 disc was issued for attachment to the anti-gas respirator. If a man were killed, the No. 1 disc remained with the body and the No. 2 was turned into headquarters. Soldiers' lore relates that the colorings helped soldiers remember which tag remained and which was turned in: red meant blood and was to be taken, since the soldier was dead; green meant grass and was to stay with the body. The only information stamped on the discs was the soldier's army number, initials, and surname, and religious denomination. Marking practices differed slightly between Commonwealth nations. Australian discs were additionally marked "AUST," New Zealander "NZ," and Canadian "CDN." Early discs were made of compressed fibreboard. These deteriorated easily, especially in the desert and tropics, plus were destroyed by fire. Stainless steel discs of the same shapes were introduced by 1944, but were not colored.

**Deuce, the**          The second-in-command. Second only to the "Trump," the CO. (Australian.) See "Two I/C."

**di-da-di**          Morse code from the short (dots) and long (dashes) signals. A wireless set or anything related.

**diffy**          Deficient or troublesome. "His rifle was diffy."

**dig**          Loss of privileges owing to charges. A mild disciplinary action.

**Digger hat**          The distinctive wool felt slouch hat worn by Australian troops with a wide pleated puggaree (hat band) and the left side of the brim (leaf) turned up. "Slouch" refers to the rest of the brim.

**Diggers**          Australian troops, but also referred to Australian civilians. It is claimed that New Zealander troops coined the term, being derived from "gumdigger" (one who digs for fossilized kauri gum), but was used by Aussies from 1916. Alternatively, some said it came from the Australian reputation for digging trenches, connected to Australian gold mining in the 1850s.

**dig out**          To perform hard work, work with extra effort.

**dimout**          Partial blackout of questionable effect imposed on Australian cities with the beginning of the Pacific War.

**dim type**          Stupid or dull person.

**dingbat**          An officer's batman, personal servant. (Australian)

**dinger**          Backside. "Dinger drill" – sleeping. (Australian)

**Dingo**          Daimler Mk I and II scout cars, light four-wheeled armored reconnaissance vehicles. The Canadian-built versions were the Lynx Mk I, II, and III.

**dinkey di**          Gospel truth, hence was often used when exaggerating. (Australian)

| | |
|---|---|
| **dinkum** | 1) Reliable person.<br>2) Reliable, good information, "fair dinkum."<br>"Dinkum oil" – accurate, truthful report.<br>(Australian) |
| **dinkum digger** | Solid, reliable soldier or veteran. (Australian) |
| **disasters** | Egyptian currency, piastres. |
| **Div, the** | New Zealand Division, redesignated 2nd (NZ) Division on June 29, 1942 as the successor of the 1916 New Zealand Division. |
| **dixie** | Small oval cooking pot with a frying-pan lid. Used for section and crew cooking, and also for carrying food to forward positions. Came to mean any receptacle for food. From Hindustani *degchi* (small pot). |
| **dixie bashing** | Cleaning pots and pans on kitchen fatigue. |
| **do a 406** | Complete a vehicle inspection. Army Book 406 was a log stating a vehicle's condition, repairs, defects, etc. |
| **doddle** | A job that is easy to perform. "This'll be a doddle." Derived from Low German *dudeltopf* meaning fool, hence an easy task any old simpleton can do. |
| **dodge the column** | Inventively avoiding unwanted duties. Derived from the old practice of individuals making the sick list or finding other duties preventing them from accompanying the column of troops departing for an exercise or campaign. |
| **dog's legs** | NCO's chevrons. |
| **domani** | Tomorrow. Italian word used in North Africa and Italy. |
| **done over** | Wounded or exhausted. (Australian) |

| | |
|---|---|
| **Don-Five** | D.5 field telephone. "Don" being the phonetic letter for "D." |
| **donga** | 1) Improvised dugout or shelter. (Australian) 2) A steep-sided water course, usually dry. Also a "wadi" or "mullah." |
| **donkey's breakfast** | Straw-filled palliasse (mattress), much like a donkey's feedsack. |
| **donnybrook** | A fight. (Irish origin.) |
| **Don R** | Motorcycle dispatch rider, from the phonetic alphabet. |
| **doodlebug** | German V1 (Vergeltungswaffe-1). The doodlebug is an Australian insect which makes an irritating buzzing noise as did the V1. See also "buzz bomb." |
| **doover** | Useful word for any item with an unremembered name. (Australian) |
| **doover hole** | Dugout or slit trench. Mainly used in North Africa. (Australian) |
| **Dorchester** | Armored command vehicle assigned to armored brigade headquarters. It was a roomy and comfortable vehicle hence the name derived from London's luxurious Dorchester hotel. |
| **dragon** | Full-tracked vehicle for towing ("haulage") artillery. |
| **draw the crabs** | To attract enemy attention and draw fire. (Australian) |
| **draw the crow** | To be assigned an undesired fatigue party or task. (Australian) |
| **dressed up like a dog's dinner** | Wearing one's best uniform for an occasion. |

| | |
|---|---|
| **drill pig** | A drill sergeant. |
| **driver op** | Artillery tractor driver who doubled as the radio operator. This term was applied to any drivers who operated a radio as required. |
| **drome** | Short for aerodrome. |
| **drop** | To get into trouble. |
| **drop a bullock** | A serious blunder, to let someone down or get him into trouble. |
| **duck** | General aquatic nickname for a Japanese floatplane. |
| **duffy** | A quaint and understated name for the mind-breaking horror of a jungle close-quarters fire-fight. (Australian) |
| **dug-in job** | Firmly set in a job, usually a cushy base assignment. |
| **dugout** | A small personnel shelter dug into the side of a trench, gully, hillside, etc. |
| **dug-outs** | Retired soldiers, sometimes WWI veterans, recalled to the colors after being "dug out" of hiding in civilian life. |

# E                     Edward

| | |
|---|---|
| **eating irons** | Knife, fork, and spoon. Also "grabbling irons," "tools." Soldiers often stamped their regimental number on the handles. |
| **Egg-whipped** | Corruption of "Eg-ypt." |
| **emu parade/bob** | A line of soldiers advancing almost shoulder-to-shoulder and bobbing up and down like feeding flightless birds as they cleaned up trash in the company area. (Australian) |

| | |
|---|---|
| ersatz | Shoddy, low-grade substitute. From the German *Ersatz* for "replacement" (see Part III). |
| Esau | Bomb Disposal Service nickname for the German 1,000kg bomb. |
| Every Night Something Awful | A less than appreciative term used by troops to refer to the Entertainments National Service Association (ENSA), which provided entertainment shows to troops. They also referred to it as "Even NAAFI Stands Aghast." |
| extract the urine from | A polite phrasing of "Take the piss out of." To knock down a notch, to tell someone off, make fun of. |
| Eyetie | Derogatory term for an Italian. Also "Macaroni" and "ding bat." (Australian) |

# F — Freddie

| | |
|---|---|
| fags | Cigarettes, "smokes." Not derived from a fagot (a bundle of kindling wood) as sometimes assumed, but a "fag end" – the frayed end of a rope. |
| fart arse around | Mess around, waste time, get nothing accomplished. Most soldiers' lives consisted of boredom, so "fart arsing around" was a day well spent. |
| February | The commanding officer, as he had the power to inflict 28 days detention or other punishment. A "February" also used to indicate the sentence of 28 days. |
| feet | Infantry. |
| finito | Finished, done for. Used in Sicily and Italy. (Italian word.) |

| | |
|---|---|
| firewater | Petrol. (Canadian) |
| fitter | Maintenance vehicle. |
| five-five | The 5.5in Mk 3 gun, a corps artillery piece. |
| flap | An alarm (often false) that generated much excitement, to stir things up. |
| flashes | Regimental insignia worn on sleeves. |
| flatirons | Landing Craft Support (LCS). Heavily armed modified landing craft for fire support. The name derived from the Royal Navy gunboats on China's Yangtse River. |
| flea bag | A sleeping bag. Also lovingly referred to as a "fleapit," or "snorebag." |
| flick | Motion picture. To go to the flicks was to go to the cinema. |
| flimsies | Tissue-like paper duplicate message forms, all too easy to rip. |
| flimsy | 2- and 4-imperial gal. petrol tins. The seams split easily causing a great deal of valuable petrol wastage. Even if this didn't happen, they were generally not reusable. Salvation was found in "jerrycans" (see Part I). |
| fling one up | To give a salute, also "sling/throw one up." |
| flit gun | 25-pdr field gun howitzer. At the other end of the scale, a flit gun was also a hand-operated insect sprayer with a plunger tube and spherical repellent canister. |
| flog | To sell Army property, usually rations, fuel, clothing, blankets, and other goods useful to war-pinched civilians. |
| Florrie | Ford truck. |

| | |
|---|---|
| **flying dustbin** | The 40lb petard bomb fired from the 290mm Mk 1 non-recoiling spigot mortar on the Armoured Vehicle, Royal Engineers (AVRE) (Churchill Mk 3 and 4) employed by the 79th Armoured Division (see "Hobart's Funnies"). It looked like a flying small garbage can and was used to blast gaps in obstacles and destroy field fortifications. |
| **Flying Flea** *or* **Flea** | Royal Enfield WD/RE lightweight motorcycle used by airborne troops. |
| **flying fox** | A cable tramway system used by Australians to haul equipment across streams. Named after the large species of gap-leaping bat. |
| **Foo** | Forward Observation Officer of the Royal Artillery. |
| **fore-and-aft cap** | Universal pattern field service cap. Also "forage cap," "side-cap," "splitarse cap" (split ass), and the ever-so-slightly demeaning "cunt cap." The design, also adopted by the US military during WWI (see "overseas cap," Part I), was influenced by the Scottish Glengarry. |
| **Forgotten Army** | No doubt many of the Commonwealth field armies felt they were forgotten, but the one with the strongest claim to the dubious honor is the Fourteenth Army in Burma. |
| **form** | Situation. "What is the form?" What's going on? |
| **four by two** | A 4x2in piece of white flannel for cleaning rifle and machine-gun bores. |
| **four-five** | The 4.5in Mk 1 and 2 guns. These were the divisional heavy artillery pieces. Some 4.5in howitzers were used early in the war. |
| **four-two** | The 4.2in Mk 1 and 2 mortars. The ammunition was not interchangeable with US 4.2in mortars. |

| | |
|---|---|
| **fox** | To deceive and mislead the enemy in a wily manner. Outfox the enemy. |
| **foxhole** | One- or two-man fighting hole or slit trench. |
| **Fred Karno's Army** | Home service troops and service units as described by combat units. Fred Karno was an early 1900s comedian who portrayed an incompetent bungler. |
| **free chewing gum** | Leather chin strap on the hat. (Australian) |
| **frig** | A military operation, whether a training exercise or actual combat operations. |
| **frig about** | Wander around aimlessly. |
| **frigging** | "This is a frigging (fucking) lash up!" |
| **Fritz** | 1) Bomb Disposal Service nickname for the German 1,400kg bomb. |

*"Fire-bomb Fritz" by Reginald Mount, 1942. (The National Archives, Kew, INF 3/1426)*

2) Nickname for the Germans used mainly by the British and the Soviets.

**Frog**  Long established nickname for a Frenchman.

**front the bull**  Report to the commanding officer for a good, stern reprimand or charges. (Australian)

**funkhole**  Foxhole or other position in which soldiers had to live. After a comparatively brief time conditions within became pretty grim, or "funky."

**furniture van**  Box-type body workshop and signals lorry.

**fuzzy wuzzy**  Lovingly crafted term for the indigenous peoples of Papua and New Guinea, "boongs." The term was originally applied to the Sudanese in the 1880s. The nickname is owed, predictably enough, to their tight curly hair. Thousands of natives were employed by the Australia–New Zealand Administrative Unit (AZNAU) as porters, guides, and scouts, providing extremely valuable services apart from nickname inspiration.

# G    George

**Gammon grenade**  No. 82 antitank hand grenade, consisting of a detonator and a small cloth bag that could be filled with a varied amount of explosives as required for the target. Developed by Captain Richard S. Gammon. It was widely used by US paratroopers.

**gap**  To breach an obstacle, and create a gap through which troops and vehicles can pass.

**gas face**  An anti-gas respirator, gasmask. Also "gaspirator," or "nose-bag."

| | |
|---|---|
| **gen** | Information regarding upcoming operations. "Pukka gen" – correct or authentic information, "phoney gen" – questionable information, "duff gen" – incorrect information. |
| **gen king/wallah/ man** | One who usually provides correct or valuable information. Often this was a clerk in ops, intel, or sigs. |
| **get a have on** | Give someone a difficult time. |
| **get a rift on** | Move on, hurry up, get cracking. |
| **getaway man** | A man who follows a short distance behind a patrol. He provides rear security, but his main function is to race off to friendly lines if the patrol is ambushed to report what happened. |
| **get cracking** | Get moving, do something. |
| **get fell in** | Purposely shocking grammar ordering troops to "fall in." |
| **get marched** | To be marched into the commanding officer's office to answer a charge or to formally make a complaint. |
| **get off my back** | Leave me alone, go away. (Australian) |
| **get your finger out** | Get busy, quit loafing, get your finger out of your arse (a position that would obviously limit one's work possibilities). (Australian) |
| **get your knees brown** | Gain experience. Suggestion to a replacement in North Africa whose legs were white between his short cuffs and socks and not yet suntanned. |
| **gharry** | Any type of vehicle in North Africa. From the Hindustani word *gari* (cart). |
| **ghost gun** | Vickers machine-gun operated remotely by a cable. The enemy could fire on it, but was of course unable to kill the crew. |

**giggle hat** Floppy fatigue uniform hat, which had a sloppy, comic appearance. (Australian)

**giggle juice** Liquor. (Australian)

**giggle suit** Fatigue uniform or working dress. (Australian)

**gippo**
1) Gravy.
2) Arab, used principally of Egyptians.

**give me a break** Give me another chance, ease up. (Australian)

**give the game away** Spoil the plan, give away the plan prematurely. (Australian)

**glamour**
1) Service and walking-out dress uniforms.
2) Hair cream, maximizing one's chances of attracting female attention. "He's applying glamour."

**Glasshouse** Detention barracks. Originally applied to Aldershot Command Detention Barracks owing to its glazed roof, but later applied to any such facility.

**going recce** Embarking on a reconnaissance to determine ground or road conditions in advance of the main body.

**goldfish** Tinned sardines.

**gone for six** Dead. From cricket, when the bowler delivers six pitches during an over and is allowed no more – it is the end.

**gong** A circular medal or decoration suspended from a ribbon. However, it was also applied to other shaped medals such as stars. To be "gonged" was to receive a decoration.

**good guts** Information, guts being the core of the matter.

**goonskin** A sleeveless sheepskin-lined vest. "Battle jerkins" were fitted with numerous pockets

|  | for weapon magazines and equipment. See "teddy bear." |
| **go phut/phutt** | A mechanical breakdown. "The bleedin' lorry went phut." |
| **gravel basher** | Drill instructor or physical training instructor. |
| **gravel bashing** | Marching or weapons drill in the barracks square, "square bashing." |
| **Greco** | A Greek. (Italian word.) |
| **green foods** | Jungle rations, owing to their being packaged in green containers and packages for camouflage purposes. |
| **grey back** | A British soldier in India owing to the gray shirts formerly issued to them. |
| **griff** | Reliable information. |
| **Groppi Gong** | The Africa Star for service in North and East Africa between June 10, 1940, and May 12, 1943. "Groppi" was a Cairo confectioner and the name suggested that the award could be earned by merely frequenting the less savory districts of the city. |
| **Groppi's Light Horse** | Rear base troops in the Cairo area. |
| **grub stakes** | An individual's share of field rations. |
| **GSI Medal** | The 1939–45 Star for service between September 3, 1939, and August 15, 1945, presented to all who served during WWII. "GSI" meant "Got Some [service] In." |
| **gunbuster** | A Royal Army Ordnance Corps weapons artificer. |
| **gup** | Information. Derived from "gossip." |
| **gutbash** | A self-inflicted stomach-ache resulting from eating too much. |

| | |
|---|---|
| **gyppo** | Anything hot or liquid out of the cookhouse – tea, soup, stew, custard. |
| **gyppy tummy** | Diarrhea accompanied by a sharp stomach-ache, always a convenient illness when conducting military operations. |

# H Harry

| | |
|---|---|
| **half-section** | Literally half of a section (equivalent to a US squad), but in slang it meant only one man, a companion. |
| **half shot** | Half drunk, and often striving for the goal of being completely shot. |
| **harbour** | A night position or halt site for an armored column. |
| **hardtack** | 1) Army biscuit.<br>2) Tinned rations. |
| **hash with broken biscuit** | The ever-available bully beef diced up and cooked with crumbed biscuit, rather than vegetables, to make a form of "hash." |
| **have a bang** | Give it a try, take a crack at it. |
| **Hawkins grenade** | No. 75 antitank grenade-mine. Small land mine that could be used as an antitank grenade or hand-delivered demolition charge. |
| **Hebron coat** | Locally acquired shaggy goatskin coat used in the Western Desert. |
| **hedgehog** | Strongpoint with all-round defenses and obstacles. |
| **hedge-hoppers** | Low-flying German fighters which strafed troops and attacked antiaircraft batteries. |

**Henderson cocktail** An oil drum filled with explosives, scrap metal fragmentation, and fitted with a 7-second delay fuse. South Africans rolled these alarmingly nasty weapons over the cliffs at Halfaya Pass to drive the enemy from their cave hide-outs.

**Hermann** Bomb Disposal Service nickname for the German 1,000kg bomb. Named after Hermann Göring.

**hide** A position in low ground or behind low ridges in the desert offering concealment from enemy observation. This would be reinforced by camouflage nets and judicious use of what spiky, sun-bleached vegetation was available. Also "hole up," or "harbour."

**Hitler War** World War II.

**Hobart's Funnies** See box overleaf.

**holdall** A pouch or bag for carrying small items, "ditty bag."

**homer** A wound serious enough to send a man home.

**homework** A girlfriend, and obviously something requiring daily effort to keep out of trouble.

**Honey** Nickname for the US-made General Stuart M3 series light tanks.

**hoo-ha** Confused talking, arguments, disagreements. It often described the angry-sounding babble in command posts.

**hooks** NCO chevrons. (Canadian)

**hospital blues** A royal blue single-breasted civilian suit-type jacket and trousers, white shirt, and red necktie (Union Jack colors) worn by convalescent

# HOBART'S FUNNIES

The disastrous August 1942 Dieppe Raid demonstrated shortcomings in the capabilities of tanks assaulting a fortified coastline and in their ability to overcome beach and inland obstacles. A variety of specialized Armoured Fighting Vehicles (AFVs) were developed, tested, and organized into unique tank and Royal Engineer units. The 79th Armoured Division was founded in October 1942 and in March 1943 was about to be disbanded owing to a lack of resources. Instead, it was placed under the command of the impressively named Major-General Sir Percy Cleghorn Stanley Hobart (1885–1957) and assigned to manage, train, and employ these varied specialist units. It was not long before the division and its unusual menagerie of AFVs became known as "Hobart's Funnies." Its units were to support the Commonwealth landings during the June 1944 Normandy invasion.

The AFVs included modified Churchill and Sherman tanks such as the Crocodile flamethrower tank; Armoured Vehicle, Royal Engineers (AVRE) with a demolition gun (they were also fitted with mineploughs, ditch-crossing fascines, assault bridges, and other obstacle-crossing/breeching aids); Crab rotating mine-flail tank; Ark armoured ramp carrier; Beach Armoured Recovery Vehicle (BARV); Duplex Drive (DD) amphibious tanks; Landing Vehicle, Tracked (LVT) amphibian tractors; armoured bulldozers; and, later, tank-mounted Canal Defence Lights (blinding searchlights). The 79th did not operate a signal formation, but its elements were attached to the assault units. Hobart's Funnies were instrumental in the Normandy assault's success, even though supported commanders were sometimes reluctant to employ unfamiliar, strange, or downright wacky-looking vehicles. After the Normandy landing the division supported Allied forces in the battle for the Roer Triangle and the crossings of the Rhine and Elbe rivers. The division was disbanded in August 1945, although some "funnies" remained in service.

patients without any form of insignia. It was considered ghastly apparel, with often mismatched colors, and was entirely unsuited to successful flirtation with nurses.

**housewife**  A small pouch holdall containing a sewing kit issued to each man. Also used by US troops.

# I  Ink

**igri** *or* **iggry**  Hurry up. (Arab word.)

**immature**  A recruit, young soldier.

**iron lung**  Nissen hut, simply "Nissen." Prefabricated and unloved hutment constructed of corrugated iron arches and able to be quickly erected by inexperienced troops. They were used as quarters and administrative buildings. Developed by Peter N. Nissen, a Canadian mining engineer. See "tin town."

**Ironsides**  A Bedford 30-cwt lorry converted into a ridiculously crude armored car by adding boilerplate. Also used for the Humber light reconnaissance car.

**"I" tank**  Infantry tank. Heavily armored, slow-moving tanks intended for infantry support, namely the Matilda, Valentine, and Churchill.

# J  Johnnie

**jab**  Inoculation, "needle," "sting."

**Jambo!**  Hello! Used in North Africa. (Swahili word.)

**jam on it**  A cynical response when someone requested more supplies or something unobtainable. "Do you want jam on it?" Always better when delivered with a lofty sneer.

| | |
|---|---|
| **jankers** | Confined to camp and given extra drill or fatigues. |
| **jankers king** | Provost Marshal or Provost Sergeant or another sergeant in charge of the Service Police. |
| **Japper grog** | "Liberated" Japanese sake (rice wine) cut with lemon crystals (flavoring) from the jungle ration. (Australian) |
| **jeepable** | A track or terrain only a jeep could negotiate. |
| **Jerry** | Term used by British and US troops for German troops. Originated in WWI, but was widely used in WWII, especially among the British. Reported to be derived from the common German given name Gerhart, but may simply be a contraction and modification of "German," which may explain why it was sometimes incorrectly spelt "Gerry." Another, more pungent, theory is that "jerry" is British slang for a chamber pot. |
| **jerrycan** | Petrol and water can captured from the Germans. These were ordered to be turned in for reuse. Later the British made their own. See "jerrycan," Part I. |
| **Jock** | A member of a Scottish regiment, who may not necessarily have been Scottish. |
| **Jock column** | Motorized units conducting raids behind enemy lines in the desert. Named after their founder, Lieutenant-Colonel John C. "Jock" Campbell of the 7th Armoured Division. |
| **Joe Soap** | Dim-witted or uncomplaining man given unwanted work assignments or one doing another's work; "carrying the can." Also "Joe." |

| | |
|---|---|
| Johnny | An Arab. Arabs consequently called Commonwealth soldiers "Johnny." Used in WWI for Turks, "Johnny Turk." |
| joker | Chap, fellow. (New Zealand) |
| jonnick/jonnock | Straightforward, customary, fair. |
| joysticks | The pair of steering levers in tanks and other full-tracked vehicles. |
| jungle green | A dark-green drill clothing designated "Khaki Drill No. 4 (green)" or "Standard Camouflage Colour 19." Jungle green began replacing brown khaki drill jungle clothing in 1942. |
| jungle juice | Home brewed or cheap liquor. |
| jungle wireless/ telephone | The method by which rumors and gossip quickly spread. Derived from rapidly spread native drum communications in Africa. Mainly used in Burma and New Guinea. |

# K     King

| | |
|---|---|
| kag | A tank crew's equipment, bedding, rolled shelter tent, rations, jerrycans, etc. stowed externally on the tank, especially on the turret sides (there to be swept off by trees, buildings, gunfire etc). The term was mainly used in Burma. |
| keep the eye down | Keep one's head down, stay under cover. |
| khaki marines | Royal Marine Commandos as opposed to the "blue marines" aboard ships. |
| kilt-apron | Kilt cover. Ochre-colored cover worn over kilts for camouflage and cleanliness purposes. Scottish kilts had been restricted from field wear from late 1939 to early 1942. |

| king | A regal title appended to anyone's job, especially those with a powerful control over a specific item, e.g. "rations king." |

| King's corporal | A fictitious rank for honorary corporals promoted in the field. |

| King's Regs | *The King's Regulation for the Army and the Royal Army Reserve 1940: Reprint Incorporating Amendments (Nos. 1 to 44) 1945.* The regulations governing the British Army. The "Red Book." |

| kipper | British service personnel of any branch, though originally sailors. |

| knackered | Tired, worn out. |

| knocked up | Tired, worn out. "To knock-up" is to awaken one. (Australian) |

| koalas | Conscripted Australian soldiers who were not required to serve overseas until 1943. Like the lovable koala bear they were not to be exported or shot at. See "chocko," and "weekend warriors." |

| kriegy | Prisoner of war held by the Germans. Derived from *Kriegsgefangener* (war prisoner). |

# L   London

| lance jack | Lance-corporal, "lance." One chevron, junior to a corporal. |

| lashings | An abundance of anything, "lashings of ammo." From an obsolete word for "lavish." |

| last bullet, last man | A desperate last-ditch order in a forlorn defense, which in the interests of self-preservation was seldom taken literally. |

| last three | The last three digits of a soldier's regimental/corps number was usually sufficient |

in identifying a soldier on a roster or form within his unit.

**lat**    A latrine.

**latrinagram**    Latrine rumor. Rapidly spread word of mouth rumors sating the soldier's gossipy appetite for information, whether it was fact or fiction. Also "latrinogram," "latrino," or "latrine wireless."

**leaf**    Leave, "the privilege that is not a right."

**leaguer**    A site to harbor vehicles, specifically a defensive position in the desert occupied at night. The act of "leaguering" or "haboring" by a combat unit, with tanks, artillery, and other AFVs facing outward. Derived from the 19th-century Boer practice of enclosing a camp with wagons. From the Cape Dutch *Laager*.

**leap frog**    The fire-and-maneuver tactic of one subunit providing covering fire as another subunit advances ("leap frogs") past or through the first. The first subunit then provides covering fire as the second subunit leap frogs.

**lemon squeezer**    Stiff-brimmed wool felt hat worn by New Zealander troops, which featured a high pointed crown with four creases making a shape reminiscent of a lemon squeezer.

**lifebuoy**    The Mk 1 and 2 portable flamethrowers, owing to the circular life ring-like fuel tank. Also "ack pack."

**limey**    British sailor. A shortened form of the 19th-century phrase "lime-juicer," owing to the Royal Navy issuing lime and lemon juice (mixed with rum and water = grog). The Australians began applying the term to any Briton in the 1880s.

| | |
|---|---|
| **Little Blitz** | A second brief period in which London was bombed, from January 21 to April 8, 1944. |
| **Little Stalingrad** | Battle of Ortona, Italy, December 1943, fought by the 1st Canadian Infantry Division. |
| **Lizzie** | Westland Lysander Mk I, II, and III army cooperation, liaison, and special mission aircraft. |
| **load of guff** | Unmitigated rubbish. |
| **LOB** | Left Out of Battle. Troops remaining in the rear during action due to illness, injuries, or special duties, such as having to hold back in order to help reconstitute a battalion after a battle (this later became an unaffordable luxury). |
| **L of C swine** | Unfavorably judged lines-of-communications rear service troops. |
| **loot** | 1) Lieutenant (pronounced "lef-ten'ent"). <br> 2) Pay disbursed during pay parade. <br> 3) Anything "liberated" or found. |
| **Lord Haw-Haw** | This was the nickname for the presenter of a propaganda programme called *Germany Calling*, broadcast by Radio Hamburg to Britain and America. While a Briton, William Joyce, was the principal Lord Haw-Haw, there had previously been a German affecting a caricature British accent who began broadcasting propaganda in 1939. He was soon replaced by Joyce. Joyce was American-born and raised in Ireland. Involved with a fascist organization, he falsely acquired a British passport to be able to vote. He defected to Germany after the beginning of the war to flee internment and became a German citizen. His broadcasts were made from late 1939 to April 1945. Tried for treason, owing to his |

obtaining a British passport (even though falsely), he was hanged in 1946. The nickname was attributed to both a British radio critic and newspaper cartoonist.

| | |
|---|---|
| **lorry hopping** | Hitchhiking a lorry ride along lines-of-communications. |
| **lurk men** | Men who constantly avoided work details; they lurked around trying to hide out. (Australian) |

# M     Monkey

| | |
|---|---|
| **M&V** | Tinned Maconochie's meat and vegetable stew. |
| **Maconochie's** | A tinned stewed steak from ration packs that was, unusually for military rations, considered quite good. Term dates from WWI and 'Maconochie's M&V' (meat and vegetables). |
| **Mad Mick** | A pick-axe. |
| **mad mile** | A bowel-unsettling stretch of road on the line-of-communications or a main supply route, regardless of its actual length, exposed to enemy artillery fire. |
| **mad minute** | The bayonet assault course, owing to its required speed, rigorous activity, and psychotic mindset. (Australian) |
| **Maggie** | Machine-gun nest. |
| **magnoon/magnune** | Eccentric, disturbed, peculiar, queer. (Australian) |
| **mahleesh/mahlish** | A dismissal, "forget it," "it doesn't matter." (Australian) |
| **mallum** | "Understand?" "Yes, mallum" – fair enough. "Use your mallum" – commonsense. (Australian) |
| **Mammut** | Mammoth truck-like armored command vehicle. |

**Mandrake**      The issue waterproof cape so called because of its wizard-like similarity to Mandrake the Magician's cape. The rubberized cape was actually a not so brilliantly designed condensation trap, which caused an active wearer to sweat and become just as wet inside as on the outside. It was also used as a groundsheet and, when two were fastened together, a very poor shelter tent – "basha."

**Markers steady**      A drill command for the base man in each subunit to remain in place. It was used to mean everything was under control, that all was steady.

**married patch**      Married troops' quarters for their families on a military base.

## CLOTHING & GEAR

| | |
|---|---|
| bailout kit | housewife |
| banjo | kag |
| bone sack | kilt-apron |
| British warm | lemon squeezer |
| chagal | Mad Mick |
| Chapplies | Mandrake |
| Christmas tree order | pixie suit |
| coal scuttle helmet | pulp helmet |
| creepers | skeleton equipment |
| dah | smalls |
| gas face | teddy bear |
| giggle suit | topi |
| glamour | Tropal |
| goonskin | turtle helmet |
| Hebron coat | Yukon pack |

| | |
|---|---|
| **marry up** | For elements in the field to link up, to make contact. |
| **Matador** | The AEC 10-ton capacity 4x4 truck-like tractor for towing heavy artillery and an armored command vehicle. |
| **matchbox** | Airspeed AS.51 Horsa and other gliders, which were largely made of wood and canvas. |
| **mate** | A close friend, pal. An Australian term used to a lesser extent by other nationalities. |
| **Mauser** | Any German bolt-action rifle. The standard was the 7.9mm Kar 98k carbine. |
| **MEMAS** | Middle East Mutual Admiration Society – pronounced "me-maas." Referred to Australian officers returning from North Africa to serve in the southwest Pacific or at home. |
| **mess tin** | Two deep, nesting rectangular pans with folding handles; officially "pan set, messing." |
| **Met** | Motor Transport, used by the Eighth Army. Derived from "MT," the official abbreviation. |
| **MFU** | Military Fuck (Frig) Up. A larger-scale military frig up was known as an IMFU, conducted on a truly "Imperial" scale. |
| **Mick** | A term, considered derogatory, for an Irishman or Irish soldier. Irish personnel served in the British Army even though Ireland (Eire), then part of the Commonwealth, was officially neutral. |
| **moaning minnies** | German multiple-tube/rail rocket launchers of various calibres known as the *Nebelwerfer*. Also "nebs." Significant characteristics of the rockets were their large caliber, slow flight, heavy blast and the loud screaming noise they made which inspired the nickname. |

**mob**  A unit, not necessarily uncomplimentary. Australian from a "mob of brumbies" – herd of wild horses.

**Monty**  Field Marshal Lord Montgomery of Alamein.

**montygram**  A message signal written by Montgomery.

**Mountbatten pink**  A shade of light pink applied to landing craft recommended by Lord Louis Mountbatten. It blended into fog and haze and at night. Also "barmaid's blush." It was actually, to be picky, medium grey with a small amount of Venetian red and appeared as a dark mauve.

**mouse-hole**  A man-sized hole knocked or blasted through interior and exterior walls and crawled through when attacking defended buildings.

**mouse-hole charge**  A prefabricated wooden frame with demolition charges on each corner and the centre to blast "mouse-holes" through walls.

**muck**  Foul, dirty weather with extremely poor visibility.

**muckin**  Butter.

**mucking-in spud**  Sharing everything with a pal.

**muckstick**  A rifle.

**mud walloper**  Troops working in the mud or accustomed to it.

**mungaree/manjaree**  Food. Also "grit," "momgey," "mungaria," "munga," and "munger."

**muscle factory**  Gymnasium.

**mush**  1) A pal, friend.
2) Jail cell, "spud hole."

**musical chair**  Latrine pit with a pole or plank on which to sit.

# N                Nuts

**Naafi** *or* **Narfy**  The NAAFI (Navy, Army, and Air Force Institutes), pronounced "na-fi," His Majesty's Forces' official trading organization. The NAAFI operated clubs, shops, canteens, and other facilities on British military bases.

**Naafi Gong/Medal**  Any of the campaign awards bestowed for merely being present. It especially applied to the 1939–45 Star (WWII service), as its suspension ribbon was the same dark blue, red, and light blue as the arm flash worn by Naafi girls. Also "Spam Medal."

**Naafi Romeo**  One who treated female service personnel to Naafi refreshments, with clear intentions.

**Naafi time**  Refreshment break at a Naafi canteen.

**Naafi wagon**  Mobile canteen trucks serving troops in the field.

**NABU, SABU, TABU**  A set of useful acronyms standing for Non-adjustable Balls Up, Self-adjustable Balls Up, Typical Army Balls Up. "Balls up" means a muddled mess, a "cock up."

**Nackeroos**  2/1st North Australia Observer Unit. Operated observation posts and conducted patrols to warn of any Japanese landings.

**Nack it!**  Stop it! Shut up!

**Nippo**  Japanese. There were many other derogatory terms including: "Jap," "Japper," "Jampans" (name given by East African troops in Burma), "Nip," "Tojo" and "Tojo-lander" (after Hideki Tojo, Prime Minister and Minister of War), "little men," and "little yellow men."

| | |
|---|---|
| No. 9 | To be "Number 9" was to be ill. It was a laxative pill given out freely by medical officers, especially to those classified M&D (medicine and duty) or NYD (not yet diagnosed). |
| Not a sausage | Meaning not to have anything of value, such as money, cigarettes, food, etc. |
| Not worth a crumpet | Worthless, especially refers to a person. |
| nullah | A watercourse, gully, or stream in India. (Hindustani word.) Also "chaung" in Burma and "wadi" or "donga" in the Middle East and North Africa. |

# O                    Orange

| | |
|---|---|
| old black men | Native African troops from West or East Africa. |
| old sweat | A veteran soldier, who could be at the ripe old age of his mid-20s. |
| one–pause–two course | A drill instructor's order when instructing basic drill movements. It referred to the basic training given to new officers at Officer Cadet Training Units (OCTU – pronounced "oc-tu"). |
| one-pipper | A 2nd Lieutenant, owing to the single star rank badge (pip). |
| on one's chinstrap | On one's last leg. "He came in on his chinstrap," implying that the soldier was pulling himself along, completely knackered. |
| on stag | Sentry duty. From a stag (male deer) who travels alone. |
| on the hooks | On charge, "on the pegs." One in trouble, hung on the hooks like meat. |
| on the nose | Smelly, disagreeable. (Australian) |

| | |
|---|---|
| **O-Pip** | Artillery observation post (OP), "orange pip." |
| **oppo** | Opposite number. One's section mate. Men paired up for sharing foxholes, meals, sentry duty, etc. |
| **ops** | Operations. The operations officer or combat operations. |
| **orderly dog** | Orderly corporal, but also applied to orderly sergeant or orderly officer, which was actually incorrect usage of "orderly dog," but nonetheless applied by unknowing conscripts. "Orderly buff" (orderly corporal) and the cutting "orderly pig" (orderly officer) saw less use. |
| **orderly stooge** | Orderly sergeants and officers. |
| **Orstralian** | Australian, but delivered with an aristocratic air. |
| **Overfed, overpaid, oversexed, and over here** | A common complaint about Americans stationed in Britain during the war. |
| **overs** | Any form of fire that passed over the intended target, be it friendly or enemy. |

# P      Pip

| | |
|---|---|
| **packdrill** | Exercises or marches with full pack and equipment as a muscle-sapping form of punishment. |
| **packet** | 1) A wound.<br>2) A serious telling off, a chewing out.<br>3) A dose of VD. |
| **pack in/pack it in** | Give up, relinquish. Pack in one's stripes. "He's packing it in" – giving up. |
| **Padre** | A chaplain in the army taken from the Spanish and Italian word for "Father." |
| **pahny/parny** | Water. (Hindustani word.) |

| | |
|---|---|
| **panga** | A machete. (Swahili word used throughout Africa.) |
| **panic artists** | Easily excitable soldiers, especially officers and NCOs feeling the heat. (Australian) |
| **paras** | Members of the Parachute Regiment, "paraboys." Applied to other parachute units as well. |
| **parascooter** | Excelsior Welbike, a miniature air-droppable motor scooter used by airborne troops. |
| **passion wagon** | A lorry transporting single-minded men on pass to town. |
| **pass the can** | Pass or shelf responsibility. |
| **PBI** | Sympathetic acronym meaning Poor Bloody Infantry. Anything was better than infantry service, which suffered the highest casualty rate. |
| **pecker up** | Chin up, "Keep your pecker up." (Australian) |
| **pen** | Prisoner of war holding area. |
| **pencil line** | The shortest distance between two points. |
| **Pheasant** | The 17/25-pdr antitank gun. When attached to its ammunition limber it was a "Pheasant with beak." The "17/25" was an early weapon mounted on a 25-pdr gun-howitzer carriage in order to field the gun rapidly. |
| **Phoney War** | The period from October 1939 to April 1940, the lull between the Polish campaign and the invasion of France and the Low Countries. The BEF called it the "twilight war." The French called it the *drôle de guerre* (lit. funny war – similar to the British saying "it's a funny old war"). |
| **piassaba** | Gun cleaning bore brush. Piassaba is a stiff, coarse fibre rope made in Brazil. |

| | |
|---|---|
| Piccadilly Commandos | Prostitutes and "good-time girls" who frequented US servicemen's clubs, turning Mayfair and the West End in London into what the police described as an "American colony." |
| pig-sticker | A bayonet. |
| pike off | To depart, to go away. |
| pills | Artillery ammunition. |
| pip | Four-pointed star used to indicate officer ranks, except majors, along with other devices. |
| pissaphone | Tastefully nicknamed urinal tube set in the ground. |
| piss pocket | An insincere, condescending, or dishonest person. The phrase "don't piss in my pocket" meant "don't bull shit me, mate." (Australian) |
| pit | 1) A slit trench or open position for riflemen, "rifle pit." 2) A machine-gun, antitank gun, or other crew-served weapon. |
| pixie suit | Insulated coveralls worn by tank and self-propelled gun crews, so named because of the fairytale transformation of the wearer when he put up the integral hood. Also "tank suit," or "zoot suit." |
| plastic | Nobel's 704B and 823 plastic explosives (PE). Also "plasticine." |
| poke the bronx | Poking fun at someone. (Australian/New Zealand) |
| pommy *or* pommie | Australian term for a British citizen since 1912. It was a combination of "pomegranate" and "immigrant," and was said to refer to an Englishman's red cheeks, like pomegranates. Also "Pongo." It was not considered derogatory by Australians. The rumor that it is derived from |

POME – Prisoner of Mother England – said to be marked on the headstones of convicts deported to Australia, is unfounded.

**pom-pom**    Small caliber fully automatic antiaircraft gun. Originally referred to the turn-of-the-century Maxim 2-pdr automatic gun introduced during the Boer War. Its name was owed to the sound of its firing.

**pontoon**    Twenty-one years' service. Derived from the pontoon card game, which was in turn derived from *vingt-et-un* (twenty-one).

**pooch**    Common pronunciation for "pouch," as in ammunition pouch or "wallet" as they were sometimes called.

**popsey/popsie**    Girlfriend.

**portée**    A means of transporting an antitank gun or light artillery piece in the back of a lorry. Frequently the gun could be fired from the back of the lorry, which itself was called a "portée." The term came from the French for "carried."

**possie**    Position, meaning a fighting position or sleeping dugout.

**potato masher**    German stick hand grenade. The term was also used by US troops.

**poultice**    Concentrated artillery fire, which really plastered the ground.

**pozzie**    Jam or jelly.

**Puddlejumper**    Taylor-Young Aeroplane Company Auster air observation post (AOP), employed for artillery spotting and liaison. It was a licence-built version of the American Tylorcraft. This type of aircraft was referred to as an "army cooperation aeroplane."

**puff**            Lady's man.

**puggled**         Description of a very drunk person, exhibiting all the mental dexterity of a sleepy toddler. Also "stitched," or "well-bottled."

**pukka**           Something good, reliable, top notch. "Pukka gen" is good information. (Hindustani word. Not to be confused with "Pucka," nickname for Puckapunyal Army Base near Melbourne.)

**pull a flanker**  1) To execute a flanking attack.
                    2) To surprise someone to one's own advantage or to put the other person in a disadvantageous position.
                    3) To pass an unpleasant assignment to another. Also "work a flanker."

**pull his Scotch** To pull one's leg, a gag.

**pull in your head** As a turtle might when faced with unwanted attention, meaning "Back off," "leave me alone," "shut up." (Australian)

*Sometimes holes were just not deep enough.*

**pulp helmet**    Dispatch rider's crash helmet made of strengthened papier-mâché. It was replaced by a steel version.

**punji**    Pointed wooden and bamboo stakes emplaced by the Japanese and British as booby traps. The points were impregnated with bully-beef, which quickly caused raging septicaemia. The term originated in the Punjab region of northwest India.

**purge**    Strict discipline. A "purger" is a constant complainer.

**purple death**    Nickname of a destructively effective wine found in North Africa.

**put in the book**    To enter one in the charge book for an infraction. Put up on charges.

# Q    Queen

**"Q" Staff**    Quartermaster staff officers responsible for supplies and transport. "Q" – Quartermaster.

**Q-stores**    Quartermaster's stores.

**quad**    The Morris Commercial C8 and the less successful Guy Ant 4x4 field artillery tractors (FATs), designed for towing 25-pdr gun-howitzers.

**Queen Mary**    The Bedford OXC heavy tractor with a 40ft trailer for transporting tanks. The tractor and trailer loaded with a tank looked as large and unwieldy as the RMS *Queen Mary*.

**quisling**    A traitor. Named after Vidkum Quisling, the German puppet Prime Minister of Norway. While normally identifying higher level traitors, in the Army it was merely a barracks snitch.

# R — Robert

**rabbiting**
Bomb Disposal Service technique requiring cast-iron nerves, of digging a hole or tunnel to gain access to a buried unexploded bomb to determine the type and to defuse it. "The BD squad rabbited for the bomb."

**rainbow**
Replacements arriving after the main action, green troops. "There's a rainbow after the storm." (Australian)

**rajpot**
A dopey or daft fellow.

**ranker**
An officer who rose through the enlisted ranks. More experienced and practical than other junior officers, they were not necessarily softer on the troops, as they knew all the tricks and excuses.

**rattler**
Handheld rattle device to sound the alarm for chemical attacks.

**recce**
Reconnaissance or reconnoitre, pronounced "recky."

**red and black, to mix the**
To assault an officer. An officer's desk would be equipped with red and black ink bottles. If an enlisted man were to lunge at an officer over his desk, the ink would be spilt. The term didn't just refer to office assaults.

**red beret**
A paratrooper due to the maroon beret of the parachute troops. The color is said to have been selected by the wife of Major-General F. A. M. "Boy" Browning, General Officer Commanding Airborne Forces, as it had been one of his school colors.

**Red Caps *or* redcaps**
Corps of Military Police (Provost), owing to their red service cap covers.

| | |
|---|---|
| **red devils** | Italian Mod. 35 hand grenades. These were impact-detonated grenades with a high blind (dud) rate. The blinds often detonated if disturbed, which, coupled with their red-painted bodies, led to their nickname. Captured grenades were used by the Commonwealth. |
| **red flannel** | Senior officers, colonels and up, owing to their red cap bands and gorgets. Also known as "red tabs." |
| **red ink** | Red wine. |
| **reds** | Red tunic worn by Guards and Household Cavalry regiments with full parade dress. |
| **regimental** | Used, not too politely, of a soldier who was too strict of a disciplinarian or too "by the book." |
| **Regimentals** | Uniforms bearing specific style designs, head-dress, insignia, accoutrements, and other distinctions authorized for the different regiments and corps. Many of these were long-held, jealously guarded traditions. |
| **reinstoushment** | Reinforcement, a play on "reinforcement" and "stoush" – to beat up or fight. (Australian) |
| **rep** | Reprimand. To give or receive a reprimand. A "severe rep" is unlikely to be pleasant. |
| **Rising Sun Badge** | The General Service Badge worn by Australian Commonwealth Military Forces, and so inscribed on caps and hats since 1904. A half-rising sunburst bearing a crown and title scrolls. |
| **Rock, the** | The Rock of Gibraltar. Also "Gib." |
| **Rock College** | Military detention centre. |
| **rocket** | A reprimand, to "give someone a rocket." |
| **roller skates** | Tanks. |

| | |
|---|---|
| **Rommel's Auxiliary Supply Column** | Alternative name for the Royal Army Service Corps (RASC), owing to the capture of abandoned British supply lorries. Also, uncharitably, "Run Away, Someone's Coming." |
| **roof spotters** | Royal Observer Corps volunteer aircraft spotters atop buildings in the British Isles. |
| **rooti** | Bread in the Indian Army. |
| **Rooti Gong/Medal** | Long Service Medal. Given to one who had consumed a great deal of Army bread (rooti). |
| **ropey** | Slack, poor appearance, or something suspiciously substandard. |
| **rose bowl** | Temporary latrine, either a hole dug in the ground or a can used as a "chamber pot." A term subtly toying with ideas of fragrance. |
| **rosella** | Staff officers, owing to their brightly colored-badges, much like the brightly colored Australian Rosella parrot. |
| **rubber bungy** | Parachute training helmet, owing to it being constructed of cloth-covered sorbo rubber. |
| **rubber heels** | Hard, rubbery fried eggs. |
| **runflats** | Very useful vehicle tyres capable of being driven a short distance after being punctured by small-arms fire or splinters. |
| **running rabbit** | The wire-suspended target on a machine-gun range, which is pulled at the speed of a man walking or running, giving gunners laying and traversing practice. |
| **running repairs** | Hasty repairs made to vehicles or equipment, or the mending of clothing in the field to keep the item serviceable. |
| **RV** | Rendezvous, a link-up point. |

# S

# Sugar

**sabre and baton**
Crossed saber and baton device identifying general officers' rank.

**saida**
From the Arabic *sah-ee-da* (lit. "Go with God"), a greeting. Soldiers used "saida" as a morning greeting.

**salvage**
To misappropriate items. Also "souvenir" – "The bleedin' sods souvenired me boots."

**sand happy**
Someone turned eccentric or a bit odd after long, brain-heating service in the desert.

**sand in the hair**
One acclimatized and accustomed to the desert.

**sangar**
When positions could not be dug in hard ground, rocks were stacked in low circular walls to make a protected positioned called a sangar. These saw wide use in North Africa and Italy. It is a Kashmiri term used since the Northwest India Frontier days of the 19th century.

**sango**
Sandwich. (Australian)

**sarn-major**
Poor, but common pronunciation of "sergeant-major."

**sarnt** *or* **sarn**
Equally poor, but equally common pronunciation of "sergeant." "Sarge" was not permitted.

**Satan**
Bomb Disposal Service nickname for the German 1,800kg bomb.

**Saturday afternoon soldiers**
Home Guardsmen who undertook training on Saturdays. Initially they were designated Local Defence Volunteers, but two months after its May 1940 establishment the organization was renamed the Home Guard.

**scarper**    To move quickly. Derived from Italian *scarpare* (to escape). (Australian)

**scoff**    1) To eat.
2) To kill or get rid of.

**scratcher**    Bed. Possibly referred to the sleep-depriving discomfort of a lice-infested bed.

**scrounge**    1) To borrow or wangle something, to obtain items by any means.
2) To avoid fatigue parties or any form of work.

**sergeant-major's**    An extremely strong and heavy-on-the-sugar brew of tea, as preferred by indomitable sergeant-majors.

**seven-two**    The 7.2in Mk 1 through 6 howitzers, a corps artillery piece.

## WEAPONS

| | |
|---|---|
| Archies | Henderson cocktail |
| bakelite grenade | lifebuoy |
| bandook | moaning minnies |
| blockbuster | muckstick |
| Bofors | panga |
| Boys rifle | Pheasant |
| butterfly bomb | pig-sticker |
| buzz bomb | potato masher |
| Chicago piano | red devils |
| Cross Cocktail | Satan |
| flying dustbin | smelly |
| Fritz | sticky bomb |
| Gammon grenade | tank buster |
| ghost gun | thermos flask grenade |
| Hawkins grenade | Tommy gun |

| | |
|---|---|
| **SFA** | Sweet Fuck All or, when women or children were present, Sweet Fanny Adams. Meaning there's nothing, zero. (Australian) |
| **shagged** | Worn out, tired. |
| **shark bait** | Said of an unpopular officer or NCO, or enlisted man for that matter, who might inexplicably "fall" overboard while on a troop transport. (Australian) |
| **Shepard's Short Range Group** | GHQ, Cairo. Shepard's Hotel was one of the more unsavory haunts of rear-area types. A sarcastic play on the Long Range Desert Group designation. |
| **shit scared** | Terrified to the point of defecating or coming close. Also "shit bricks." |
| **shit wallah** | Sanitary orderly. |
| **Shop, the** | Royal Military Academy Woolwich, where artillery, engineer, signals, and other technical officers were trained. |
| **Shot, the** | Aldershot Garrison. A complex of military bases, barracks, and training facilities in southern England. |
| **show** | A battle or operation. |
| **showing a medal** | A trouser fly button left undone. |
| **shy-grog** | Australian bootleg booze, illegal liquor. |
| **sick bunk** | Regimental aid post. |
| **side kick** | Close friend, "cobber." (Australian) |
| **sig/sigs** | Signals. Anything related to the Royal Corps of Signals (R Sigs). |
| **signal basher** | Signalman. |

**Signalman Jimmy** The Mercury (messenger of the gods) badge of the Royal Corps of Signals.

**sinkers** Sinkers are a type of doughnut, strips of dough deep fried in fat to form stripes, twists, or rings.

**SIP grenade** No. 76 Self-Igniting Phosphorous antitank hand grenade, or "Albright and Wilson" ("AW") grenade, was a phosphorous-filled 1-imperial pint milk bottle. The flammable liquid was a horrible, sickly, yellow-brown color.

**sitrep** Situation report.

**skeleton equipment** Web belt and braces (equipment suspenders).

**skipper** Captain.

**skirt patrol** A lusty reconnaissance action, undertaken by soldiers targeting women while on pass.

**slittie** Slit trench. Life in a slit was not fun.

**slug** Solid armor-piercing shot for antitank guns.

**smalls** Underwear, officially called "smallclothes."

**smelly** Play on SMLE – [Rifle], Short, Magazine, Lee-Enfield, No. 1 Mk 3 and similar marks.

**Smoke/Big Smoke** London, called the "Smoke" owing to the hundreds of thousands of smoking chimneys.

**Snip** Regimental tailor.

**Snob** Unit cobbler, derived from an old British slang term for cobbler.

**snow drops** American military police in Britain owing to their white helmets.

**soft number** An easy or cushy job.

**Soldier's Friend** A pink tablet to be rubbed on brass (after spitting on it or applying water) to polish it.

| | |
|---|---|
| **Some Bloke's Choke** | Very strong compressed tea tablets called SBC, "Service Blend, Compressed," and said to have the odor and flavor of old socks. |
| **sound spotting** | Estimating the range to enemy artillery by timing the interval between sighting the muzzle flash or smoke to the sound of the report arriving. |
| **sow** | To lay mines. |
| **spag** | Spaghetti. |
| **spare file** | Individual with no specific duties, "spare wank." No doubt an NCO found something to occupy the spare file's time. |
| **Sparks** | Electrician. |
| **Speedy** | Assigned name for the different lines–of–communications (roads) in Italy. The different roads were designated "Speedy 1," "Speedy 2," etc. |
| **spine bashing** | Sleeping, "kip." |
| **spit and polish** | Maintenance of equipment, doing things for appearance's sake. |
| **spit and polish parade** | Parade inspection. |
| **splinter** | Fragmentation or shrapnel produced by grenades or mortar shells. |
| **spotter** | 1) Air observer lookout.<br>2) A lookout on the watch for Military Police, while his mates do something they shouldn't. |
| **spout** | The barrel or muzzle of a weapon. "One up the spout" meant there was a round in the chamber, usually of a rifle. |
| **Springboks** | South African troops, named after the small native antelopes. |

| | |
|---|---|
| **sprog** | A person of lesser rank. Derived from a term for a child. |
| **spud basher** | Potato-peeler, on kitchen fatigue. |
| **squaddie** | A recruit, as in a drill squad. |
| **square** | Parade ground, regardless of its shape. |
| **square bashing** | Dismounted drill. |
| **square-head** | Derogatory term for a German referring to a dumb or dense person. Related to "boxhead" or "blockhead." |
| **squitters** | Dysentery. Also "skitters." |
| **staff** | Staff-sergeant. |
| **stand on everything** | Hit the brakes hard to halt a vehicle immediately. |
| **star** | Illumination shell or rifle-discharged signal grenade. |
| **steel chest** | A hardened soldier. |
| **Stella** | The brand name of a popular Egyptian beer. Was used to refer to any Egyptian beer. |
| **stick it** | "Stick it up your arse" – the last three words were added to beef up the insult. "Shove it" was also used. |
| **stickman** | The best turned-out soldier at guard mount. He was assigned duties to assist the officer and sergeant of the guard and did not stand a guard post. |
| **sticks** | A drummer. |
| **sticky** | An understated description of a difficult or dangerous situation. |
| **sticky bomb** | No. 74 antitank hand grenade. The grenade was covered with especially sticky glue and was |

supposed to stick to a tank when thrown. It was withdrawn from use owing to its unfortunate habit of sticking to the thrower, or not sticking to wet, oily, or dirty target surfaces. The glue also dried out in storage, and limited effectiveness.

| | |
|---|---|
| **stinking** | Completely and utterly drunk. |
| **Stirling and Stirling** | Reputed to be the actual meaning of "SAS" (Special Air Service), as the founder was David Stirling and the 2nd SAS Battalion was commanded by his brother Bill Stirling. |
| **stonk** | 1) Artillery or mortar fire, firing a linear barrage or a very heavy concentration for a short duration – may be to support or initiate a surprise local attack.<br>2) A "regimental shoot" with all guns on line barraging the target area. |
| **stonkered** | Exhausted or drunk. |
| **stooge** | An assistant or deputy. |
| **stop one** | Hit by a bullet or splinter. |
| **Strike me pink!** | Long-popular Australian exclamation of surprise or disbelief. British vernacular of the early 1900s. |
| **stripes** | Point-down chevrons worn by lance-corporals, corporals, and all sergeant grades other than sergeant-majors. |
| **stripped** | Reduced in rank. |
| **success signal** | Colored flare(s) signalling that the objective has been seized or that another mission has been accomplished. |

| | |
|---|---|
| suicide squad | Often said of reconnaissance, machine-gun, antitank gun, and other troops in high-risk battlefield professions. |
| swaddy | Long in use as slang for a soldier, "swatty," "swoddy," "swoddie." |
| swede basher | Country bumpkin, known apparently for his rough handling of vegetables. |
| swing | Boasting. |
| switch | No. 10 time pencil. These were chemical delay fuses available in different delay times ranging from 10 minutes to 24 hours. |

# T                          ## Toc

| | |
|---|---|
| tabs | Feet. |
| take felt | To don a bowler hat when discharged from the service. |
| take the King's shilling | See box overleaf. |
| talc | Transparent cellulose sheet covering map boards on which one could mark unit positions and activities with grease pencils. |
| tank buster | An antitank gun. |
| tankie | Tanker, member of a tank crew or unit. |
| tank island | An area defended by numerous antitank weapons, mines, and manmade obstacles, and situated on "tank-proof" terrain. |
| tank proof | An area of terrain impassable to tanks or difficult for tanks to penetrate, such as dense woods, rocky ground, mud, swamps, gullies, steep hills, etc. |

| | |
|---|---|
| **tea blocks** | Compressed compo block of tea, powdered milk ("whitener"), and sugar. |
| **teddy bear** | Goatskin-lined jerkin. See "goonskin." |
| **teed up, getting** | Getting everything ready for an operation. A borrowed golf term. |
| **tell the tale** | To exaggerate or offer excuses. |
| **Terriers** | Members of the Territorial Army, the pre-war part-time militia. |

## TAKE THE KING'S SHILLING

"When you take the King's shilling, you are the King's man." This phrase dates back to the early 1800s, perhaps earlier, when recruiting parties were paid a bounty for enlisting recruits. If the recruiters could not convince a potential soldier to enlist voluntarily, usually through a liberal application of ale and stories of a soldier's carefree life, quick promotion, and how women were sexually magnetized by the red coat, they resorted to subterfuge. A recruiting sergeant of the era recounted, "Your last recourse was to get him drunk, and then slip a shilling in his pocket, get him home to your billet, and next morning swear he enlisted, bring all your party to prove it, get him persuaded to pass the doctor. Should he pass, you must try every means in your power to get him to drink, blow him up with a fine story, get him inveigled to the magistrates, in some shape or other, and get him attested (swearing he was not already in the Army or Navy, or an apprentice); but by no means let him out of your hands." The shilling (one twentieth of a pound), was sort of an advance on his enlistment bonus of two months' pay. There were two enlistment options – seven years or life. Of course, by WWII recruiting practices had much changed, but when enlisting in the British Army it was still described as "taking the King's shilling." Conscription was re-introduced in April 1939.

| | |
|---|---|
| tewt | Tactical Exercise without troops, pronounced "toot"). A field exercise in which commanders and leaders participated without troops (who were conducting other training). A form of practice exercises training leaders in their duties and signals. |
| thermos bomb | Italian AR-4 anti-personnel fragmentation bomb, which was the size and shape of a thermos bottle. |
| thermos flask grenade | No. 73 antitank hand grenade, "hand percussion grenade," again the size and shape of a small thermos bottle. |
| three-pipper | Captain, owing to his three stars (pips). |
| three-seven | The 3.7in Mk 1, 2, 3, and 6 quick-firing heavy antiaircraft guns. |
| three-striper | Sergeant. (Certain units used four-stripe specialty sergeant ranks.) |
| Tilly | Utility truck. Light pick-up trucks converted from civilian Austin, Hillman, and Morris trucks. |
| time-expired man | A soldier whose time in service had expired and who was awaiting discharge. |
| tin hat | Helmet, "titfa," "titfer," "panic hat" (Australian). Brodie-pattern Mk 1 and 2 steel helmets used since 1916. |
| tinny | Incredibly lucky. (Australian) |
| tin-openers | Tank-destroying fighters such as rocket-armed Hurricanes and Typhoons. |
| tin tanks | Americans. Cockney Rhyming Slang for "Yanks." (Australian) |
| tin town | A camp of Nissen huts. |
| toggle rope | A 6ft rope with a loop in one end and a wooden handle on the other. Worn wrapped around the |

waists of commandos, they could be linked together as a single rope to enter buildings, climb ravine sides, scale walls, etc.

**Tojoland**     Japan, from the Japanese Prime Minister Hideki Tojo.

**Tommy**       The British soldier, so called by himself, his allies, and his enemies. From Tommy Atkins, the generic name for the common soldier and used on example forms since 1815. As Rudyard Kipling said, "O it's Tommy this, an' Tommy that, an' 'Tommy, go away.' But it's 'Saviour of 'is country' when the guns begin to shoot."

**Tommy armour**     Tough, unexciting issue biscuit, hardtack. Also
**plates**         "tile," and "Anzac biscuit." Issued in two types, equally bland: "biscuit, enriched" and "biscuit, plain."

**Tommy cooker**     Small field tri-fold stove fuelled by solidified spirits (alcohol), "hexi-cooker." There were also similar commercial stoves such as the Tommy's Cooker, and the Blackie.

**Tommy gun**     US-made .45-cal. M1928 submachine-gun used in large numbers by Commonwealth forces.

**topi**          Foreign service helmet, pith helmet. (From Hindustani for "hat.") The cloth-covered cork helmets were designed to offer protection from the sun, with the cork providing insulation from the heat. Regardless of the pith helmet's association with hunters and explorers in Africa, it was developed by the British in India. See "Bombay bowler."

**tourist**       Australian serviceman serving overseas.

**tradesmen**     Other rankers, specialists identified by special cuff badges.

| | |
|---|---|
| **trooper** | The ever-luxurious troop transport ship. |
| **Tropal/poshteen** | Full-length sheepskin or kapok-lined orange-brown canvas overcoat issued for guard duty in cold climates. |
| **troppo** | Jungle happy, one having spent too much time rotting in the tropics. |
| **Trump, the** | The commanding officer, or the second-in-command. From "trumps" in cards. (Australian) |
| **tucker** | Food. (Australian) |
| **turtle helmet** | The Mk 3 steel helmet, which was adopted in 1941 but did not see widespread issue until 1944. So named owing to its domed design, different from the traditional "tin hat." |
| **twillip** | A dumb or unpleasant person. |
| **two-five-two** | Form 252, charge sheet. |
| **Two I/C** *or* **2iC** | Second-in-command, pronounced "two-I-see," "two-icky," "the Deuce." |
| **two-nine-five** | Form 295, leave or pass form. |
| **two-pipper** | A lieutenant, owing to the two stars (pips). |
| **two-striper** | A corporal, with the familiar double stripes on his arm. |
| **Two Types** | A cartoon that appeared in the Eighth Army newspaper from 1943 to 1946 in some 300 installments. While the cartoon did not appear until the Eighth Army was in Italy, the two officers featured often reminisced about their Western Desert days and continued to sport their exaggerated mustachios and distinctively eccentric desert garb. The "Two Types" was drawn by Captain John J. "Jon" Philpin (1913–92). The phrase was used in a humorous |

way to refer to a pair of men with similar characteristics who were inseparable. See cartoon opposite.

**type**  An officer.

**typewrite**  To fire a Vickers or Bren gun in short bursts.

# U  Uncle

**unbuttoned**  Unprepared, as in the case of one's trousers fly left unbuttoned.

**Uncle Bill**  Field Marshal William Joseph Slim, 1st Viscount Slim (1891–1970), commander of the Fourteenth Army in Burma. It is sometimes assumed that "Slim" was a nickname, but it was actually his surname, which served as a nickname.

**unstick**  The hernia-inducing toil of extracting a vehicle stuck in sand or mud. "Unsticking gear" included sand channels, sand mats, and airfield matting (see "Marston matting," Part I) to provide traction for tyres.

**up shit creek**  In a rather difficult position. Often "without a paddle" was appended to emphasize that matters had really gone "tits up." Another version was "up shit creek in a barbed wire rowboat." (Australian, obviously.)

**US**  Unserviceable. U/S or u/s was the official abbreviation. Meant to be mildly derogatory toward the United States.

**Use your loaf!**  Use your brains!

**ute**  Public Utility (PU) truck. A pickup truck (hybrid car/truck) of Australian origin.

# V      Vic

**valise**      Officer's bedroll or OR's large field pack.

**vino**      The widely adopted Italian word for wine.

**V's**      A brand of Indian-made cigarettes. Packets were marked with a "V" and the Morse code . . . – for Victory.

# W      William

**wad**      Bun or cake. A "cuppa char and a wad" were often ordered during canteen breaks in training and instruction.

**wadi**      A watercourse or gulley in North Africa. They could become inundated by flash-flooding, but were mostly dry and often used for a dusty cover and concealment. From the Arabic word *wādī*.

**waffle**      Indecisive, "dither," rambling talk.

**wakee, wakee!**      Orderly corporal's annoying reveille cry to awaken.

*"She says she IS Lili Marlene." (Captain John J. Philpin)*

197

**walk with a spade, take a**  Going for a walk with a spade to dig a hasty latrine.

**wallah**  Chap, fellow. An Indian term used in connection with many duties. Also "signals wallah," "transport wallah," and "char wallah." Compare to "basher."

**wash-out**  1) A complete miss on the rifle range.
2) A failed operation.

**weekend warriors**  Australian Citizens Military Force (CMF). In peacetime they trained one weekend a month. Also "Militia," "Australian Militia Forces," and "Citizen's Forces" – all unofficial terms. Like conscripts, Militia units could not serve outside of Australia or its territories. Some did fight in New Guinea and Papua, though.

**Western Desert**  Area of operations comprising Egypt and Libya.

**wet one's stripes**  To celebrate an NCO's promotion with the assistance of beer or other libations.

**Willy's**  US ¼-ton 4x4 truck, a "Willys jeep," which was widely used by Commonwealth forces. Also "blitz buggy." The British rated its capacity as 5-cwt.

**Wind in your neck!**  Close the door.

**wings**  Referred to the Parachute Badge, SAS Qualification Badge, and Army Flying Badge. The last of these was worn by air observation post (spotter plane) and glider pilots. A Second Glider Pilot Badge (for co-pilots) was authorized in 1944.

**Winnie**  Prime Minister Sir Winston S. Churchill (1874–1965).

**wog**

Derogatory racial epithet allegedly meaning "wily oriental gentleman" or "wards of government," or "westernized oriental gentleman." It has been used to describe dark skinned peoples from India through the Middle East to North Africa and the Mediterranean fringe.

**Woolworth gun**

The various marks of 9mm machine-carbines (submachine-guns) commonly known as the "Sten gun" – the "St" was derived from the designers, Major Reginald Shepherd and Harold Turpin, and "en" from Enfield, its place of development. Also "plumber's delight," "plumber's nightmare," "plumber's abortion," and "Stench gun." These names, along with "Woolworth gun," were given because of the Sten's cheap construction and gloomy performance.

**Wouldn't it!**

Exclamation of frustration, exasperation, revulsion. Shortened form of "wouldn't you know it!" For example, "What? You lost the bloody Don-Five! Wouldn't it!"

**wuff**

Kill an enemy or destroy a tank or other vehicle.

# X        X-ray

# Y        Yoker

**Yank**

An American. Also "colonist," or "colonial."

**Yukon pack**

A pack frame for carrying heavy equipment and supplies. It was especially useful in the mountains to man-pack ammunition, rations, and supplies to forward positions.

# Z          Zebra

**zambuk**      Medical orderly (MO). Named after "Zambuk" athletic healing salve.

**zizz**        A nap. Derived from the cartoonist practice of depicting snoring with "Z-Z-Z-Z."

**zombie**      Conscripted Canadian soldier who did not volunteer for overseas service. Only volunteers could be sent overseas. Zombies were considered to be the living dead because they allegedly had no souls owing to their refusal to deploy overseas. Because of the severe infantry replacement shortage in late 1944, almost 13,000 of the 60,000 "zombies" were deployed overseas with only 2,400 actually assigned to infantry battalions (69 were killed and fewer than 250 wounded).

**zop**         An officer with little experience or who thought of himself in lofty terms. (*Zopp* is Maltese for "prick.")

## UNIT NICKNAMES

| | |
|---|---|
| Black Button Mob | Fred Karno's Army |
| Broomstick Army | Groppi's Light Horse |
| Buck Guard | Nackeroos |
| Bullocks | paras |
| Chindits | Red Caps |
| Desert Rats | Red Devils |
| the Div | Terriers |
| Forgotten Army | weekend warriors |

# PART III

# LANDSERDEUTSCH –
# GERMAN ARMY SLANG

# BACKGROUND

What is variously referred to as soldiers' German (*Landserdeutsch*), soldiers' speech (*Landersprache*), or soldiers' expressions (*Landserausdrücke*) is an intriguing aspect of the life of the German soldier, the *Landser*. The *Landser* was much more politically indoctrinated than soldiers of the Western Allies, and this can be seen in his speech, which contained many ideologically and politically driven terms and phrases. The Germans also made extensive use of acronyms and abbreviations (*Abkürzungen*) and some of these were used as a form of slang in their own right. Certain slang terms were restricted to specific theaters, where it was not uncommon to borrow local words. Some standard terms are also included in order to describe the context in which they were used, which might be different from that assumed in the English context. As in all armies, terms dating from previous wars were sometimes retained in the soldier's vocabulary. It is important to note that, for clarity's sake, the term Wehrmacht is frequently mistranslated as "army." Wehrmacht means Defense Force and was comprised of the Heer (Army), Kriegsmarine (War Navy) and Luftwaffe (Air Force). The Waffen-SS was not a component of the Wehrmacht.

# A      Anton
# Ä      Ärger

**Aal**

Eel, slippery customer. A perfect illustration of how every side had soldiers who knew how to wangle their way out of unpleasant duties.

**abbauen**

To dismantle. Disengage from the front without the enemy becoming aware of it.

**Abzug**

Trigger, as in triggerman. A machine-gunner (*Maschinengewehr-Schütze*).

**Acht–Acht**

Eight-eight. The 8.8cm Flak 18, 36, 37, and 41 antiaircraft guns. While sometimes employed as an antitank gun, it was *not* the standard field artillery piece and was not used as indirect-fire artillery. Also *Otto-Otto*.

**Affe**

Ape. The cowhide-covered flap (*Tornisterklappe*) of the old-type backpack (*Tornister*). The hide was unshaved and the hair helped waterproof the pack. The term was retained for the later model backpack, even though the hide flap was replaced by one of canvas.

**Affenschaukel**

Monkey swing. (A girl's hairstyle consisting of looped plaits). Any kind of *fourragère* or shoulder cord worn by officers (service dress), adjutants, marksmen, etc.

**Afrikaner**

African. 1) A member of the Wehrmacht who served in North Africa. Contrary to popular conception, not all *Heer* personnel serving in North Africa were members of the Deutsches Afrika-Korps (DAK). There were divisions and smaller units in Africa outside the DAK serving under 5. Panzer-Armee Afrika.

2) A German prisoner of war captured in North Africa, the term was self-bestowed by prisoners.

**Alles Gute** — All the best, good luck. Often, no doubt, spoken cheerily before comrades set off on a semi-suicidal mission.

**Alles in die Waagschale werfen** — Lit. "to throw everything into the scale pan." To use everything that you have, to risk everything to win. When all subunits are placed in the front line and no reserve is held owing to reduced manpower or broad frontages.

**alte Kämpfer** — Old Fighters. A distinction designating members of the SS who had served in Nazi organizations prior to January 30, 1933. (Members of Austrian Nazi organizations serving prior to February 12, 1938, were also authorized to wear the chevron.) They were identified by a silver point-down chevron *Ehrenwinkel für alte Kämpfer* (Honor Chevron for Old Fighters) on the upper right uniform sleeve.

**alte Landser** — Old soldier. *Landser* is a slang term for a German soldier. Veteran "old" soldiers.

**Alter** — Old superior or old man. Mostly applied to the *Kompaniechef* (company/battery chief). See *Vater*.

**alter Hase** — Old hare. An old hand, a combat veteran who was sprightly enough to have managed to stay alive.

**alter Mann** — Old man. The encouraging nickname for Italian-issue tinned beef consumed by German troops in Africa, Sicily, and Italy. Also known as, and reflecting poorly on the taste, *Arsch Mussolini* (Mussolini's ass) or *armer Mussolini* (poor

Mussolini). The nickname is derived from the "AM" stamped on the meat cans, meaning *Amministrazione Militare* (Military Administration) in Italian. The Italians said it meant *Arabo Mòrto* (Dead Arab), *Asino Mòrto* (Dead Donkey), or *Anale Mussolini* (Mussolini's Ass).

**Ami, Amis**      Contraction of *Amerikaner* (American).

**Angstbrosche**      Lit. "brooch of fear" The *Parteiabzeichen der NSDAP* (Nazi Party Badge), as some members were motivated by gnawing fear rather than proud ideology.

**Anno Scheiße**      Year shit – WWI.

**anscheißen**      Shit on. To be chewed out by one's commander.

**Apfelsinenorden**      Orange medal (owing to the ribbon color). Refers to the *Medaille für den Italienisch-Deutschen Feldzug in Afrika* or any other worthless decoration. See also *Sandsturm Orden*.

**Arsch**      Arse – a simple word with myriad uses, including: *am Arsch der Welt* (at the arse-end of the world – any isolated or forward position); *beim Arsch kriegen* (get by the arse – make someone responsible for); *den Arsch schonen* (protect the arse – to vomit/throw up); *den Arsch verlöten* (solder the arse – beat up); *den Arsch zukneifen* (clench the arse – be killed in action); *kalter Arsch mit Schneegestöber* (cold arse with snow flurry – a bad meal); *Schütze Arsch* (rifleman arse – simple soldier); *sich den Arsch auskugeln* (dislocate one's arse – be killed in action).

**Arschlecker**      Ass-licker, brown-noser.

**Aspirinjesus**

Aspirin Jesus. A substandard physician. Often this was not so much the fault of the physician as due to the serious lack of medical supplies and shortage of medications.

**aufgewärmte Leiche**

Warmed-up corpse. Member of a no doubt highly functional unit made up of the disabled, such as a *Magenbataillon* (stomach battalion), comprising soldiers with stomach complaints or other gastrointestinal ailments.

**Aufriß**

Split. Glancing shot or flesh wound.

**Ausmister**

Mucker-out. Rear-area officer charged with identifying, locating, and scraping out soldiers (and, towards the end of war, also civilians) suitable for frontline duty.

**ausradieren**

Rub out. To wipe out or totally destroy a position, vehicle, or installation.

**aussteigen**

To alight. Leave a damaged tank, aircraft, or ship as if your trousers were on fire.

**automatische Artillerie**

Automatic artillery. Referred to the high rate and volume of fire maintained by US field artillery.

# B Bertha (Bruno)

**Backofen**

Baking oven. Any hotly contested position. Also a generic term for armored vehicles (whose interior temperatures rose rapidly in combat or when in hot climes).

**Bandhändler**

Ribbon-dealer. A soldier wearing a large number of ribbons and other decorations. Reminiscent of the old practice of actual ribbon dealers, who displayed samples fastened to their coats.

| | |
|---|---|
| **Banditen** | Bandits. 1) Euphemism for partisans. The High Command of the Army issued a directive on August 23, 1942, stating that for psychological reasons *Partisan* would not be used, but rather *Bandit*. Other terms included *bewaffnete Bänder* (armed gangs), *Bolshewistische Aufwiegler* (Bolshevik agitators), *Saboteure* (saboteurs), and *Soldaten in Zivilkleidung* (soldiers in civilian clothes), implying they were acting illegally along the lines of a spy and in violation of the Geneva Convention. This meant, to the Germans, that such people fell neatly outside the rules of war and could be freely tortured and executed.<br><br>2) *Banditen* was also used in conjunction with other terms, such as *englische Banditen*, to describe supposed enemy war criminals. |
| **Barackenpferd** | Barrack stallion. A woman-chaser of some skill. |
| **Bau** | Building, construction. Arrest or detention cell, e.g. *Zwei Wochen Bau* (lit. "two weeks in the cells"). |
| **Bauchbinde** | Bellyband. Enlisted man's black leather belt (*Koppel*), later made of substitute materials or webbing. |
| **Beerdigungs-komiker** | Comedian at a funeral. Military chaplain delivering a stultifyingly boring sermon. |
| **Behandlung, die** | The treatment. Delivering or receiving heavy fire, especially artillery fire. |
| **Beichtwebel** | Combination of *Beichte* (confession) and *Feldwebel* (sergeant). A Catholic military chaplain. |
| **bepflastern** | To plaster (cover with cobblestones). To bombard with artillery or bomb an enemy position heavily. |

Also used to describe the not so gentle treatment
of the wounded in field dressing stations.

**Berge des Mondes** Mountains of the Moon. Nickname of the
*Grafenwöhr Truppen-Übungsplatz* (Troops Training
Area) because of its remoteness. This was a
major training area where part of the Afrika-
Korps trained.

**Besteck** A complete set of cutlery – knife, fork, and
spoon. Slang for a *Ritterkreuz des Eisernen Kreuzes
mit dem Eichenlaub mit Schwertern* (Knight's Cross
of the Iron Cross with Swords), simply called the
*Ritterkreuz*. Also *Blechkrawatte* (tin-necktie), as it
was worn suspended from a neck ribbon, and
*Halseisen* (neck-iron). See also *Halsschmerzen*.

**Betonorden** Concrete order. *Deutsches Schützwall-Ehreuzeichen*
(German Defenses Decoration) for participating
in the construction of the *Westwall* (Siegfried
Line) and Atlantic Wall defences.

**Beutegermanen** Booty-Germans. *Volksdeutschen* (ethnic Germans)
or foreign volunteers in the Wehrmacht or
Waffen-SS; booty in the sense of war-booty, as
their home country was taken over by Germany.
*Volksdeutschen* outside of Germany were exempt
from conscription, but eligible for recruitment
by the Waffen-SS.

**Bienenvater** Beekeeper. Soldier infested with lice. See also
*Läusehaus*.

**Bifteck** Used to mean British (also *Engländer*). Little
used and probably derived from the French
nickname for the English – *beafsteak*.

**Bildungskanone** Education cannon. Truck delivering reading
material to troops at the front. Also bookshops
for the German military in occupied territories.

**bimsen**
To bounce. Hard, leg-stomping drill in the company area, be it practice drills with weapons or marching.

**Birne**
Pear. To refer to someone's head as a "pear" is, surprisingly, uncomplimentary.

**blau**
Blue. Drunk. Alcoholism was more widespread within the *Heer* than many realized, with combat troops having a particular fondness for drink.

**Blaue-Bohnen-Eintopf**
Blue bean soup. Heavy machine-gun fire.

**Blaue Max, der**
Blue Maximum, the imperial *Orden Pour le Mérite* (Order for Merit), Prussia's highest decoration through WWI. It was supplanted as a military order by the *Ritterkreuz des Eisernen Kreuzes* (Knight's Cross of the Iron Cross) in 1939, but a civil order of the *Blaue Max* remained in use and still exists today in Germany as the *Orden Pour le Mérite für Wissenschaft und Künste* (Order for Merit for Science and Arts). It was established in 1667 as the *Ordre pour la Générosité* (Order for Generosity) and was renamed in 1740. The *Blaue Max* was so named because its cross was blue-enameled and the *Max* came from *Maximum*, meaning the highest decoration. Those who had been awarded the decoration in WWI were permitted to wear it along with other imperial awards under the Nazi regime. It bore a French title as it was instituted by Frederick the Great (Frederick II, 1712–86), who spoke only French.

**Blech**
Sheet metal trinkets or "tin-wear." Metal badges worn on the uniform such as the various assault, combat, and wound badges.

**Blechhut**

Tin-hat. Specifically the Stahlhelm 35 (steel helmet M1935), the standard helmet of the Wehrmacht. Also *Hurratüte* (lit. "hurrah paper-bag," a party hat), and *Parteihut* (party hat).

**Blitzmädchen,**
**Blitzmaus,**
**Blitznutte**

Lightning girls, lightning mouse, lightning prostitute. All expressions for *Nachrichtenhelferinnen* female signals auxiliaries (both army and air force), derived from the lightning flash insignia on the sleeves of their uniforms.

**Blumenkohl**

Cauliflower. Oak Leaves, officially *das Eichenlaub zum Ritterkreuz des Eisernen Kreuze*s (the Oak Leaves to the Knight's Cross of the Iron Cross). Also *Salat* (Salad).

*The Germans seemed to have a fascination for big guns.*

**Blumenkrieg**

Flower War. The peaceful occupation and annexation of the Saar in January 1935, Rhineland in March 1936, Austria in March 1938, and Sudetenland in October 1938. So named because of the enthusiastic welcome German occupation troops received.

**Bolschewisten/ Bolschewiken**

Communists (*Kommunisten*), Soviets (*Sowjets*). The Germans did not generally use the term *Sowjet* to refer to individuals. See also *Stalinisten*.

**Bonzen**

Bigwigs or stuffed shirts. Commanders and staff, senior officers or officials. See *Bronzen*.

**Bronzen**

Bronzes. Commanders and staff. Used in a similar context to the American "Brass." See *Bonzen*.

**Brotbeutel, der**

The bread bag. The small ration haversack attached to the belt over the right hip. The Waffen-SS' slightly patronizing nickname for the *Heer*, although little used in this context.

**Bruno**

Bruno-Kanone (Br.Kan.). General nickname for 28cm railroad guns (*Eisenbahngeschütze*). See also *Theodor* and *Robert und Leopold*.

**brustkrank**

Suffering from chest trouble. Used to describe anyone with an unhealthy yearning for medals or decorations. See also *Halsschmerzen*.

**Bubi**

Diminutive of *Bube*, a "boy" or "lad." A nick-name for any fresh-faced youngster or the youngest member of the unit. It could also be used to suggest that someone was a homosexual.

**Bückware**

Lit. "stooping ware." *Schwarzer Markt* (black market) items sold from under the counter, necessitating a furtive bend.

**Bude**            A civilian slang term for a room. Sometimes used by the military to refer to a group (squad) barracks room.

**Bulle**           Bull. The Soviet Yakovlev Yak-1, 3, 7, and 9 fighters because they were as dangerous as raging bulls.

**Bummel**          "Pub-crawl," a drinking binge.

**Butterfront**     Butter front. Any occupied area (e.g. France) where supplies were plentiful, there was no fighting, and life was rosy.

# C            Cäsar
# Ch           Charlotte

**Capau** *or* **Kapau**   A Russian barn, often used as troop quarters. Derived from the Russian Cyrillic spelling for "barn," pronounced "ssaraj."

**Charly**          Enemy reconnaissance or spotter aircraft.

**Chef**            Chief. Commanding officer of a small unit, for example, *Kompaniechef*. Sometimes used to describe any leader at the small unit-level, as in *der Chef* – "the boss."

## WHAT'S COOKING?

| | |
|---|---|
| alter Mann | Mussolini-Kartoffeln |
| Churchill-Pimmel | Nazibohnen |
| Dachschwein | Quatschschwein |
| Drahtverhau | Rückzugspastete |
| Frontkameradensuppe | russische Schokoladen |
| Horse Wessel-Suppe | Stalintorte |
| Karo einfach | Wassersuppe |

**Churchill-Pimmel**  Churchill's dick. Solidly crafted nickname for *Blutwurst* (blood sausage).

# D  Dora

**Dachschaden**  Roof damage. Evocative term for a head shot, or head wound.

**Dachschwein**  Roof pig. A cat lovingly raised as food by desperate civilians suffering meat shortages. Compare to *Quatschschwein*.

**Dauerurlaubs-schein**  Permanent leave pass. *Einen Dauerurlaubsschein kriegen*: get a permanent leave pass – be killed in action.

**Deutsch-amerikaner**  German–American. Refers to an unexploded American bomb "residing" in Germany.

**Dödel**  Dick. Refers to the *Ritterkreuz des Eisernen Kreuzes* (Knight's Cross of the Iron Cross).

**Donnerbalken**  Thunder-beam. Used in reference to a luxurious sanitation construction consisting of plank or pole on which one sat over a temporary pit-type latrine.

**Doppelladung**  Double charge. Two demolition charges with a delay fuse connected by a short length of wire and thrown over a tank's main gun barrel.

**Dopplegranate**  Double grenade. Two stick or egg hand grenades taped together, one activated, and thrown into rooms or pillboxes to provide an even more horrible blast and fragmentation effect.

**"Dora und Gustav"**  Dora and Gustav. Individual nicknames for the two massive 80cm railroad mobile guns. Gustav saw action at Sebastopol and Dora was deployed outside Stalingrad, but never saw action.

**Drahtverhau**  Barbed-wire entanglement, but in this case meaning *Gemüse* (mixed dried vegetables), which tended to be hard and lumpy if insufficiently cooked after reconstituting with water. These were issued separately or as a component of *Eiserne Portion* ("iron rations").

**dran sein**  His time is up, which could be followed ominously by *ich bin dran* (it is my turn). This term was used when undertaking a dangerous mission or patrol.

**Druckposten**  Pressing assignment. An assignment important enough to allow one away from duties in the front line. A cushy rear-area job.

**d.u.**  Official abbreviation for *dienstunfähig* (unfit for duty). Said by troops to mean *dauernd unsichtbar* (permanently invisible), *dauernd urlaubsverwendungsfähig* (permanently eligible for leave), or *dauernd unterwegs* (permanently on the move).

**Dünnschißkanone**  Lit. "diarrhea cannon." A machine-gun, the nickname possibly deriving from the physiological effect of encountering one, or from the unhealthy spray of bullets.

**durchaus gefestigt**  A solid Nazi supporter, as opposed to a *Spießer* (bourgeois) critical of the goverment.

**D-Zug**  Contraction of *Durchgangszug* ([troop] express train). Also known as a *Fronturlaubzug* (front leave [special] train). See *Partisanenexpress*.

# E    Emil

**Eau de Pologne**  Corruption of *Eau de Cologne*. Liquid manure, any patch of stinking mud.

| | |
|---|---|
| **Ehrenkeule** | Honor cudgel. A *Generalfeldmarschallen Stab* (general field marshal's baton). |
| **Eiserne Ivan** | Iron Ivan. The nickname for the twin-engined Soviet Petlyakov Pe-2 ground-attack aircraft. Soviet crews affectionately called it the *Peshka* (Pawn). |
| **Eiserne Kuh** | Iron cow. The staple *Büchsenmilch* (canned milk) or *Kondensmilch* (condensed/evaporated milk). |
| **Energietropfen** | Energy drops. Alcohol issued before an attack to spur soldiers on (i.e. render them numb). |
| **englische Krankheit** | English disease. Rickets (vitamin D deficiency) blamed on the poor diet caused by the British blockade of Germany. Dates from WWI. The expression also stood for homosexuality, in the time-honored tradition of questioning the other side's sexual leanings. |
| **Entfettungskur** | Slimming course. Time spent in a prisoner-of-war camp. |
| **Ersatz-Landser** | Substitute soldier. Unemployed Luftwaffe and Kriegsmarine personnel transferred, naturally just when they thought they were safe, to the *Heer* to serve in combat or service positions. Note: an *Ersatz* unit (Grenadier-Ersatz-Regiment, for example) was a replacement troops processing unit. |
| **Ersatzreserveersatz** | Replacement reserve. Derogatory term for the *Volkssturm* (People's Assault), civilians conscripted for a last-ditch defense in the closing months of the war. |
| **Esak** | Abbreviation for *Evangelische Sünden-Abwehr-Kanone* (lit. "Protestant Anti-Sin Gun"), i.e. a Protestant Chaplain. A word-play on such accepted terms as *Flak* (antiaircraft gun) and *Pak* (antitank gun). |

**E-schein**　　Contraction for *Entlausungsschein* (delousing certificate), which was issued by *Entlausungsstationen* (delousing stations). Its possession was mandatory before a soldier could depart the Eastern Front on leave, to avoid Russian lice taking a vacation back to Germany.

**Eselsohren**　　Donkey ears. The 6x30 Sf.14Z *Scherenfernrohr* (scissors binoculars); known as a battery commander's scope in the United States.

**Eßbesteck**　　Eating (*essen*) cutlery. Combination interlocking knife, fork, spoon, and can-opener set.

**Etappenschweine**　　Rear swine. Frontline troops' name for rear service troops. Combat soldiers generally despised the rear service troops, a common sentiment in all armies, but especially prevalent in the German forces and even more so on the Eastern Front. Compare to *Frontschweine*.

*Rear service troops were despised in all armies, but they seemed to be even more hated in the German Army.*

**Etappenhengst**  Rear stallion. 1) *Ersatzheer* (Replacement Army) soldiers or rear service troops, particularly those remaining within Germany.
2) Rear service troops who claimed they desired frontline service.

**Ewige Rottenführer, der**  Lit. "the eternal senior private." Rottenführer was the Waffen-SS equivalent of the Heer Gefreiter rank. It means one who was never promoted to SS-Unterscharführer or Heer Unteroffizier (corporal), and probably never would be.

# F  Friedrich (Fritz)

**Fahrkarte**  Ticket. An artillery projectile fired at a distant target and its impact unobserved; a "lost round."

**faule Hünde**  Lazy dogs, loafers.

**Faust**  Fist. From *Panzerfaust* (armor fist). The general term for a series of single-shot, shoulder-fired, disposable, recoilless antiarmor weapons: *Panzerfaust klein* (small), 30, 60, 100, and 150 (the designations refer to the weapons' effective range). The Finns, to whom the Germans provided the *Panzerfaust*, called it the *Panssarikauhu*.

**Feger**  Sweeper. Good-looking, woman-hungry man, sweeping up all females who crossed his path.

**Feldküchensturm-abzeichen**  Field Kitchen Assault Badge. *Kriegsverdienstkreuz* (War Merit Cross), which was mainly awarded to non-combatants such as rear service troops, administrative units, and those at higher headquarters. It is apparent from the number of disparaging nicknames for this decoration that *Frontsoldaten* thought little of it. Also known as

|  | *Kantinenorden* (Order of the Canteen) and *Kriegsverlängerungskreuz* (War Prolongment Cross). See also *Nichteinmischungsorden mit Eßbesteck*. |
|---|---|
| **Feldmäuse** | Field mice. Applied mockingly to *Feldgendarmerie* (field military police). |
| **Feuerpause** | Firebreak, the formal term for temporary "cease-fire." A cigarette break or rest break. Also *Marschpause*. |
| **Feuerzauber** | Magic fire. A sudden barrage inexplicably received from the ever-eager American artillery. This may have been due to good target acquisition or simply random harassing and interdiction fire. |
| **Flamingo** | Flamingo. A *Generaloffizier* (general officer). Refers to a general's double red trouser stripes, red tabs, and other red adornments. |
| **flammen** | To kick someone's backside, figuratively or physically. |
| **Flandernzaun** | Flanders fence. Double-apron barbed-wire fence known as the *doppelt verstärkter Zaun*. Term dates from WWI. |
| **Fliegerei** | Lit. "flying," but specifically the Luftwaffe. Also *Flieger* (flyers). |
| **Flintenweib** | Lit. "shotgun-woman." Nickname for female partisans, known to be tough and generally good with guns. |
| **Fohlen** | Foals. New recruits. |
| **Franzmann** *or* **Franzose** | Frenchman. 1) *Franzmänner* or *Franzosen* – Frenchmen, *französisch* – French. The stereotypical *Schneckenfresser* (snail devourer) was in limited use. |

2) *Französen* – German prisoners of war captured in France. This term was self-bestowed by prisoners.

**Frauen aus der Hölle**
Ladies from Hell. Scottish units of the British Army, because of their skirt-like kilts combined with a ferocious fighting spirit, together forming a truly alarming vision. Originated in WWI.

**Frontbummel**
Lit. "front stroll." Reconnaissance patrol.

**Frontkameraden-suppe**
Front comrades soup. Stew of beans, potatoes, and ham – "the comrades." The concoction would keep well in cold/cool weather and was edible when cold (preferred hot, of course). In hot/warm weather vinegar was added to preserve it. It was sometimes prepared for later use and carried in the mess kit during the day.

**Frontschweine**
Front pigs. Rear service troops' name for *Frontsoldaten* (front soldiers). It was derived using *Schweine*, as in *wir armen Schweine* (lit. "we poor pigs"), a self-deprecating, but distinguishing nickname. *Frontsoldaten* sometimes referred to themselves with this nickname.

**Führergeschenk**
Leader's gift (referring to Hitler). Food parcels given to soldiers at railroad stations while in transit. Contained preserved food such as tinned sausage, cheese, marmalade, hard biscuit, cigarettes, etc.

**Furzfänger**
Fart catcher. Belted service or parade dress tunic.

**Fußlappen**
Foot-cloth. This term was usd for boiled cabbage, as it was flat and smelled bad, alluding to its similarity to richly scented foot-wraps. A *Fußlappen* was actually a square of fabric, which was wrapped over a sock to preserve it and for added warmth.

**Fußlappenindianer** Lit. "foot-cloth Indian." An *Infanterist* (infantryman), also known as a *Sandlatscher* (sand-traipser) and *Stoppelhopser* (stubble-jumper).

**Fußvolk** Foot people. Infantrymen and pioneers. In the infantry division virtually all personnel rode on motor vehicles, motorcycles, bicycles, wagons, or horses, all that is except the 27 rifle, nine machine-gun, and three pioneer companies – they walked.

# G Gustav

**Gähnappell** Yawn parade. Church parade in the field, which obviously inspired deep spiritual concentration. Also any period of boring classroom instruction.

**Gangster** Adopted American word. Used in German propaganda to refer to American soldiers or politicians.

**Gartenspritzer** Garden sprinkler. Light machine-gun, quick-firing cannon, or light flak gun.

**Gebetbuch** Prayer book. Company/battery reporting NCO's report book carried in a small *Meldetasche* (black leather case) inserted between the first and third front closure buttons of the tunic, the second being unbuttoned. A man had best pray hard if his name was entered in the book. See *Spieß, der*.

**Gebirgsmarine** Mountain navy. Any hastily assembled military unit, made up of nervous personnel from any or all branches of the services, usually thrown into action as a stop-gap measure in times of crisis.

**Gefrierfleischorden** Frozen Meat Order. *Medaille Winterschlacht im Osten 1941/42* (Winter Battle Medal in the East

1941/42). The shortened name for the decoration was the *Ostmedaille* (East Medal). Indicative of conditions in the East, it was also called *Hackfleischmedaille* (Mincemeat Medal) and *Eisbeinorden* (Ice-leg Order), the latter from *Eisbein*, a culinary dish made from knuckle of pork. It was instituted in May 1942 for soldiers who served during the brutal Eastern Front winter between November 15, 1941, and April 15, 1942. To receive the medal combatants had to serve at least 14 days in a combat zone and non-combatants at least 60 days.

**General Heldenklaue**  General Hero-Nabber. Generalleutnant Walther von Unruh, responsible for combing paramilitary organizations for personnel to be transferred to the *Heer*.

**gepanzerte Krabbe**  Armored prawn. The *fahrbare Panzerlafette* (transportable armor[ed] mount). This was a cupola-like 4-ton cast-steel two-man machine-gun pillbox that was moved on wheels. The wheels could be removed and the pillbox positioned in a pre-dug pit, and camouflaged. First used on the Eastern Front in 1943 and later in Italy and on the Western Front. Also known as a *fahrbarer Bunker* (transportable bunker) or *Panzernest* (armor nest).

**Gesinnungsrück-strahler**  Opinion reflector. *Deutsches Kreuz in Gleb* (German Cross in Gold). The nickname was a reference to the decoration's in-your-face political design, featuring a large swastika. Also known as the *Partieabzeichen für Kurzsichtige* (Party badge for the short-sighted) on account of its resemblance to the (much smaller) early Nazi Party badge. See also *Spiegelei*.

**Goldfasan**
Golden Pheasant. Official or *politischer Leiter* (political leader) of the Nazi Party. So called owing to their light-brown uniforms hinting a golden cast, gold and red insignia, and reddish-brown leather accoutrements, altogether reminiscent of the plumage of male pheasants. Also *Pofu*, an abbreviation of *politischer Funktionär* (political functionary), also a Nazi Party member.

**Grabenschreck**
Lit. "trench shock." Any high-ranking officer turning up unexpectedly in the front line and making a thorough nuisance of himself.

**Gretchen**
Diminutive of Margaret. The Panzerfaust klein 30, the first model of the *Panzerfaust*. It had a smaller and differently shaped warhead from later models. See *Faust*.

**Gröfaz**
Contraction of *Grösster Feldherr aller Zeiten* (lit. "greatest general of all time"). Derogatory term for Hitler based on a propaganda claim attributed to Generalfeldmarschall Walter Keitel, Chief of the Wehrmacht. *Feldherr* (warlord) was an old term for general or commander.

**Grüner Elefant**
Green Elephant. Zündapp motorcycle, specifically the KS 601, with a commercial nickname owing to its matte green color. This color was often retained on those impressed into military service.

**Grünhölle**
Green hell, a term used to describe forest fighting on the Eastern Front. It was almost impossible to determine the locations of enemy lines and positions. Engagements were at extremely close range and attacks and fire could come from any direction.

**Grünpolizei**   Green Police. *Landespolizei* (State Police), owing to their green uniforms. They were absorbed into the *Heer* as infantry in 1935 and for a time retained their traditional green uniforms.

**Gulaschkanone**   Goulash cannon. *Feldküchenwagen* (field kitchen wagon), also known as a *Futterkanone* (fodder cannon). The wood, coal, or charcoal-fired stove was horse-drawn (motorized versions existed) and could be operated on the move. It was easily identifiable by its stovepipe, its "cannon." It was mainly used for cooking soups and stews in large pots, but also possessed an oven and a coffee

*The doublecross was a fitting description of the swastika.*

cauldron. Each company/battery possessed one
along with its limber carrying utensils and
cooking gear.

**Gummi**                Rubber. A condom. Also, simply stated,
                         *Gummischutz* (rubber protection).

**Gummiband**            Rubber band. A ½–1in wide section cut out of a
                         tire inner tube and placed around a steel helmet
                         to secure camouflage materials.

# H                      Heinrich

**HaBé**                 Abbreviation of *Hals- und Beinbruch!* (lit.
                         "Break your neck and leg!"), an expression of
                         encouragement, especially to one about to
                         embark on a mission that might kill him. Also
                         an oblique reference to HB (pronounced
                         "Ha-Bay"), a popular brand of cigarette.

**Halsschmerzen**        Sore-throat. Officer said to be seeking the
                         Knight's Cross of the Iron Cross at the expense
                         of the *Landser*, who only wanted to stay alive.

**Hammel**               Castrated ram. A *Rekrut* (recruit) – all bleat and
                         no balls (a lot of talk, but no experience).

**Hängekommando**        Hanging Commando. The *Feldjägerkorps*
                         (Field Hunter Corps), who were positioned at
                         river crossing sites, major road junctions, railroad
                         stations, etc. with authority to conduct
                         *Feldkriegsgerichte* (flying courts martial) and
                         summary executions of fit combat soldiers
                         deserting the front. See *Kopfjäger*.

**Hausfriedensbruch**    Trespassing. Attacking and occupying an enemy
                         position. Also *Hausfriedensbruch mit Ansage*
                         (trespassing with prior notice) – the same but
                         with a preliminary artillery bombardment.

| | |
|---|---|
| **Heeresgut** | Army Property. These words were stamped on issue packing containers. They came to mean anything belonging to the military. Similar to the US "GI" (Government Issue) or British "WD" (War Department). |
| **Heia Safari!** | Battle cry of the Deutsches Afrika-Korps (German Africa Corps) and the title of its theme song. Swahili phrase meaning "Let's go get them!" |
| **Heiliger Geist** | Holy Spirit. Barracks "justice" meted out by soldiers against one whose misbehavior or mistakes led to group punishment. The rest of the soldiers might collectively beat the offender in a nighttime attack. When asked who conducted the attack the barracks replied cooperatively, *Der Heilige Geist*. |
| **Heimatschuß** | Lit. "home wound." Wound that gets one sent home. |
| **Heimkrieger** | Home warrior. Rear service troops who never left Germany. Sometimes referred to as the *Heimatheer* (Home Army). |
| **Heldenkeller** | Hero's cellar. Air raid shelter or bunker, where even the brave headed when bombed. |
| **Heldenklau** | Hero thief. *Klau* is a slang term for a thief. *Heldenklau* was an officer collecting stragglers or commandeering rear service troops for frontline combat duty or to form an *ad hoc* unit. Often soldiers on their way to or from leave were commandeered for such units at railroad stations. |
| **Hermann Meiermütze** | Hermann Meier cap. *Tropenschirmmütze* (tropical peaked cap) issued for Luftwaffe use in Africa and southern Europe from 1941. Its nickname is attributed to Reichsmarschall Hermann Göring's misplaced boast that enemy bombers would |

never reach the Ruhr River and if they did, "you can call me Meier." Also, *der Dicke* (the Fat One).

**Henker, der**
The Hangman. Nickname for SS-Obergruppenführer und General der Polizei Reinhard Heydrich (1904–42), chief of the *Reichssicherheitshauptamt* (National Security Main Office) and *Reichsprotektor von Böhmen und Mähren* (National Protector of Bohemia and Moravia), as well as a principal architect of the Final Solution. Other affectionate nicknames include *Henker Heydrich* (Hangman Heydrich), *das blonde Vieh* (the Blonde Beast), and Butcher of Prague (by non-Germans).

**Himmelfahrts-kommando**
Ascension Day Commando. A "journey to heaven mission," "suicide mission." Although not necessarily deliberately suicidal in the literal sense, it referred to high-risk missions, especially rearguard actions, as well as reconnaissance patrols, raids, counterattacks, and mine and bomb clearing. (Ascension Day commemorates the ascension of Christ into heaven, 40 days after the Resurrection and ten days before Pentecost.)

**hinrotzen**
Lit. "evading snot." An unpleasant image evoking the equally unpleasant activity of running for cover and avoiding fire.

**Hitlermühle**
Hitler mill. The *Schlüsselgerät* (cipher equipment) SG.41, issued in small numbers late in the war to replace the Enigma cipher equipment. *Mühle* (mill) is slang for typewriter.

**Hitlersäge**
Hitler's saw. The 7.9mm MG42 machine-gun. Also *Hitlergeige* (Hitler violin). Its cyclic rate of fire was 1,100–1,200rpm, while the MG34 had an 800–900rpm rate. Most American machine-

guns fired at 450–500rpm. Neither term was
widely used.

**Hiwi** *or* **HiWi**     Acronym for *Hilfswillige* (Auxiliary Volunteer).
After the invasion of the USSR thousands of
captured Soviet soldiers volunteered to fight
against the Soviet regime. Initially the Germans
declined their employment, but because of
mounting casualties accepted them in non-
combat roles, especially engineer and supply
troops, and large numbers were later assigned to
combat units. See also *Osttruppen* and *Kawi*.

**HJ-Spätlese**     Late-vintage *Hitler-Jugend* (HJ, Hitler Youths).
The *Volkssturm* (People's Assault) last-ditch
home defense militia was established in
September 1944 and consisted mainly of men
aged between 16 and 60, previously regarded
unfit for regular military service. So ran the joke:
"The government is commandeering all prams."
"Why?" "To transport the born in 1943 class
to the front." See also *Krüppelgarde*, *Magen-
Bataillone*, and *V3*.

**Hoffnungsbalken**     Hopeful boards. *Offiziersanwärter* (officer
aspirant) shoulder straps. This was the individual
NCO's rank shoulder straps, with the addition
of two 9mm wide braid loops at the base of the
strap. Refers to the aspirants' desire for
promotion to officer rank.

**Höllenabwehr-      Lit. "anti-hell gun." Military padre (see also
kanone**             *Esak*).

**Horst Wessel-Suppe**     Horst Wessel soup. A meatless, flavorless soup, in
other words with nothing to it, just as there was

little to the over-inflated Nazi martyrdom of Horst Wessel.* See also *Wassersuppe*.

**Hosenscheisser**
Trousers shitter. Self-explanatory and nicely descriptive term for a coward.

**Hühneralarm**
Chicken alarm – first the egg, then the cackle. Alarm sounded after the damage had been done, for example, an air raid siren sounding after the first bombs struck.

**Hummelhunde**
Lit. "tomboy-dogs." "The lads" – newly assigned replacements or recruits.

**Hundemarke**
Dog tag. *Erkennungsmarke* (oval identity tag) worn around the neck on a cord. It was perforated with each half bearing the individual's unit designation, *Stammrollennummer* (unit roster number), and blood group. If the wearer were killed the bottom half of the tag was broken off and turned into the unit and the other half remained with the body.

# I     Ida

**Infanterie**
Infantry. Could also stand for an insect infestation, e.g. *leichte Infanterie* (light infantry) – fleas; *schwere Infanterie* (heavy infantry) – bed bugs.

**Intelligenzstreifen**
Intelligence stripes. *Generalstab* (General Staff) officers wore crimson red double stripes on their trousers and breeches (two 33mm wide stripes separated by 5mm on either side of the 2mm wide seam piping). The term "intelligence

---

\* *Horst Wessel (1907–30) was a member of the Nazi Party murdered by political opponents and made into a martyr by the Nazis. A propaganda song bearing his name was popularized along with a later parody,* Horst Wessel Lügen *(Horst Wessel Lied).*

stripes" sarcastically commented on the qualities required of General Staff officers. General officers wore similar stripes in bright red.

**Irrenanstalt**  Lunatic asylum. Referred to the *Führerhauptquartier* (Führer HQ).

**Isba**  Russian peasant "log cabin." Usually small and crude, with one or two rooms, but at least gave shelter from the awful Russian weather.

**Iwan, Iwans**  1) *Russischer Soldat* (Russian soldiers). Also *Popov, Popovs*. See *Russe*.
2) Soviet Mikoyan–Gurevich MiG-3 fighter.

# J  Julius

**Jabo**  Acronym for *Jagdbomber* (fighter-bomber) and the nickname for Allied ground-attack fighter-bombers. This is an interesting combination of German and English words, *Jagd* (fighter) and "bomber." See also *Tiefflieger*. *Jagd* is another word for "the hunt."

**Jagdpferderlaubnis**  Hunter's license. Certificate issued by a physician stating a soldier with a serious head wound was not responsible for his actions or what he said. Obviously, seldom issued.

# K  Konrad (Kurfurst)

**"K" *or* "S" Rolle**  Concertina wire. Coiled spring steel wire used as an obstacle; "K"– *Klardraht* (plain wire), "S"- *Stacheldraht* (barbed wire).

**Kaffee-Ersatz**  Substitute coffee. Coffee became scarce, but chicory was also grown in Europe and had long been blended with coffee. It was a popular beverage prior to the turn of the century. Pure

chicory "coffee," though, was bitter and lacked
the caffeine and calories to give soldiers their
early-morning zip. Other entirely inadequate
substitutes (*Kaffee-Ersatz-Ersatz*) included roasted
and ground acorns, beechnuts, barley, chick peas,
and oats. There was also *Tee-Ersatz* (substitute tea)
made from strawberry leaves, *braunstielige* ferns,
and many other plants. Without sugar these
substitutes were pretty grim.

**Kaffeemühle**  Coffee grinder. Light machine-gun. Also Soviet
Polikarpov PO-2/U-2 ground-attack aircraft.

**Kamerad**  Comrade. 1) Friend, comrade-in-arms.
*Kameraden* – comrades. *Kameradschaft*
(comradeship) had a deep and serious meaning
within the Wehrmacht, implying the strong bond
forged between men who fought together.
2) *Kameraden!* was shouted by German soldiers
to indicate they were surrendering and meaning
"Friends!" in this context, although they might
have been blasting away moments before. For
this reason they often followed with *Nicht
schießen!* (Do not shoot).

**Kameradenhelfer**  Comrade's helper. *Nähzeug* (sewing kit) or
*Nadelpackung* (needle packet).

**Kamerad
Schnürschuh**  Lit. "comrade laced-shoe." Refers to former
*Bundesheer der Republik Österreich* (Federal Army
of the Republic of Austria) soldiers, who wore
laced boots rather than jackboots, and who were
absorbed into the *Deutsches Heer* after the 1938
*Anschluß* (annexation).

**Kängaruh**  Kangaroo. The spread-winged *das Hoheitszeichen*
(eagle and swastika insignia) worn on the right
breast of the tunic as national identification.

**Kaninchenmedaille**
**or Kaninchenorden**
Rabbit Medal or Order. The *Ehrenkreuz der deutschen Mutter* (Honor Cross for the German Mother). German mothers were presented with this award for their dutiful talent of producing children: 1st Class – eight or more, 2nd Class – six or seven, 3rd Class – one to five. The meaning of its nickname is patently obvious. The award was part of an official effort to increase Germany's population. Typically, German families were small, and officially sex was for reproduction and not pleasure. Also known as the *Mutterkreuz* (Mother's Cross).

**Kapo**
Derived from Latin *capo*, meaning "head [man]." (*Capo* was used by the Italians to designate an NCO leader.)

Kameraden *were inseparable no matter what the situation was.*

1) Used to identify *Heer* Unteroffiziere and
SS-Unterführer ranks (corporals). Its use in this
sense pre-dates WWI.
2) A title given to concentration camp inmate
barracks or block leaders who were required to
maintain control over other inmates.

**"Karl"**    Carl. The nickname for both the 60cm (Gerät
040) and 54cm (Gerät 041) full-tracked self-
propelled siege mortars. Both were incorrectly
called *Thor*, but this was the nickname of an
individual 60cm mortar.

**Karo einfach**    Simple diamond. *Trockenes Brot* or *Dauerbrot* (dry
bread). Also simply *Karo*. Officially this issue
black rye bread, preserved with cinnamon, was
called *Kommißbrot* (commissariat bread). *Karo
einfach* is the lowest opening bid in the German
card game of Skat (where diamonds are the
lowest of the four suits). See also *Stalintorte*.

**Kartoffelstampfer**    Potato masher. The Stielhandgranate 24 (stick
grenade), owing to its resemblance to said
kitchen implement.

**Kattun**    Calico. To receive heavy fire. The relationship to
the word calico (a coarse cloth printed with
bright designs) is undetermined, though it may
possibly refer to the bright flashes of artillery fire.

**Kaugummisoldaten**    Chewing-gum soldiers. Propaganda term for
American soldiers implying they chewed gum
constantly like *Wiederkäuer* (cows chewing cud).
Apparently little used by *Landser*.

**Kawi**    Acronym for *Kampfwillige* (battle volunteers).
Former Soviet soldiers volunteering to serve
under German command in security and combat

units. The term was little used, with *Hiwi* being more common. See *Hiwi* and *Osttruppen*.

**Kerl, ein ganzer**    A complete fellow – a real guy. Similar to a buddy (American) or bloke or chap (British).

**Kesselraum**    Boiler room. Interior (fighting compartment) of a tank, known for being extremely hot.

**Kettenhund**    Chained dog. *Feldgendarmerie* (Field Gendarme), military police. Refers to their identifying metal gorget plate worn on the upper chest suspended from a neck chain.

**Kindersarg**    Children's coffin. A dark nickname for a small wooden antipersonnel mine. It did not imply it was intended to target children, but that it was a small casket-like box.

**Kiste**    Crate. An airplane.

**Klamotten**    Civilian slang for clothing, sometimes used by soldiers.

**Klavier**    Piano. Carrying case for a 2.7cm flare pistol cartridges, owing to its shape.

**Kleiderpartisanen**    Lit. "clothes partisans." Those ever-present lice.

**Kleinhaus**    Little house. A small *Unterschlupf* (dugout shelter).

**klotzen**    "Clumping." Throwing (firing) everything at a target.

**klotzen nicht kleckern**    Lit. "clump don't scatter." A caution to avoid the practice of too widely dispersing a unit thereby preventing its elements from supporting each other.

**klug**    Clever. Slang for a clever fellow. Believed to be the word from which today's computer-related term, "kludge," is derived, meaning something neither smart nor attractive.

**Klugscheisser**
Lit. "wise-shitter." A standard-issue, lying through his teeth, bull-shitter.

**Klumpfuß Goebbels**
Clubfoot Goebbels. A derogatory nickname for Joseph Goebbels (1897–1945), *Reichsminister* for Public Enlightenment and Propaganda. He actually was clubfooted.

**Knackmandel**
Lit. "almond in the shell." Egg hand grenade or any explosive or hollow-charge munition.

**Knobelbecher**
Lit. "toss-pots." High-topped leather marching boots, *Marschstiefel* (jackboots). The phrase alludes to boots being used to toss dice. Dates from WWI. See also *Würfelbecher*.

**Knochensack**
Bone-sack. The *Fallschirmjägerbluse* (paratrooper's blouse), a waterproof protective jacket, usually with a camouflage pattern, worn over the uniform and combat equipment when conducting parachute jumps. It was habitually retained for ground combat.

**Knochen-sammlung**
Bone collection. A burial party. Searching a battlefield for dead and wounded.

**Koffer**
Suitcase. Heavy artillery projectile in its wicker shipping container.

**Kohlenklau**
Coal thief. *Klau* is a slang term for thief, and was also a poster character with a walrus-like face, a squinting eye, worker's cap, and a furtively acquired sack of coal over his shoulder. The posters were part of an energy conservation campaign commencing in June 1942, and it warned that those hording or wasting coal denied German industry and soldiers the coal for industrial production, electricity, cooking, and heating.

**Kolbenringe**   Piston rings. Two 9mm-wide braid cuff bands worn by *Hauptfeldwebel* (chief field sergeants), who were the company/battery reporting NCOs, the equivalent of a US company/battery 1st sergeant or Commonwealth company/battery sergeant-major. See *der Spieß*.

**Komintern, Kommies**   Communists, "commies." A general term for Soviets.

**Kommiß**   Contraction of *Kommissariat* (commissariat) or *Kommissar* (commissary). An old term for the administrative service, which sometimes remained in use. The contemporary term was *Intendantur* (intendant).

*The* Kohlenklau *and anyone hording or squandering resources was pictured as an enemy of the State and the People.*

**Kopfjäger**  Headhunter. The *Feldjägerkorps* (Field Hunter Corps). A special military police force raised in November 1943 to apprehend deserters, collect stragglers and detached personnel, and organize them into *ad hoc* units or send them to stiffen combat-depleted units. See *Hängekommando*.

**Krämer**  Shop, but meaning a unit store. Also *Kantine* (canteen), *Marketenderei* (unit store). Similar to a US post exchange (PX).

**Kriegie**  Prisoner of war. Derived from *Kriegsgefangener* (war prisoner). Term was adopted by Western Allied prisoners to describe themselves.

**Kriegsgericht**  Court martial. It was used to mean a poor meal, the diner being "condemned to eat poor food." *Gericht* means either a tribunal or a dish or course.

**Kriegsgerichts-automat**  Court martial automat. Frightening mobile courts martial carrying out Hitler's death sentences. To be avoided at all costs.

**Kreuz, das**  The Cross. General term for the various grades of *das Eiserne Kreuz* (the Iron Cross), specifically the Iron Crosses 1st and 2nd Class.

**Krüppelgarde**  Crippled guard. Wry term for the *Volkssturm* (People's Assault), the last-ditch militia manned by mostly elderly men. See also *HJ-Spätlese*, *Magenbataillone*, *V3* and *Ersatzreserveersatz*.

**Kübel**  Tub. Refers to the similarity of the old prewar SdKfz 13 *Adler* (Eagle) and the later SdKfz 221 and SdKfz 222 *leichter Panzerspähwagen* (light armored reconnaissance vehicle), because their low, open-topped, boxy bodies were reminiscent of a bathtub.

**Kübelwagen**  Bucket car. The Volkswagen Typ 82 light field car. Refers to its bucket-type seats. There were other models of light field car bearing this name as well.

**Küchenbulle**  Kitchen bull. Cook (*Koch*).

**Kugel**  Ball. Bullet. In the same context that a standard bullet, as opposed to special-purpose ammunition such as tracer and armor-piercing, is referred to as "ball" ammunition.

**Kugelerlaß**  Bullet Decree. Hitler's March 4, 1944, decree that recaptured escaped officer and NCO prisoners of war (other than those from the Commonwealth and United States) were to be sent to concentration camps to be worked to death or executed. However, some recaptured Commonwealth officers were still executed under this decree.

**Kugelspritz**  Bullet-squirter. A term giving all the seriousness of a child's toy to the *Maschinenpistole* (machine pistol – submachine-gun), specifically 9mm MP18/I, MP28/II, MP34/I, MP38, MP40. To the Allies the MP38 and MP40 were known as "burp guns" because of the sound of their high rate of fire. See also "Kraut burp gun," Part I.

**Kumpel**  Buddy, pal. Also *Kumpan* (friend).

**Kusselgelände**  Russian brush land, of which the average German soldier on the Eastern Front saw alarming, endless amounts.

# L  Ludwig

**Lakeitel**  Contraction of *Lakai* (lackey or footman) and *Keitel*. Another name for Generalfeldmarschall Walter Keitel (1882-1945), *Oberbefehlshaber des Heeres* (Senior Commander of the Army), owing to his unbending support for Hitler's increasingly wacky ideas and agenda. Keitel was also known as the *Nickesel* (Nodding Donkey), a "yes man."

**Lametta**  Tinsel. Medals, decorations, and rank insignia; uniform adornments.

**Landser**  Traditional term for a soldier or soldiers. It is derived from the term *Landsknecht* (mercenary). The *Landsknechte* were western German lowlands soldiers of the Holy Roman Empire from the late 1400s to the early 1600s, renowned as pikemen.

**langmachen**  Literally "to make oneself long." To take cover by stretching out on the ground, an entertaining earth-hugging pastime when being bombed or shelled to oblivion.

**Latrinen-kommando**  Latrine commando. Latrine cleaning detail.

**Latrinenparole**  Latrine password. Rumors, *Klatsch* (gossip).

**latsches**  Colloquial for "go."

**Laura**  Rifle or carbine. Laura, a woman's name, implied that the rifle was a soldier's wife or girlfriend. He would certainly see more of it than a real partner.

**Läusehaus**  Louse house. *Heereshemd* – the pullover long-sleeve Army undershirt. It was worn for long periods and tended to harbor lice. See *Kleiderpartisanen*.

**Läuse und Scharfschützen**  Lice and snipers. The two worst things that characterized Russia, bar the climate. A general phrase for anything that was a nuisance.

| | |
|---|---|
| **Leithammel** | Bellwether. An NCO, specifically one who lacked the respect of, or credibility with, his men. Also referred to an Unteroffizier as they were newly promoted to an NCO grade and may not have yet been accepted by the troops. |

## LILI MARLEEN

*Das Lied eines jungen Soldaten auf der Wacht* (The Song of a Young Soldier on Watch) was known to Allied and Axis soldiers alike as *Lili Marleen*, arguably the most popular soldiers' song of WWII. Its lyrics originated from the 1915 poem *Mädchen unter der Laterne* (The Girl Under the Lantern) by Hans Leip (1893–1983), a veteran soldier. It was not published until 1937 in a book of his writings and was set to music in 1938 by Norbert Schultze. Sung by Lale Andersen (1905–72), it did not become popular until broadcast over *Soldatensender Belgrad* to German troops in North Africa in its 1941 program *Belgrader Wachtposten* (Belgrade Sentry Post). Frau Andersen herself, an already popular Danish singer, was known as the *Engel der Soldaten* (Angel of the Soldiers), and the song proved to be just as popular with Commonwealth soldiers as with their German counterparts. At least one British general urged that it not be played over the BBC as it affected morale, while Rommel requested that it continue to be played for the Afrika-Korps. Joseph Goebbels was not a fan of the song and he banned it in 1943 for its "portentous character." However, the outcry from soldiers returned it to the airwaves. An Italian version appeared in 1943 and English lyrics were composed in 1944 by J. J. Philips and sung by Ann Shelton. Later, other singers, including Marlene Dietrich, Bing Crosby, and Perry Como performed it with many variations of the lyrics. When asked why it was so popular and enduring (released in 48 languages and into the 1980s), Lale Andersen answered, "Can the wind explain why it is a storm?"

A bellwether is a castrated ram with a bell hung around its neck that leads a flock of sheep.

**Lili Marleen** — A phrase which came to mean a longing for home. See box on previous page.

**Lippenstiftbrigade** — Lipstick brigade. Civilian women employed by the military (e.g., in counter-intelligence).

**LSR** — A sign indicating the location of, or direction to, a *Luftschutzraum* (air protection room – air raid shelter). As the Soviets approached Berlin the abbreviation was said to mean *lernt schnell russisch* (learned Russian quickly).

**Lumpi** — A common dog's name. When someone has a dog-like pleading expression.

**Lysol** — Absinthe liqueur, particularly a cheap, sharp-tasting brand found in France with all the qualities of Lysol, a strong, nasty smelling disinfectant.

**Lysolmäuschen** — Little Lysol mouse. A nurse, again the term playing on the name of Lysol disinfectant.

# M     Martha

**Mädchen für Alles** — "Maids of all work." Said of the *Pioniertruppen* (Pioneer Troops – engineers) owing to the bewildering variety of tasks they performed.

**Magenbataillone** — Stomach battalions. *Volkssturm* (People's Assault) units with obviously eager-to-fight older men (45–55) requiring special diets owing to ailments. Individuals with lung and ear ailments fell into this category.

**Marabu** — Marabou stork. Any high-ranking officer such as an army commander or general staff officer.

**Marketenderwaren** Market items. Parcel of food items sent from home. These were restricted from being sent to the Eastern Front because of space limitations aboard trains, resulting in a lively local *schwarzer Markt* (black market).

**Maultier** Mule. A series of heavy halftracked cargo carriers (SdKfz 3).

**Mauseloch** Mouse-hole. Holes knocked or blasted through walls and floors to connect rooms within defended buildings.

**meine Kinder** My children. Officers and NCOs sometimes referred to their men as such. Company officers and NCOs were expected to emulate the German concept of the strong father figure who looked out for the well being of his family. In return the troops were expected to perform well. See also *Mutter* and *Vater*.

**MG** *Maschinengewehr* (machine-gun). The abbreviation used in machine-gun designations (MG08, MG15, MG34, MG42) and the common soldier's term.

**Molotow-Cocktail** Molotov cocktail. Petrol-filled bottle used (as a last resort) to combat enemy armor.

**Molotow-Gitarre** Molotov guitar. Soviet 7.62mm PPSh 41 submachine-gun.

**Moorsoldaten** See box overleaf.

**Motschuppe** Mot(orized) dandruff. Head lice.

**MP** *Maschinenpistole* (machine pistol – submachine-gun). Abbreviation used in machine pistol designations (MP28/II, MP34, MP38, MP40) and the common soldier's term for the weapon.

# MOORSOLDATEN – UNWORTHY TO BEAR ARMS

Soldiers convicted of particularly serious military, civil, or political crimes were declared *Wehrunwürdig* (unworthy to bear arms), and were imprisoned in special camps in the bleak peat bog moors of the Ems River area (*Emsland*), becoming known as *Moorsoldaten*. The 15 *Emslandlager* (Ems area camps) had been established by the *Sturmabteilung* (SA) in 1933 for political prisoners, religious objectors, Jews, habitual criminals, and certain military offenders. Closed in 1936, they were reopened in 1939 for prisoners of war until regular camps were established, and were then used for the incarceration of Wehrmacht prisoners. The camps were operated by the National Justice Ministry. A postwar song was written in their memory, *Die Moorsoldaten*. The prisoners also referred to themselves as *die Blauen Dragonen* (the Blue Dragoons).

Other soldiers were sentenced to penal units (*Bewährungsbataillon* – probationary battalion). Such units were numbered in the 500 series, resulting in their soldiers being referred to as *fünfhundert* (500). *Bewährungstruppen* units, generally known as *Sonderbataillone* (special battalions) or *Bataillone zur besonderen Verwendung* (*z.b.V.* – battalions for special employment), were numbered in the 300 series and as 999 *Afrika* and *Festung* (fortress). These units were for soldiers convicted of more serious crimes than the 500-series units. One such unit was the 999 Afrika-Division, of which a brigade served in North Africa. It was led by handpicked officers and NCOs, and the men could redeem themselves in combat or through other difficult service and eventually be reinstated in regular units. Another term for these soldiers was *Soldaten zweiter Klasse* (soldiers second-class – also *Soldat 2. Klasse*). Besides *Bewährungstruppen* units they could be assigned to the cheerily titled *Organisation Todt* (Organization Death) for hard labor. They were treated to a harsher *Strafvollzug* (infliction of punishment) than soldiers assigned to 500-series *Bewährungstruppen* units, who were convicted of less serious crimes.

**Mündungsschoner** Muzzle protector. A worthless soldier, who never quite motivated himself to fire his weapon. Refers to a metal cap placed on a carbine's muzzle to keep the weapon's bore clean.

**Mussolini-Kartoffeln** Mussolini potatoes. Pasta, e.g. macaroni, spaghetti.

**Mutter** Mother. The company/battery reporting NCO (*der Spieß*) was sometimes referred to as *die Mutter der Kompanie* (the "mother" of the company/ battery) with the "father" (*Vater*) being the company/battery commander. Also *Mutti* – Mummy.

# N     Nordpol

**Nabelschnur** Umbilical cord. Vital telephone or telegraph line/cable linking headquarters to forward units or other headquarters.

**Nachthexen** Night Witches. Nickname for the Soviet 588th Night Bomber Regiment, which was crewed by females flying U-2 ground-attack aircraft. The women from these units are said to have proudly adopted the title.

**Nähmaschine** Sewing Machine. Soviet Polikarpov U-2 (redesignated Po-2 in 1944) two-seat biplane, originally a trainer, used for night harassing attacks. Arguably bestowed with more nicknames than any other aircraft: *Unteroffizier vom Dienst* (*UvD* – Duty NCO), *Rollbahnkrähe* (Highway Crow), *Eisenbahnkrähe* (Railway Crow), *Iwan vom Dienst* (*IvD* – Duty Ivan), *Kaffeemühle* (Coffee Grinder), *Petroleumkocher* (Petroleum Cooker), *Mitternachtbomber* (Midnight Bomber), *Sperrholzbomber* (Plywood Bomber), and *rus-veneer* ("Russian veneer," referring to plywood). The Soviets nicknamed it the *Kukuruznik*

(Corn-harvester) or *Maizer* (Corn-cutter). The
North Koreans used the Po-2 for the same
ground-attack role during the 1950–53 Korean
War and the Americans nicknamed it "Bed
Check Charlie," "Washing Machine Charlie,"
and "Maytag Messerschmitt."

Napoleon-
Gedächtnis-Rennen

Napoleon memorial race. The German
retreat from Russia, replaying some unfortunate
moments from European history.

Nazibohnen

Nazi beans. *Sojabohnen* (soybeans). The NSDAP
promoted healthy foods, and soy beans,
previously unpopular in Germany, were one of
these.

Nichteinmischungs-
orden mit
Eßbesteck

Lit. "non-interference medal with cutlery." The
*Kriegsverdienstkreuz mit Schwertern* (War Service
Cross with Swords), introduced October 18, 1939.

Nußschale

Nutshell. The steel *Fallschirmhelm* (paratrooper's
helmet). It was of a simple domed design, lacking
the characteristic ear and neck protection of the
standard German helmet.

Nutte

Colloquial for prostitute. Also *Hure* (whore). The
armed services operated *Bordelle* (brothels) for
troops in occupied counties, employing racially
acceptable local women who were periodically
medically examined. Also *Offiziersdecke* (officer's
blanket), a woman employed in the finer
position of officer's prostitute.

O       Otto
Ö       Ödipus

Oberschnäpser

Drunken waiter, a type of character in comedies.
A term for someone who has a job but is

incompetent. Applied to Obergefreiter (senior private).

**Offiziersmatratzen** Lit. "officer's mattresses." Wry term for *Wehrmachtshelferinnen* (Defense Force Female Auxiliaries). While there were no doubt occasional instances of illicit liaisons, these appear to be more of an assumption than fact, as the women were held to high standards of conduct and well supervised by their *Führerinnen* (female leaders). See *Blitzmädchen*.

**Ostheer** East Army. *Heer* forces on the Eastern Front; not an official designation. The *Landser* of the Ostheer viewed himself differently from the rest of the *Heer* deployed in the West and South. More of the *Heer* was committed to the Eastern Front than all other fronts combined – nine out of ten German soldiers killed in combat or lost to illness died there.

**Osttruppen** East[ern] Troops. *Ostvolk* and *Turkicvolk* (Turkish People), in German military service. Russian auxiliary troops (*russische Hilfstruppen*). See also *Hiwi*, and *Kawi*.

**Ostvolk** East[ern] People. A collective term for Cossacks, Caucasians, and Slavs from the USSR. Specifically referred to those employed in German military service.

# P     Paula

**Pakfront** Armor defense gun front. A position of concentrated antitank guns located to halt tank breakthroughs. Originated on the Eastern Front in 1943.

**Paknest**     Contraction of *Panzerabwehrkanonennest*
                (antiarmor gun nest), an antitank gun firing
                position.

**Panje**       Small Russian two- or four-wheel, single-horse-
                drawn cart (*Panjewagen*) or sleigh adopted by the
                Germans on the Eastern Front to haul unit
                supplies. It actually refers to the small, hardy
                Russian Bashkir ponies. (Russian term.)

**Panje-Division**  Play on words referring to *Panzer* divisions in
                early 1942 on the Eastern Front, which had lost
                most of their motorized transport and tanks and
                relied on *Panje* columns to supply the troops,
                who were now fighting as infantry.

**Panzeranklopfgerät**  Lit. "tank door-knocker." Derogatory term for
                the ineffectual 37mm antitank gun (3.7cm PAK
                35/36), whose shells simply bounced off heavily
                armored tanks and did little more than helpfully
                announce to the enemy crew that there was
                somebody outside.

**Panzerknacker**  Armor-cracker (akin to a nutcracker). The Haft-
                Hohlladung 3kg (Magnetic Hollow-charge 3kg),
                hand-emplaced antiarmor mine with a delay
                fuse. (*Haften* means to cling or stick to.)

**Panzerknacker-abzeichen**  Armor-cracker badge. The highly specific
                *Sonderabzeichen für das Niederkämpfen von
                Panzerkampfwagen durch Einzelkämpfer* (Special
                Badge for the Close Combat of a Tank by
                Single Combat), awarded to soldiers for
                knocking out a tank with a *Panzerfaust*,
                *Panzerschreck*, hand or rifle grenade,
                satchel charge, hand mine, etc. Also
                *Panzervernichtungsabzeichen* (Armor
                Destruction Badge)

**Panzerschreck**

Armor-terror. 1) 8.8cm R.PzB 43 or R.PzB 54 reloadable bazooka-type rocket launchers. Also known as the *Ofenrohr* (stovepipe) and officially as a *Rakete Panzerbüchse* (armor-burster rocket – R.PzB.).
2) The fear of enemy tanks that could cause troops to descend into panic and retreat upon their appearance.

**Panzerturm**

Armor turret. The *Panzerstellung* (armor position) incorporated the turret removed from a battle-damaged, captured, or obsolete tank and emplaced atop a concrete or prefabricated steel below-ground fortification, with only the turret exposed. The below-ground portion served as shelter from heavy fire, and provided crew quarters and ammunition storage space. They were mainly used in coastal defenses, but were also found in inland defensive lines. "Turret" in this context referred to a castle's turret, even though tank turrets were used. Also *Panzer-Ringstand* (armor circular mount). See *Tobruchstellung*.

**Papierkrieg**

Paper-war. Administrative paperwork, red tape.

**Papieroffizier**

Paper officer. A *Propagandakompanie* (propaganda company) member, a war correspondent.

**Papiersoldat**

Paper-soldier. Soldier clerk.

**Pappkamerad**

Cardboard comrade. Man-shaped, waist-up silhouette target used for practice range firing.

**Partisanen**

Partisans. A nickname for *Läuse* (lice), which gives a sense of how truly irritating they were. See *Banditen*.

**Partisanenexpress**  Partisan express. Troop trains en route to the Eastern Front. So named because they often ran a gauntlet of Soviet partisan attacks and railroad track destruction.

**Plünnen**  Civilian slang for dirty laundry. This term was sometimes used by soldiers.

**Polacken**  Derogatory term for Poles. Derived from *polska*.

**Polska, Polskas**  Neutral term for *Pole* (Poles), *polnisch* (Polish).

**pommes frites**  Fried potatoes. Germans used this French term for both French fries (chips) and Frenchmen.

**Post bekommen**  To receive mail. 1) To be chewed out. 2) To receive artillery fire.

**Pulk**  Small sled, which was adopted by the Germans on the Eastern Front to haul unit supplies and equipment when deep snows made the use of wheeled vehicles impossible. They were drawn by one or two tough little Bashkir ponies. Often attributed as Russian for "sled," the term is actually Finnish.

**pumpen**  Pumping. Deep knee bends with a rifle or push-ups, both being punishments on the drill field.

**Püppchen**  Dolly or Little Doll. 8.8cm Raketenwerfer 43 rocket launcher (*R-Werfer*). Small rocket antiarmor weapon mounted on a two-wheel carriage.

**Putz- und Flickstunde**  Clean and patch hour. Time designated for cleaning and making clothing repairs in the barracks. Came to mean taking care of small details.

# Q Quelle

**Quatschschwein**  Balcony pig. Unfortunate rabbits raised on balconies and porches by civilians as food owing to meat shortages. Compare to *Dachschwein*.

**Querschläger**  Ricochet, but here meaning an unpopular soldier. Also *Querschießer* (wrongheaded fellow).

# R Richard

**Rabatz**  Fuss. A euphemism generally used to describe really unpleasant situations, major disorder, or heavy enemy fire.

**rasputitza**  Russian autumn rains beginning in mid-September, which turned the poor roads and landscape into boot- and wheel-sucking quagmires that severely hampered troop movements. *Rasputitza* was the Russian term for "big mud," and it also referred to the spring rains. While the spring rains were heavy, most spring mud was caused by snowmelt.

**Rata und Super Rata**  Rat and Super Rat. Soviet Polikarpov I-16 and Lavochkin La-5 fighters, respectively. The nickname *Rata* was bestowed by Nationalist forces during the Spanish Civil War, because like a rat the I-16 was fast, agile, and came as a nasty surprise when encountered. When the La-5 entered service in the middle of WWII it was dubbed *Super Rata* because its bulky radial engine gave it a superficial resemblance to the earlier *Rata*.

**Ratschbumm**  Lit. "crash-boom." Soviet-made 76.2mm M1936 field gun impressed into German service from 1942 as the 7.62cm Pak 36(r) antiarmor gun.

Large numbers were captured and used by the Germans to the extent that it was virtually a standard weapon. The nickname alludes to the sound of its firing and almost instant impact, owing to its high velocity.

**Rattenkrieg**

Rat's war. The nasty business of combat in cities (i.e. house-to-house fighting), specifically Stalingrad.

**Reißaus-Armee**

Runaway Army. Uncomplimentary term for the Italian 1st Army (1° Armata) in North Africa.

**RJF Seife**

A widespread rumor reported that the Nazis were rendering fat from murdered Jews for soap, which was said to be distributed in ghettos and concentration camps. RJF was said to mean *Rein Jüdisches Fett* (Pure Jewish Fat). No such undertaking occurred. The abbreviation was actually "RIF" – uppercase Gothic script "I" and "J" are identical in appearance, hence the confusion. "RIF" was *Reichsstelle für Industrielle Fettversorgung* (National Agency for Industrial Fat Provisioning) responsible for the allocating and conserving of fat, and developing no-fat substitute products. RIF soap, a poor-quality, nearly sudless soap substitute containing no fat, was issued to the Wehrmacht, Party organizations, and civilians.

**robben**

Lit. "to seal" (from *Robbe* – seal), that is, to low-crawl like a seal, wriggling across the ground, usually with the principal aim of avoiding enemy fire.

**Robert und Leopold**

Robert and Leopold. Individual nicknames for the two 28cm K5 railroad guns employed against the Allies at Anzio, Italy. To the Allies they were

together known as "Anzio Annie." A total of 25
were produced.

**Rommelspargel**    Rommel asparagus. Ten-foot wooden posts set
vertically in open fields and interconnected by
barbed wire to serve as anti-paratrooper and anti-
glider obstacles. For extra chaos some were topped
with contact-detonating artillery projectiles.

**Roten Teufel, die**    The Red Devils. British parachute troops of the
1st and 6th Airborne Divisions. British Paras and
German *Fallschirmjäger* first faced one other in
North Africa in November 1942. The British
Paras wore maroon berets and sleeve insignia.

**Rotkäppchen**    Little Red Riding Hood, otherwise a French
soldier. Believed to derive from the red *képis*
worn by some French troops in WWI. See also
*Franzmann*, and *pommes frites*.

**Rückzugs-**    Lit. "retreat gaiters." Short *Gamaschen* (canvas
**gamaschen**    leggings) issued with short, laced *Schnürschuhe*
(marching boots) from mid-1942. The German
soldier said that when short ankle boots began to

*A* Schütze *(rifleman) and* Abzug *("trigger") or* Maschinengewehr-Schütze
*(machine-gunner) undertake a* Robben *(low seal-like crawl).*

251

be issued in lieu of the traditional high-top jackboots, material resources had obviously dwindled and Germany would soon be defeated. Dates from WWI.

**Rückzugspastete**    Retreat pastry. Italian tomato sauce. A reference to the idea that the Italians were seen to have a propensity for retreating.

**Russe**    A Russian (*russisch*). This term was applied to all Slavic citizens of the USSR. The German soldier was not motivated to differentiate between ethnic or nationalistic groups such as Ukrainians, Byelorussians, etc., hence *Russe* also had a double meaning – it is a slang term for a cockroach. See *Iwan, Iwans*.

**russische Schokoladen**    Russian chocolates. Sunflower seeds, nicknamed because of their black color. They were a popular snack consumed by Russian peasants and often the only foodstuffs left after German soldiers had been looting. Peasants seemed to eat the seeds endlessly, an activity that the Germans ridiculed.

**russische Tresse**    Russian braid. The chevron (*Soutacheschnur* – soutache) of narrow *Waffenfarbe* (arm of service color) braid worn on the front of the field cap. It was so called as it was reminiscent of the flamboyant braid worn by the Russian Imperial Army. See *Schiffchenmütze*.

**Russischloch *or* Rusloch**    Russian hole. A hastily dug, shallow, circular, one-man rifleman's position.

**russische Krankheit**    Russian sickness. The dreaded *Ruhr* (dysentery), making soldiers' lives that extra bit miserable on the Eastern Front and elsewhere.

**russki**    Common adjective for anything Russian, e.g. *russki Soldat* – Russian soldier.

| S | Siegfried |
| Sch | Schule |

**Sahariana**  Saharan. A sand-colored Italian-style tropical tunic worn by some German officers in North Africa. (Italian term.)

**Sandsturm-Orden**  Sandstorm Order. *Medaille für den Italienisch-Deutschen Feldzug in Afrika* (Medal for the Italian–German Campaign in Africa) awarded to members of the Deutsches Afrika-Korps and the Panzerarmee Afrika. See also *Apfelsinenorden*.

**Sanitöter**  Wordplay combining *Sanitäter* (medical orderly) and *Töter* (killer) resulting in a not particularly reassuring term for a medic.

**Saukopf**  Sow's head. The gun mantlet of an assault gun or tank, especially if armed with a short-barreled gun. Specifically refers to the streamlined gun mantlet of the 7.5cm Stu.G 40 assault gun. Also *Saukopfblende* (pig's head mantlet) and *Topfblende* (pot mantlet).

**Schanzzeug**  Entrenching tool. Also used for *Gabel-Löffel* (combination folding fork and spoon) and *Löffel* (spoon).

**scheißen**  Shits – diarrhea. A classic soldier's curse.

**Scheißhaus**  Shithouse. 1) Latrine.
2) Abort a mission. The second use is mainly a Luftwaffe term, but was used elsewhere.

**Scheißhaus-jahrgang**  Lit. 'shit-house age-group'. Age-groups were indicated by the year they were born: e.g. '00' for 1900. As '00' on a door indicated a toilet, this charming phrase clearly shows regard for one's elders among young German soldiers.

**Scheißkopf**  Shit-head. Basic but effective civilian insult for someone doing something stupid or wrong, hence widely used in the armed forces. *Dummscheiß* (dumb-shit) and *Dummkopf* (dumb-head) were used for less severe infractions.

**Scheißpapier**  Shit-paper. *Toilettenpapier* (toilet paper) – often in short supply at the front and less comfortable substitutes were common, such as newspaper and enemy propaganda leaflets.

**Scheunentor**  Barn door. The 8.8cm Pak 43/41 antitank gun, so nicknamed because of the size of its large gun shield. The nickname was probably first bestowed on the earlier 8.8cm Pak 43, which had even a larger shield. Both weapons were large and cumbersome.

**Schiffchenmütze**  Little boat cap. The peakless Feldmütze 38 (M38 field cap). Also *Schiffchen* and *Krätzchen* (little scratch), owing to the turn-up that could be lowered to protect the neck and ears against the cold.

**Schikane**  Nasty trick. Harassment meted out by training NCOs.

**Schleifer**  Polisher. 1) An NCO specializing in cruel training.
2) A tank in need of repair.

**Schlipssoldaten**  Necktie soldiers. Army term for members of the Luftwaffe, the only branch of the services to wear collars and ties as part of its uniform.

**Schlitzaugen**  Slit-eyes. Predictable nickname for orientals. Referred to *Turkicvolk* (Turkish People) from the south-central USSR in German service. Many of these people were of Mongolian descent.

**Schlumpschütze**  Slob shooter. One who basically couldn't hit a barn door at close range.

**Schmalspurhengst**  Narrow-gauge stallion. *Wehrmachtbeamten* (Defense Forces administrative officials) and *Sonderführer* (special leaders) wore shoulder cords narrower than those of regular officers, and they were considered a sort of phallic symbol because of their shape. The term referred to officials making a big show of their importance, but having little real authority. Also *Schmalspuroffizier* (narrow-gauge officer).

**Schnabus**  Slang for *Schnapps*. See *Zielwasser*.

**Schnatterpuste**  Lit. "chatter breath." Machine-gun.

**Schubertiani**  German-raised Greek anti-communist militia on Crete in the 1942–43 period, named after their German leader, Feldwebel Fritz Schubert of the *Geheime Feldpolizei*.

**Schurke**  Rogue. While translated as a "devious rogue" today, during the war it was considered a serious insult.

**Schwarz-Divisionen** Black divisions. Soviet *ad hoc* divisions consisting of gulag inmates transferred to the Red Army in the summer of 1941, the nickname owing to their black worker's uniforms. Also *schwarz gekleidete-Soldaten* (black-clad soldiers).

**Schwarze Jesuit, der**  The Black Jesuit. Nickname for Heinrich Himmler (1900–45), Reichsführer-SS (National Leader of the SS) because of his black uniform and his dogmatic devotion to Nazi ideology. He was also called, less fearfully, *Reichsheini* (the Reich's numbskull). Heini is a diminuative of Heinrich, but also means "dolt" or "numbskull."

**Schwarzen, die**    The Blacks. *Panzertruppen* (armor troops – tank crewmen), owing to their black *Sonderbekleidung der Panzertruppen* (special uniforms for armor troops).

**Schwarzen**    The Black Devils. 1) Combined US and
**Teufel, die**    Canadian 1st Special Service Force. This brigade-sized amphibious–parachute–commando unit was known for its aggressive night combat patrols and the black face camouflage they wore at Anzio, Italy.
2) Also applied to the *Koninklijk Nederlands Korps Mariners* (Royal Netherlands Marine Corps) and the *Morskaya Pekhota* (Soviet Naval Infantry), both because of their black uniforms and ferocity.

**Schwarze Pioniere**    Black Pioneers. Pioneers or assault engineers wore black arm of service color, and this term differentiated them from pioneer units assigned to infantry regiments, who wore infantry white.

**Schwarzhemden**    Black Shirts. 1) Italian fascist militia, *Milizia Volontaria per la Sicurezza Nazionale* (MVSN; Volunteer Militia of National Security). Black Shirt (in Italian, *camicie nere*) units were sometimes incorporated into Italian Army divisions. While they have been classed as a paramilitary organization parallel to the Waffen-SS, they were usually of marginal quality.
2) Little-used early nickname for the prewar SS. Both organizations wore black shirts and other similarly morbid uniform components.

**Schwarztod**    Black Death. Soviet Ilyushin Il-2 *Shturmovik* (Germanized as *Sturmowik* – Stormer) ground-attack aircraft. They were often painted black and operated at night. Other nicknames included

*Schlachter* (Butcher), *Zement Flugzeug* (Cement Airplane), *Fliegerpanzer* (Flying Tank), *Eiserner Gustav* (Iron Gustav), *Zementbomber* (Cement Bomber), and *Fliegendes Badezimmer* (Flying Bathtub), all owing to its unusually heavy armor. See *Shturmovik*, Appendix 2.

**Schwein** *or* **Schweinehund**
Pig or pig-dog. A common insult, although *Schweinehund* is a particularly contemptuous remark.

**Schweineschnauze** Pig's snout – gasmask.

**Selbstmörder-kolonne**
Suicide column. Members of any lethally dangerous undertaking, i.e. mine clearance, combat patrols, and rearguard.

**Sieben-Fünfer**
Seventy-five. The 7.5cm tank gun, assault gun, or antiarmor gun.

**Siegfried**
Siegfried. General nickname for the earth-shaking 38cm railroad gun. Three were produced.

**Soldatenadler**
Lit. "soldier eagle." *Nationalsozialistische Führungsoffizier* (National Socialist Guidance Officer). Political indoctrination officer attached to a combat unit, who tried to make sure soldiers accepted violent death with ideological fervor. The post was instituted from December 22, 1943.

**Soldatenbraut**
Soldier's bride. A soldier's rifle or carbine. Unlike the soldier's real wife, it would never leave his side.

**Soldatenbriefe**
Soldier's letters. 1) Letters sent home by soldiers. 2) Paperback novels and textbooks provided by the German government via Switzerland to German prisoners of war held by the Western Allies.

**Sohlenschoner**    Lit. "boot-leather saver." Member of a motorized unit (i.e. troops not required to march).

**Sonderbehandlung**    Special treatment. Euphemism for the torture and/or execution of prisoners, hostages, partisan suspects, commandos, spies, and agents.

**Spaghettifresser**    Spaghetti eater. Italian soldier (also *Makaronifresser*).

**Spanienkämpfer**    Spanish Fighter. German volunteers who fought in the Spanish Civil War with the *Legion Condor* (Condor Legion) on the Nationalist side, assisting Franco's victorious fascist rebels.

**spanischer Reiter**    Spanish rider. Barbed-wire-wrapped portable wooden frame barrier for crossing gaps in barbed-wire barriers or for use as road blocks. Generally known as a knife rest or *chevaux de frise*.

**Spargelbeet**    Asparagus bed. Any area sown with antitank obstacles, e.g. the "dragon's" teeth of the *Westwall* (Siegfried Line). See also *Rommelspargel*.

**Sparlampe**    Economy lamp. Kerosene-soaked candle providing a bright light and even a bit of warmth. They were commonly used in lieu of kerosene lamps, battery lamps, and flashlights to illuminate dugouts, bunkers, tents, etc. Kerosene and batteries were always in short supply. Melted candle wax was remolded into new candles.

**Spiegel**    Lit. "mirror," meaning the matched pair of double lace *Doppellitzen-Kragen* (collar bars) worn on German Army uniforms. The practice originated in the Imperial Army, where Guard Corps units wore double collar bars to signify "protection of the Crown." The *Heer* continued the practice through WWII, hence signifying its "protection of the nation."

**Spiegelei**

Fried Egg. Referred to the *Deutsches Kreuz* in Gold (German Cross in Gold) because of its large white disc (with a black swastika) and surrounding gold sunburst design. This was also known as the *Hitler-Spiegelei* because of the dominating swastika, and *Ochsenauge* (bullseye) as its white disc was large enough to be one.

**Spieß, der**

The pike (often translated as "the spear"). Common term for a company/battery reporting NCO (*Hauptfeldwebel* – chief field sergeant),* the equivalent of a US company/battery first sergeant or Commonwealth company/battery sergeant–major. He was the *Mutter* (mother) of the company with the *Vater* (father) being the company/battery commander. *Spieß* refers to the time when NCOs carried pikes to keep men in position in formations advancing into enemy fire. See *Kolbenringe*, *Mutter*, and *Vater*.

**Spund**

Plug, as in a bottle plug. A *junger Soldat* (young soldier), a *Rekrut* (recruit). Thought to refer to the screw-on cap of the *Feldflasche* (field flask – water bottle).

**Stacheldraht-Krankheit**

Barbed-wire sickness. Psychological illness affecting German prisoners of war understandably homesick and worried about their families.

**Stalinhäcksel**

Stalin's chaff. Finely chopped Russian tobacco mixed with the readily available sawdust. Russians

---

\* *Hauptfeldwebel was a duty position rather than a rank and held by an NCO from the rank of Unteroffizier to Oberfeldwebel, although more senior NCOs usually held the position. In the Waffen-SS this grade was known as an SS-Stabsscharführer (staff band leader – "band" used in the sense of a small grouping of troops).*

called it *Machorka*. Usually rolled in a fat tube of newspaper, it created a great deal of smoke.

| | |
|---|---|
| **Stalinisten** | Stalinists. Propaganda term for communists. See *Bolschewisten/ Bolschewiken*. |
| **Stalinorgel** | Stalin's organ. Soviet *Katyusha* (see Appendix 2) truck-mounted multiple rocket launchers in general, but specifically the BM-13 (132mm, 16 launch rails). The Germans also used the term *Katjuscha*. |
| **Stalintorte** | Stalin's pastry. Tasteless, but filling, army-issue black dry bread. See *Karo einfach*. |
| **Steppenmantel** | Steppe greatcoat. Issue greatcoat lined with fur, or overcoat made completely of fur hides with the fur on the inside. Issued to vehicle drivers and guards for protection against the Russian Winter. Also *Wachtmantel* (guard greatcoat). |
| **stiften gehen** | To step out, meaning to escape from a tank or other vehicle. |
| **Stoppelhopser** | Stubble hopper. The infantryman. |
| **Strippenzieher** | Line-puller. A *Nachrichtensoldat* (signals soldier), in reference to endless plugging and unplugging of field telephone switchboard circuits. |
| **Stuka zu Fuß** | Lit. "Stuka-on-foot." The SdKfz 251 *Schützenpanzerwagen* medium halftrack with three Wurfrahmen 40 (launcher frame) 28/32cm rocket launcher racks fitted externally on both sides. A play on the old term of *Artillerie zu Fuß* (foot artillery – light artillery accompanying infantry). |
| **Stummelwerfer** | Literally "stump projector/launcher." The "stumpy mortar," an 8cm kurzer Granatwerfer 42 (kz.Gr.W.42). A shortened version of the standard 8cm schwerer Granatwerfer 34 |

(s. Gr. W. 34) – heavy 8cm mortar. Both were actually 81mm and could fire US ammunition.

**Stumpf**

Stumpy. The short-barreled 7.5cm gun mounted on early versions of the PzKpfw IV (Mk IV) tank. The term also referred to the tank itself.

# T     Theodor (Toni)

**Tante Ju**

Aunt Ju. Junkers Ju 52 three-engine transport aircraft. Also *Alte eiserne Tante* (Old Iron Aunt), *Judula* (Julia).

**Tarnausweis**

Lit. "camouflage identity card." *Feindflugausweis* (combat mission identity card), meaning an individual identity card carried by *Fallschirmtruppen* (paratroopers) and air crewmen in lieu of the *Soldbuch* (pay book) when conducting operations over enemy territory.

**Taschenflak**

Pocket air defense cannon, a round-about way of saying pistol.

**Tee-Salon**

Tea salon. The Soviet T-34 tank, far more scary to the Germans than the name implies.

**Teilzeitdeutsche**

Part-time Germans. Ethnic Germans living outside of Germany, but native to the country in which they resided, such as Alsace-Lorraine in France, Sudetenland in Czechoslovakia, and Galicia in Poland. *Volksdeutschen* (German peoples) was the official term.

**Terrorflieger**

Terror-flyer. A propaganda term for Allied bomber crewmen that came into general use.

**Teufelsabwehr-kanone**

Lit. "devil defense cannon." Military chaplain. See *Esak*.

**Teufelsgarten**

Devil's garden, otherwise known as a minefield.

**Theodor**  Theodore. Nickname for 24cm *Eisenbahngeschütze* (railroad guns). They were *Theodor* and *Theodor Bruno*, of which three and six were produced respectively. See *Bruno*.

**Tiefflieger**  Low-flier. 1) A not very smart person. 2) A low-flying aircraft, a fighter bomber, *Jabo*.

**Tobruchstellung**  Tobruk position, called a Tobruk pit by the Allies. Small circular, open-topped concrete machine-gun position with its rim flush with the ground. The German design was proposed in April 1941 and redesignated as a *Ringstand* (circular mount) in November 1942. It was developed by the Italians for the Libyan defenses of Tobruk and Bardia, and was widely used by the Germans elsewhere. See *Panzerturm*.

**Tommy**  Tommy. The Germans often referred to British soldiers by their own nickname. See *Bifteck*.

**Tommykocher**  Tommy cooker. M4 Sherman tank, on account of its propensity for catching fire when hit. "One hit and they boil" was a fairly accurate description.

**Totensonntag**  Lit. "Sunday of the Dead." Refers to November 23, 1941, the battle of Sidi Rezegh, Libya, when the Afrika-Korps was seriously battered by Commonwealth forces. Other engagements resulting in heavy losses and occurring on a Sunday were sometimes bestowed with this name.

**Trek**  Refugee column. From the Dutch word for travel or journey.

**Tropf**  Simpleton.

**troßkrank**  Lit. "train sick," meaning a convalescent soldier placed on light duty and detailed to work in the company/battery baggage train (*Troß* – supply section or rear echelon).

**Tunisgrad**

Melancholy combination of Tunisia and Stalingrad. The name applied to the May 1943 German mass surrender in Tunisia, which followed the February 1943 Stalingrad surrender.

**Turkicvolk**

Turkistan People, south-central Asians from the Soviet Union. Specifically referred to those in German service, and included Turkestanies, Uzbecks, Kasachs, Kirghiz, Karakulpaks, and Tatshiks. Only the *Turkicvolk*, Cossacks, and Crimean Tartars were approved to serve side-by-side with Germans.

**Türklopfer**

Doorknocker. 1) 3.7cm Pak 35/36 antiarmor gun, as it was ineffective against the better Soviet tanks such as the KV series and T-34.
2) Stick hand grenade, in the context of it being thrown through a door into a room, thus "announcing" one's presence in very clear terms. It is interesting that Soviet soldiers also referred to the German stick grenade as the "doorknocker" (*kolotushka*) and may have applied the same term to the 3.7cm Pak.

# U     Ulrich
# Ü     Übel

**Untergefreiter**

Junior private. No such rank existed in the German forces – it referred to a civilian, of even lower status than a private. (Interestingly this is the opposite outlook to that of the American soldier, who regarded a civilian as "outranking" a soldier and a "rank" to be desired.)

# V                Viktor

**V3**

*Volkssturm* (People's Assault), the late-war last-
resort militia. Nicknamed the V3 in jest as a new
*Wunderwaffe* (wonder weapon) to defeat the
Allies. The V1 and V2 were guided missiles, the
"V" meaning *Vergeltungswaffen* (vengeance
weapon). See *HJ-Spätlese*, *Krüppelgarde*, and
*Magenbataillone*.

**Vater**

Father. A company/battery commander was often
known as the "Father of the company/battery."
Some especially popular commanders, including
those commanding higher echelon units, were
called *Vater* or *Papa* followed by their name, for
example, *Papa Ramcke* (Generalmajor Hermann
Ramcke of the *Fallschirmtruppen*). Compare to
*Mutter*.

**Vati**

Daddy or Pops. An endearing term for a
respected older soldier, who may have been only
a couple of years older than his comrades. See
*alte Landser*.

**Verbrecheralbum**

Lit. "criminal album." The rogues' gallery that was
the punishment book, a list of wrongdoers jotted
down in the adjutant or senior NCO's notebook.

**verheizen**

Burn-up. Senseless sacrificing of troops in an
attack or other action.

**Versager-1 (V1)**

Failure No. 1. A strategically accurate name for
the V1 rocket bomb. It was intended to have a
massively destructive and serious effect on
British morale, but was actually far better at
sucking up German war resources. A play on
the V1's designation, *Vergeltungswaffe* (vengeance
weapon). Also *Volksverdummung-1* (People's
Stultification-1), implying that the public was

not entirely in possession of the facts regarding the *Wunderwaffen* (wonder weapon).

**Versuchssoldat**   Experimental soldier. Member of the *Volkssturm* (People's Assault), no doubt "experimentally" used as cannon fodder. See *Ersatzreserveersatz*.

**Vierling**   Quad. Specifically the four-barrel 2cm Flak 38 antiaircraft gun. Also *Flakvierling*. (There were other German multi-barrel antiaircraft weapons, including the twin 12.8cm Flakzwilling 40/2 and the three-barrel 15mm MG 151/15 and 2cm MG 151/20 Flakdrilling.)

**Vitamin B**   Vitamin B, but rather than meaning "thiamine" the "B" stood for *Beziehungen* (connections), implying that well-connected Nazi officials and their families would nourish themselves well, avoiding the hardships and shortages experienced by others.

**vollrotzen**   Lit. "full snot," meaning to fire everything at the target.

**Vomag**   Contraction of *Volksoffizier mit Arbeiter Gesicht* – a "people's [meaning a common man] officer with a laborer's face." Regardless of the supposed Nazi classless society, the German officer corps resented "commoners" entering their ranks, many being former NCOs. Officers were expected to "look like officers" and maintain a certain decorum and bearing.

**von der anderen**   Lit. "from the other field post [office] number."
**Feldpostnummer**   Receiving fire from an enemy position. The expression was also used to describe the enemy in general. Derived from a Field Post stamp on letters.

# W

# Wilhelm

**warmer Bruder**

Warm brother. A rather cosy expression for a homosexual soldier. *Schwichtl* (faggot) was less polite. *Homosexualität* (homosexuality) was illegal in Germany and punishable by death, but nonetheless it was encountered within the Wehrmacht.

**Wassersuppe**

Water soup. Soup with so few ingredients that it was little more than flavored hot water. See *Horst Wessel-Suppe*.

**Wehrbeitrag**

Defense contribution. Fathering a child while on leave, doubtless a conscious decision to add to the Reich's manpower.

**Weiche Birne**

Dim bulb or soft pear. Refers to a person of low intelligence – not too bright.

**Weißer Reiter**

White rider. Cavalry units wore gold-yellow *Waffenfarbe* (arm of service color), but some infantry units, which displayed white *Waffenfarbe*, employed small mounted units for reconnaissance which were known as "white riders."

**Wenn schon, denn schon**

"If it is worth doing, it is worth over-doing." An Army saying referring to attention to detail, making every effort to get it right the first time.

**Windei**

Lit. "a soft shelled egg." Something that failed or was canceled, i.e. was easily bust open.

**Wohnbunker**

Dwelling bunker. Small *Unterschlupfe* (dugout shelter) protecting 1–6 men. See *Kleinhaus*.

**Wolchow-Stock**

Volkhov stick. Originating in the Volkhov River area of Russia, these short walking sticks with intricately carved designs along the length of their shafts were carried by many officers on the Eastern Front. The carving was an ideal means of passing time and the sticks were often presented to officers by their unit as a memento.

**Wolfsgrabhügel**
Wolf's barrow. One- or two-man rifleman's position, analogous to a foxhole.

**Würfelbecher**
Dice shakers. High-topped *Marschstiefel* (marching boots) – jackboots. The phrase alludes to boots being used to toss dice. See *Knobelbecher*.

**Wüstenfuchs**
Desert Fox. Nickname bestowed on Generalfeldmarschall Erwin Rommel (1891–1944) by the British in North Africa in 1941. The nickname was taken up by the German media and the *Landser*.

**Wutmilch**
Lit. "anger milk." Aggression- and courage-inspiring alcohol issued before an attack. See *Energietropfen*.

# X    Xanthippe

# Y    Ypsilon (Ypern)

# Z    Zeppelin

**Zahlmops**
Lit. "paying pug" or "money pincher." A *Zahlmeister* (paymaster) who enjoyed an easy life in the rear.

**zahmer Tommy**
Tame Tommy. Shell or bomb that had, thankfully for bystanders, failed to explode.

**Zielwasser**
Lit. "target water." An alcoholic drink that really hit the spot (i.e. made you feel pleasantly drunk) specifically *Schnaps* (schnapps, a brandy). The term also referred to any alcoholic beverage, the most common available being *Kognak* (cognac) and *Wodka* (vodka).

**Zigarettenbüchse**   Cigarette box. The *Tragbüchse für Gasmaske* (carrying case for gas mask) was a robust, fluted steel, waterproof canister put to better use for stowing cigarettes and matches. Socks, foot wraps, and writing materials were also carried in the container. This application of the canister was a prohibited, but nonetheless widespread practice.

**Zwo**   Corruption of *zwei* (two). Nickname for the No. 2 of a weapon crew, such as a 2. *Maschinengewehr-Schütze* (assistant machine-gunner).

**Zwölfender**   Lit. "twelver." A soldier who assumed an obligation for 12 years' active military service as an NCO. In peacetime only 25 percent of NCOs could extend their service beyond 12 years. The others were discharged and offered a choice of civil service employment, *Wehrmachtsbeamten* (Wehrmacht administrative official) positions, farm loans, or training to enter a trade.

## INSULTING NAMES

| | |
|---|---|
| Aal | Hammel |
| Arschlecker | der Henker |
| Aspirinjesus | Hosenscheisser |
| Bonzen | Klumpfuß Goebbels |
| Ersatzreserveersatz | Querschläger |
| Etappenschweine | Scheißkopf |
| faule Hünde | Schlumpschütze |
| Frontschweine | Schurke |
| Grabenschreck | Schwein |
| Gröfaz | Tropf |
| Halsschmerzen | Weiche Birne |

# APPENDICES

# APPENDIX 1
## IMPERIAL JAPANESE ARMY SLANG

The *nihon-jin* (Japanese) *heitai* (soldier) had his own slang and nicknames. Much use was made of contractions, especially for weapon designations, and these were used in the same manner as slang. The following is a selection of the slang used by the Japanese military.

**akagami**
Red paper. Conscription notification cards were printed on red paper. When more men were needed the Military Administration Bureau merely mailed more postcards with a free train ticket to the garrison where the recruit would be trained.

**akatsuki butai**
Dawn units. *Akatsuki* (dawn) was the codename for *sempaku* (shipping transport) troop. They operated Army embarkation ports in Japan, overseas debarkation ports, anchorages in operational areas, and barge bases, and manned, loaded, or unloaded Army troop transports, landing barges, and other craft. Their name doubtless came from their unsocial hours of work.

**ameko**
Disparaging name for an *amerika-jin* (American).

**anpan**
A bun containing bean jam and the nickname of a Type 93 (1932) antitank mine, because of its shape.

**arigeta**
Alligator. General nickname for American amphibian tractors (amtrac – landing vehicle, tracked [LVT]). Only the LVT(1) was formally nicknamed the Alligator by the Americans; the LVT(2) and LVT(3) bore other nicknames.

# APPENDIX 1

**batta**       Grasshopper. Disparaging name for an
                infantryman.

**b-san**       Mister "B" or Mister Bomber. US B-29
                Superfortress heavy bomber. A Japanese fighter
                pilot said the *b-niju-ku* (B-29) flew too high,
                too fast, and he could not make enough holes
                in it.

**chankoro**    A non-complimentary name for the *chugoku-jin*
                (Chinese).

**chibi**       "TB." This was the Type 1 (1941) frangible, toxic
                gas hand grenade filled with liquid hydrocyanic
                acid. The glass grenades were captured in 1942 on
                Guadalcanal and in Burma, having been employed
                against British tanks near Imphal in the latter area.
                Japanese is read right to left so "TB" is actually
                read "BT" (*bi-chi*), which refers to the Soviet BT
                tanks encountered during the 1939 battle of
                Nomonhan in Manchuria. It was called a *chibi*,
                reversing the letters, because the BT tanks would
                be "reversed" by killing the crews.

**chosen-jin**  Korean. Chosen was the Japanese name for Korea,
                which had been under Japanese domination since
                1910. Officially Koreans were citizens of Japan,
                albeit second-class, so to call them *chosen-jin* rather
                than *nihon-jin* was an insult. The Koreans were
                forced to call their country Chosen.

**ga-to**       Starvation (*ga*) Island (*to*), the nickname for
                *Gadarukanaru* (Guadalcanal), to which it was
                extremely difficult to ship supplies.

**gobo ken**    Burdock sword. Meiji Type 30 (1897) *juken*
                (bayonet) with a 15½in blade. Its black-painted
                steel scabbard looked like a burdock, a popular
                vegetable food.

**guraman**

American fighters were commonly called *guraman* (Grumman) regardless of the manufacturer and model. Soldiers who were annoyed with American airplanes, to put it mildly, said *nikkuki guraman* (hateful American airplane).

**hakuheisen**

Lit. "fight with drawn sword," an official phrase. The Japanese derided Americans for "hiding" behind their artillery barrages. Equivalent of the American to "fight man-to-man."

**haisen fuku**

Defeat suits. A doleful expression referring to how demobilized soldiers often continued to wear their *heitai fuku* (uniforms) owing to postwar clothing shortages. Their boots were known as *haisen kutsu* (defeat shoes).

**heitai**

*Hei* – soldier, *tai* – unit. *Heitai* originally meant "troops," but was commonly used to refer to a soldier and was roughly analogous to GI or Tommy in the US or British forces.

**hizoku**

Bandits, the colloquial term for guerrillas. Mostly used in China.

**ichioku isshin**

Lit. "one-hundred-million people, one mind," a popular slogan signifying unity, though misleading – Japan's population was 72 million (an accurate phrase wouldn't have been quite as catchy, however).

**igirisu**

English or British. The Japanese referred to *osutorariya-jin* (Australians), *kanada-jin* (Canadians), and *niyuu jirando-jin* (New Zealanders) collectively as the "British," as they viewed those British Commonwealth countries as colonies of *eikoku* (England).

**imozuru**

Sweet-potato vines. Signalmen. Alludes to telephone wires.

| | |
|---|---|
| **kamikaze no fuki sokone** | Lit. "the divine wind did not blow." Alluded to the failure of the Japanese armed forces. |
| **kankoku** | Disparaging name for Korea. See also *Chosen-jin*. |
| **kogun** | Emperor's troops, a term that included the Imperial Japanese Army and Navy. |
| **kojiki bukuro** | Begger's bag. *Seoibukuro* (tube pack) worn over the shoulder and around the back like a begger's or hobo's pack. |
| **menko** | Rice bowl. One's service time was described as *menko*, a term originating during the 1904–05 Russo-Japanese War and meaning the wooden tray on which food was served. In WWII it meant the rice cooker's side-dish pan and referred to the number of meals consumed in one's service. The number of *menko* was more important than the number of stars indicating rank on one's collar. |
| **min min zemi** | An ingeniously humiliating barracks ritual in which a recruit mimicked the cry of the *zemi* (cicada), protesting against the summer heat as he clung to an 8–10in diameter barracks roof support post, with his arms and legs wrapped around the varnished post. He might cry *min min* twice before sliding to the floor, no matter how hard he gripped the slick post. He immediately jumped up and repeated the act until completely sapped of strength. |
| **pi** | Slang for military comfort women (*jugun ianfu*) working in military brothels (*jugun ianjo*). Military comfort houses were staffed by local women in occupied territories who were forced, coerced, or deceived into prostitution. |
| **piya** | Slang for comfort house (military brothel). These were officially called *jugun ianjo* and operated by contractors. |

**roosevelt kyuyo**    Roosevelt supplies. Rations and other supplies
                       captured from the Americans. *Churchill kyuyo*
                       were captured from the Australians and British.

**rosuke**             Disparaging name for a *roshiya-jin* (Russian).

**sen'ninbari**        Belt of a thousand stitches. A white cloth belt,
                       several inches in width, wound around the waist.
                       When a man was conscripted the women in his
                       family would make the rounds in their village or
                       neighborhood, asking every woman they met to
                       sew a stitch into the belt for good fortune. The
                       black yarn stitches could be formed in straight
                       lines or into a pattern, such as a tiger. (It was said
                       the tiger would return from a far place and was
                       stitched in hopes the soldier would return.) A five-
                       *sen* coin was sometimes sewn on (it had a small
                       hole in the center) because it was higher than the
                       number *shi* (four), which also means death. It was
                       believed the belt might cause bullets to miss.

**shomohin**           Expendable article. Soldiers' term for themselves,
                       and all too often horribly accurate.

**sora no shimpei**    Soldier gods of the sky. The propaganda name
                       for the Army *rakkasan hei* (parachute troops) who
                       captured the oil refinery in Palembang, Sumatra
                       (Dutch East Indies) on January 1, 1942. Derived
                       from the titles of a motion picture and a popular
                       song.

**ta dan**             Nickname for a shaped-charge antitank
                       projectile: *ta* – antitank, *dan* – shell. The basic
                       technology came from Germany and the shell
                       was sometimes called *Hitora no okurimono* (lit.
                       "gift from Hitler"). The Japanese made limited
                       used of shaped-charge munitions.

**takoashi**

Octopus tentacles. Old-type *haino* (backpack), because of its unwieldy tangle of straps.

**takotsubo**

Octopus trap. One- and two-man *kojinyo engo* (foxholes) deep enough for a soldier to fight standing. They were called "octopus traps" after a fishing techique in which a hole was dug above the high-tide line and a jar inserted. An octopus would crawl into the jar and be trapped when the tide went out. In a comforting analogy, a soldier in a foxhole looks like an octopus trapped in a *takotsubo*.

**takotsuri**

Octopus teasing, as in boys harassing an octopus trapped in a tidal pool. Recruit harassment or hazing.

**tenposen**

Graduates of the *Rikugun Daigakko* (Army Staff College) considered themselves elite. General Staff officers were called *tenposen gumi* (Tenposen Group) after the special badge they wore, which was similar to a large coin of the Tenpo period (1830–43). *Taizuki shoko* (unit officers) who had not attended the Army Staff College were called *muten gumi* (non-badge group), and had limited prospects of career progress, unless they met good fortune in war.

**tokko**

Contraction of *tokubetsu kogeki* (special attack, i.e. suicide attack). Suicide missions were also called *kamikaze* (divine wind) and *kikusui* (floating chrysanthemums).

**uguisu-no tani-watari**

The "flight of the warbler across the valley" was a recruit hazing ritual employing the long barracks tables placed end-to-end with a 3ft gap between them. The long-suffering recruit picked to play the *uguisu* (warbler) would duck under the table when ordered to "fly" and crawl as fast as he could on all fours, popping his head up in the "valley" between the tables. He would sing out *ho ho-kekyo* mimicking the warbler's spring song as soldiers atop the tables cheerfully pelted him with shoes, sticks, and manuals.

**untai**  *Un* – chance, *tai* – unit. It is a pun on *guntai* (army). The fate of soldiers depends on chance. So, *guntai* is *untai*.

**yasukuni de aou**  Lit. "see you at Yasukuni!" Soldiers killed in combat were commemorated at the Yasukuni shrine (*yasukuni* – peaceful country) and became *kami* (national deities) protecting the Empire, as they did when they died fighting. Soldiers believed the highest honor was to die for the Empire and Emperor followed by enshrinement in Yasukuni. Soldiers going into battle would sometimes shout to one another *Yasukuni de aou!*, believing they would meet again as comrades in death.

**yasukuni jinja no kippu**  Lit. "ticket to Yasukuni Shrine." The soldier's identification tag, meaning a ticket to death. Tags were marked with the first character of the soldier's arm of service, regimental designation, and regimental number. If the soldier were killed, after the body was cremated the tag was attached to a *shiraki no hako*, a wooden box containing his ashes, which was now considered to contain the spirit of the war dead (*eirei*).

**yochin**  Iodine tincture. This most widely used antiseptic was the nickname for a medic.

**yuhei**  Useless troops. Stragglers and survivors of sunken troop transports who had made it to islands, many without weapons and of little use to the defense.

## APPENDIX 2
## RED ARMY SLANG

The slang of the *Rabochaia i Krest'sanskaia Krasnaia Armiia* (Workers' and Peasants' Red Army) of the *Soyuz Sovetskikh Sotsialisticheskikh Respublik* (Union of Soviet Socialist Republics; USSR) during the *Velikaja Otechestvennaja Vojna* (Great Patriotic War) has much in common with the slang of other soldiers. However, there is a diffident socialist-political bend to the vocabulary. The following is a taster of the Red Army slang of World War II.

| | |
|---|---|
| **Amerikosy** | American. |
| **balalaika** | A small string musical instrument considered the Russian national instrument. The Soviet government encouraged its use and formed balalaika orchestras. It was a common instrument used by soldier entertainment troupes and also gave a nickname to the 7.62mm PPSh-41 submachine-gun – *Pistolet-Pulemet Shpagina*. Also *Peh-peh-shah*. |
| **BEF** | Abbreviation for *Bei fashistov* (defeat the fascists). Commonly seen on tank turrets. |
| **Berloga** | Beast's lair. Referred to Berlin. |
| **bratskaya mogila dlya semerykh** | Lit. "communal grave for seven." Truly worrying name for a US-made M3 medium tank provided via Lend-Lease, which had a seven-man crew. Also known as "device for incinerating seven brothers" owing to the ease with which it caught fire. |
| **chemodan** | Suitcase. Heavy artillery projectile. The word was also common in the Russian Imperial Army in WWI. |

**Devyat gram**      Nine grams (the weight of bullet). A bullet or an execution.

**emcha**      Lend-Lease US-made M4A2 Sherman tanks. Emcha was derived from *em* – "M," and the number 4, which resembled the Cyrillic letter Ч – *che*.

**Ferdinand**      After the battle of Kursk in mid-1943 all German self-propelled guns were known as Ferdinands.

**finka**      A nickname for a *pistolet-pulemet* (submachine-gun) such as the 7.62mm PPSh-41 and PPS-43. *Finka* also describes a short, broad-bladed Russian hunting knife. The word is the Finnish term for a woman, so may have been used to describe the Finns' own submachine-guns, and was then picked up by the Soviets during the Winter War (1939–40).

**Frits, fritz**      A derogatory word for "Germans," like "Kraut" or "Boche."

**Generál Moróz**      General Frost, who was an enemy of both sides and conducted chilly operations during the Russian Winter.

**govnodavy**      Shit tramper. Sturdy marching boots.

**grob**      Coffin. Any armored vehicle or aircraft especially vulnerable to enemy fire.

**Ishak**      Donkey. German *Nebelwerfer* multiple-tube/rail rocket launchers. Also *Vanyusha* (small Ivan).

**karandashi**      Pencils. Radio code for soldiers.

**Katyusha**      Truck-mounted multiple rocket launchers in general, but specifically the BM-13 (132mm, 16 launch rails). The Germans also used the term *Katjuscha* – see *Stalinorgel*. The Russian nickname is from a song by the same name about a girl longing for her far-away soldier lover and is said to refer to the song's crescendo. *Katyusha* is the diminutive of the name *Ekaterina* (Katherine). The BM-31 (also called *Andryushas*), firing 16 300mm rockets, and the BM-8, firing 36 or 48 82mm rockets, were also generally called the *Katyusha*.

**Khozyain**     The Boss. Nervous nickname for Joseph Stalin (1878–1953), General Secretary of the Central Committee of the Communist Party of the Soviet Union, the "Great Leader and Teacher."

**kolymka**     Makeshift lamp fabricated by soldering three or four small copper tubes to the lid of a tin. Hot coals were placed inside and a heated gas vented through the tubes. The tubes were lit by a match to provide light. The term derives from the mining gulags on the Siberian Kolyma Peninsula.

**korobki** *or* **korobochki**     Boxes. Radio code for tanks.

**krysa**     Rat. *Krysy* meant rear service troops, and *Tylovaya Krysa* was a derogatory term for a rear service officer.

**Kukuruznik**     Polikarpov U-2 or Po-2, a general-purpose Soviet biplane, nicknamed *Kukuruznik* from the Russian *kukuruza* (maize). It served extensively on the Eastern Front as a light ground-attack and general supply aircraft.

**kukushka**     Cuckoo. Enemy sniper in the forest.

**limonka**     Lemon. F-1 fragmentation hand grenade.

**makhorka**     Poor, cheap tobacco. Soldiers rolled their own cigarettes using *makhorka* and whatever paper they could find, usually newspaper. Before the war no Western-style cigarettes were produced. There were only *papierossi*, paper pipes half full of tobacco.

| | |
|---|---|
| **Narkomovskie 100-gramm** | The *Narodnyi Kommissariat* or *Narkom* (People's Commissariat of Defense), which issued frontline soldiers with 100 grams of vodka per day. |
| **natsmen** | Derogatory general term for the many ethnic minorities in the USSR. The concept of "national minorities" was officially non-existent in the USSR, but reality was painfully, often bloodily, different. |
| **ogurtsy** | Cucumbers. Radio code for artillery projectiles. |
| **okruzhenets** *or* **okrugénez** | Soldier who escaped from a German encirclement. |
| **opolchentsy** | Members of the *opolchenie* (volunteer militia), aged 17–55, raised early in the war to serve as last-ditch combat and labor units. |
| **Pantera** | German Panther PzKpfw V tank, also known as the T-V to the Soviets. |
| **Pevun, muzikant** | Singer, musician. The German Ju 87 Stuka dive bomber, nicknamed "singer" for its high-pitched and totally unmusical shriek when diving. |
| **podsnezhnik** | A dark pun on "snowdrop." Referred to the grisly exposure of the German dead during the spring thaw in Russia. |
| **Pokhodno-polevaya zhena (PPZh)** | Lit. "field marching wife." A play on the designation for the PPSh-41 submachine-gun (see *balalaika*) that referred to camp followers. It was a common practice for officers and soldiers to alleviate wartime discomforts by "adopting" women as mistresses. Officers would sometimes |

enter them on unit rosters and assign them duty positions for rationing purposes.

**Politsai**
From the German *Polizei* – the auxiliary police raised by the Germans in occupied territories and manned by locally recruited Soviet citizens for public order and anti-partisan operations.

**proigryvatel'**
Record-player. The 7.62mm DP and DPM light machine-guns, the standard section (squad) automatic weapons, owing to the flat turntable-like 47-round drum magazines on top of the weapons.

**proschai Rodina**
Lit. "goodbye Motherland." Referred to the 45mm M1932 and M1937 antitank guns, owing to their underpowered performance. Hence to engage a German tank was an invitation to death. A crew was expected to do its great patriotic duty by knocking out one or two tanks before it was destroyed.

**pukalka**
Wind-emitter. Any small arm or gun of poor effectiveness or penetration.

**Pustit v raskhod**
To expend someone. Execution (of prisoners, deserters etc).

**Ruzveltovskie yaitsa**
Roosevelt eggs. US powdered eggs provided via Lend-Lease. In a handy double-entendre, *yaitsa* translates to both "eggs" and "testicles."

**samostrel**
A soldier with a self-inflicted wound. A *samostrel* is a crossbow and the term is believed to be derived from the ease with which someone could shoot himself in the foot with a crossbow.

**seksot**
From *sekretnyj sotrudnik* (secret collaborator). An informer.

| | |
|---|---|
| **Shchi i kasha, pishcha nasha** | Lit. "Shchi and kasha, that's our fare." *Shchi* (cabbage soup) and *kasha* (boiled buckwheat) were two staples of a soldier's diet. |
| **Shturmovik** | Stormer. Ilyushin Il-2 ground-attack aircraft. Also *Letayushchiy* (flying tank) and *Gorbatyi* (humpbacked). See *Schwarztod*, Part III, for the German nicknames. |
| **SMERSH** | A contraction of *Smert' Shpionam* (Death to Spies), the short title for the People's Commissariat of Defense Chief Counterintelligence Directorate. The counterintelligence department was organized in 1943 to secure rear areas and arrest traitors, deserters, spies, and criminals. |
| **smertnyi** | Lit. "death medallion." A faceted wooden or bakelite capsule with a threaded cap, hung around the soldier's neck on a cord or more likely carried in a pocket. It contained a scroll-like form with the soldier's personal information and was equivalent to an identity tag. |
| **soldat buterbrod** | Soldier's sandwich. An ironic nickname for a single slice of black bread. |
| **spichechnaya korobka** | Matchbox. T-34 tanks, owing to their panic-inducing propensity to catch on fire when hit. Also because they were produced so rapidly and in large numbers, like matches. |
| **Tridsatchedverka** | Thirty-four, the T-34 tank. |
| **Trudarmee** | Worker's army. Forced labor units comprised of evicted Volga Germans and other undesirables. |
| **Vyshka** | Execution. From *vysshaya mera nakazanija* (extreme penalty). |

**Vzyat yazyka**   Lit. "Capture a tongue." Capturing an enemy soldier or officer for interrogation.

**zagradotryady**   Barrage units. Battalions and companies of regular troops formed in the summer of 1941 and tasked with blocking the retreat of frontline units, with orders to shoot "panic-mongers and cowards."

**Zapadniki**   Westerners. Referred to Soviet citizens in the western USSR, especially the German-occupied parts of Ukraine. When they were "liberated" in 1943–44 they became eligible for conscription in the Red Army, but were treated with mistrust, as were former prisoners of the Germans.

**za polevya zaslugi**   Lit. "for sexual service." A play on the phrase *za boevye zaslugi* (for military service) appended to combat decorations. Said, with usual sensitivity, of female soldiers.

**Zazhigalki**   (Cigarette) lighters. German aerial incendiary bombs.

**zhid**   Equivalent to "Yid," an insulting term for a Jew.

**Zmeya**   Snake. German 7.5cm Pak 40 antitank gun.

**Zveroboi**   Beast hunter. SU-152 and SU-122 self-propelled guns (SU – *Samokhodnaya Ustanovka* – mechanized mounting). Armed with 152mm and 122mm guns, they were quite capable of killing Tigers, Panthers, and Ferdinands.

## APPENDIX 3
## ARMORED FIGHTING VEHICLES NICKNAMES

### United States

The US military did not officially give nicknames to AFVs, although a number of nicknames were widely accepted, and some were bestowed by the manufacturer. The tanks nicknamed after generals were for the most part so named by the British. Many came into widespread American use, usually dropping the "General."

| | |
|---|---|
| **Alligator** | LVT(1) landing vehicle, tracked Mk 1. |
| **Beachmaster** | LVT(4) landing vehicle, tracked Mk 4, "Beach Buster." |
| **General Chaffee** | M24 light tank, 75mm gun. |
| **General Grant** | M3 series medium tanks, 75mm and 37mm guns. |
| **General Jackson** | M36 series tank-destroyers, 90mm gun. The "Jackson" and "Slugger" nicknames are believed to be postwar. |
| **General Pershing** | T26E3/M26 tank, 90mm gun. |
| **General Sherman** | M4 series medium tanks, 75mm, 76mm, or 105mm gun. |
| **General Stuart** | M3 series and M5 series light tanks, 37mm gun. |
| **Greyhound** | M8 armored car, 37mm gun. A British nickname not used by US troops. |
| **Hellcat** | M18 tank destroyer, 76mm gun. Bestowed at the war's end. |
| **Water Buffalo** | LVT(3) landing vehicle, tracked Mk 3. |
| **Wolverine** | M10 series tank-destroyers, 3in gun. A British nickname. |

## United Kingdom

The official nicknames of British AFVs varied greatly with no common source of names. American tanks employed by the Commonwealth were given the names of American Civil War generals. Canadian AFVs were named after animals. Few armored cars were assigned nicknames being known by their manufacturer (AEC, Daimler, Guy, Humber, Marmon-Herrington, etc.). Tank gun calibers are not designated owing to the wide variance on the same tank.

| | |
|---|---|
| Achilles | Tank destroyer (modified US M10 Wolverine). |
| Alecto | Self-propelled 6-pdr. gun or 95mm howitzer. |
| Archer | 17-pdr gun tank destroyer. |
| Ark | Bridging vehicle (modified Churchill or Sherman). |
| Cavalier | A24 cruiser tank. |
| Centaur | A27L cruiser tank. |
| Chaffee | Light tank (US M24). |
| Challenger | A30 cruiser tank. |
| Churchill | A22 infantry tank. |
| Comet | A34 cruiser tank. |
| Crocodile | Flamethrower tank (modified Churchill). "Croc." |
| Cromwell | A27M cruiser tank. |
| Crusader | A15 cruiser tank. |
| Firefly | Medium tank (British-rearmed M4 Sherman). |
| Fox | Armored car (Canadian-made). |
| Grant | Medium tank (British-modified M3 Lee). |
| Grant Scorpion | Anti-mine tank. |

| | |
|---|---|
| Greyhound | Armored car (US M8). |
| Grizzly | Medium tank (Canadian–made Sherman). |
| Kangaroo | Infantry carrier (Canadian or British conversion of Sherman and Ram tanks or Priest self-propelled guns). "Priest Kangaroo," known as a "defrocked Priest" when the howitzer was removed. |
| Lee | Medium tank (US M3–series). |
| Lotus | Light airborne tank (US M22). |
| Matilda | A12 infantry tank. |
| Matilda Frog | Flamethrower tank (Australian–made). |
| Otter | Scout car (Canadian–made Humber). |
| Priest | 105mm self-propelled howitzer (US M7–series). |
| Ram | Cruiser tank (Canadian–made based on Grant and Sherman). |
| Sexton | 25-pdr self-propelled gun-howitzer (Ram chassis). |
| Sherman | Medium tank (US M4–series). |
| Sherman Crab | Medium tank fitted with spinning mine-detonating flails. |
| Sherman Firefly | Medium tank (British-modified M4 Sherman). |
| Sherman Scorpion | Medium tank fitted with spinning mine-detonating flails. |
| Staghound | Armored car (US T17–series). |
| Stuart | Light tank (US M3–series and M5–series). "Honey." |
| Tetrarch | Light airborne tank. (No "A" designation.) |
| Valentine | Infantry tank. (No "A" designation.) |
| Wolverine | Tank destroyer (US M10). "Ajax." |

## Germany

Many, but by no means all, German AFVs were provided with official or semi-official nicknames. Some of these were widely known and even used by Allied soldiers. Others were less well known and actually came into wider postwar use by those interested in AFVs. Some nicknames were overused; for example, to many American soldiers just about every German tank reported in memoirs was a Tiger or Panther.

German *Panzerkampfwagen* (armor[ed] battle vehicles, abbreviated to PzKpfw) were designated by sequential series numbers from PzKpfw I to PzKpfw VI. The British began the practice of identifying them by Mark numbers, as they did their own vehicles and weapons (Mk I to Mk VI), and this practice was followed by the Americans. The Soviets applied a similar system, although using "T" (as they designated their own tanks) and Roman numerals (unlike their AFVs), T-I to T-VI. All German AFVs were designated by a *Sonderkraftfahrzeug* (special motor vehicle, SdKfz) number, including tanks, although they were more commonly known by their PzKpfw designation. A few AFVs were bestowed official nicknames, assigned by the Heereswaffenamt (Army Armaments Office). On January 27, 1944, Hitler ordered that certain nicknames be replaced or dropped, as he felt they were inappropriate for AFVs. Among these were *Hummel* (Bumblebee), dropped altogether, and *Ferdinand*, which was changed to *Elefant* (Elephant).

| | |
|---|---|
| **Bison** | Bison. A 15cm infantry gun mounted on an PzKpfw I chassis. Sometimes incorrectly called the "Bison I," a postwar model-builder's nickname. See *Grille* for remarks on the "Bison II." |

**Brummbär**  Grizzly Bear. A 7.5cm gun-armed Stu.H 43
(SdKfz 166) assault gun. Also informally known
as the *Grumble*, meaning Grumbling Bear, the
name of a bear in a children's story.

**Elefant**  Elephant. An 8.8cm gun mounted on the
Jagdpanzer Tiger (a highly modified Tiger tank
chassis). It was known as the *Ferdinand* prior to
January 1944. Ferdinand itself was a common
nickname for an elephant.

**Flamingo**  Flamingo. Flammpanzer II PzKpfw II(F) (SdKfz
122) flamethrower tank.

**Goliath**  Goliath. The *leichte Ladungsträger* (light charge
carrier) Ausf. A SdKfw 303 and SdKfw 304.
These small, unmanned, full-tracked vehicles
were remotely controlled via radio or cable,
respectively, and were intended to breach
obstacles, destroy fortifications, and attack enemy
AFVs with demolitions.

**Grille**  Cricket. A 15cm infantry gun mounted on a
PzKpfw II or PzKpfw 38(t) chassis. Sometimes
incorrectly called the "Bison II," a postwar
model-builder's nickname.

**Hetzer**  Chaser or Fast Hunter. A 7.5cm gun-armed
Jagdpanzer 38(t) built on a PzKpfw 38(t) tank chassis.

**Hornisse**  Hornet. See *Nashorn*.

**Hummel**  Bumblebee. A 15cm self-propelled howitzer
mounted on a Geschützwagen (gun vehicle)
III/IV (SdKfz 165) chassis. The name was
officially dropped in January 1944.

**Jagdpanther**  Hunting Panther. An 8.8cm antiarmor gun
mounted on the Jagdpanzer Panther (SdKfz 173,
a highly modified Panther tank chassis).

APPENDIX 3

| Jagdtiger | Hunting Tiger. A 12.8cm antiarmor gun mounted on the Jagdpanzer Tiger (SdKfz 186) chassis. |

Jagdtiger · Hunting Tiger. A 12.8cm antiarmor gun mounted on the Jagdpanzer Tiger (SdKfz 186) chassis.

Kugelblitz · Ball Lightning. Twin 3cm *Flakzwilling* (Flak gun) mounted on a PzKpfw IV chassis. It was the only German *Flakpanzer* with an enclosed turret; there were six examples undergoing field trials at the war's end.

Luchs · Lynx. A 2cm gun-armed reconnaissance version of the PzKpfw II (SdKfz 123) light tank.

Marder · Marten. The weasel-like animal gave its name to three types of *Panzerjäger* (tank destroyers). These mounted either a 7.5cm Pak 40 or 7.62cm Pak 36(r) gun.

Marder I · A Panzerjäger Lr.S (SdKfz 135), a highly modified French Lorraine prime-mover tractor chassis.

Marder II · A Panzerjäger II (SdKfz 131 and 132 – two variants), a highly modified PzKpfw II tank chassis.

Marder III · A Panzerjäger 38 (SdKfz 138 and 139 – two variants), a highly modified Czechoslovak PzKpfw 38(t) tank chassis. Also "Marder 38."

Möbelwagen · Furniture wagon. An unofficial name for the 3.7cm Flak 43 antiaircraft gun mounted on a PzKpfw IV (SdKfz 161/3) tank chassis. It was protected by a box-like, open-topped, drop-sided housing.

Nashorn · Rhinoceros. An 8.8cm antiarmor gun mounted on the Panzerjäger III/IV, known as the *Hornisse* (Hornet) prior to January 1944. The Panzerjäger III/IV is a highly modified chassis made from components of the PzKpfw III and IV.

Ostwind · East Wind. A 3.7cm Flak 43/1 gun mounted on a PzKpfw IV (SdKfz 161/3) chassis. The Ostwind II mounted a 3.7cm Flak 40.

The Ostwind II nickname may not have been official.

**Panther**      Panther. A 7.5cm gun-armed PzKpfw V (SdKfz 171) tank introduced in November 1942. In February 1944 it was officially redesignated PzKpfw Panther, but it was still known as the Mk V to the Allies, though it was more commonly called a "Panther."

**Puma**      Cougar. A 5cm gun-armed eight-wheel armored car (SdKfz 234/2).

**Sturmtiger**      Assault mortar Tiger. A 38cm Sturmmörser RW 61 assault rocket launcher mounted on a Tiger tank chassis.

**Tiger**      Tiger. An 8.8cm gun-armed PzKpfw VI (SdKfz181) heavy tank introduced in September 1942. Sometimes known as the Tiger I after the introduction of the Tiger II.

**Tiger II**      Tiger II. An 8.8cm gun-armed PzKfpw VI (SdKfz182), the much-improved version of the Tiger introduced in November 1943. The term *Königstiger* (King Tiger) saw some use by the Germans to identify the Tiger II, but was not official. "King Tiger" and "Royal Tiger" were principally Allied inventions. The Tiger II possessed a more streamlined turret and hull compared to the Tiger I's boxy design. Its well-sloped armor made the Tiger II appear somewhat similar to the Panther. Allied intelligence initially referred to the new design as the "Pantiger," an invented term.

**Wespe**      Wasp. A 10.5cm self-propelled howitzer on a PzKpfw II (SdKfz 124) chassis.

**Wirbelwind**      Whirlwind. Quad 2cm *Flakvierling* (Flak gun) mounted on a PzKpfw IV (Gerät 582) chassis.

ABBREVIATIONS

# ABBREVIATIONS

**AA**     antiaircraft

**AFV**    armored fighting vehicle

**cwt**    hundredweight (112lb). A British unit of measurement for truck capacity

**Flak**   *Fliegerabwehrkanone* – lit. flyer defense cannon, or antiaircraft gun

**M**      Model (US equipment designation). It is incorrect to use hyphens – it is "M1," for example, not "M-1."

**Mk**     Mark (Commonwealth and US Navy equipment designation)

**NCO**    non-commissioned officer

**NSDAP**  *National-Sozialistische Deutsches Arbeiterpartei* (National Socialist German Worker's Party). Abbreviated to Nazi Party

**NZ**     New Zealand

**OR**     Other ranks (British enlisted men)

**Pak**    *Panzerabwehrkanone* – lit. "armor defense cannon," or antitank gun

**pdr**    pounder (British gun designation system)

**PzKpfw** *Panzerkampfwagen* – lit. "armor[ed] battle vehicle," or tank

**SAS**    Special Air Service

**SdKfz**  *Sonderkraftfahrzeug* – lit. "special motor vehicle." A designation assigned to AFVs

**SS**     Schutzstaffel (Protection Unit). Waffen-SS (Armed Protection Unit)

Other abbreviations of one-time or limited use are defined in the text.

# SELECT BIBLIOGRAPHY

# SELECT BIBLIOGRAPHY

Scores of English- and German-language non-fiction books, military publications, and memoirs were searched for slang in the production of this book, as were many Internet sites, far too many to list here. The following books are of particular value as sources of World War II military slang or as reference aids to the subject:

Angolia, John R. and Schlicht, Adolf. *Uniforms and Traditions of the German Army 1933–1945*, Vol. 3 (San Jose, CA: R. James Bender Publishing, 1987)

*Army Times*, "G.I. Slang Dictionary" (Published in three parts: October 16, 23, and 30, 1943)

Beale, Paul. *Partridge's Concise Dictionary of Slang and Unconventional English* (New York: Macmillan Publishing, 1989)

Berry, Henry. *Semper Fi, Mac: Living Memories of the US Marines in World War II* (New York: Arbor House, 1982)

Brohaugh, William. *English Through the Ages* (Cincinnati: Writer's Digest Books, 1998)

Chapman, Robert L. *American Slang* (New York: Harper and Row, 1987)

Colby, Elbridge. *Army Talk: A Familiar Dictionary of Soldier Speech* (Princeton, NJ: Princeton University Press, 1942)

Davis, Brian L. *British Army Uniforms and Insignia of World War Two* (London: Arms and Armour Press, 1983)

Davis, Brian L. *German Army Uniforms and Insignia 1933–1945* (New York: World Publishing, 1972)

Dickson, Paul. *War Slang: American Fighting Words and Phrases from the Civil War to the Gulf War* (New York: Atria Publishing, 1994)

Elting, John, Cragg, Dan and Deal, Ernest. *A Dictionary of Soldier Talk* (New York: Charles Scribner's Sons, 1984)

Forty, George. *British Army Handbook 1939–1945*, Stroud, UK: Sutton Publishing Ltd, 1998

Fritz, Max. *Schwäbische Soldatensprache im Weltkrieg* (Stuttgart-N: A. E. Glaser, 1947)

Fritz, Stephen G. *Frontsoldaten: The German Soldier in World War II* (Lexington, KY: University Press of Kentucky, 1997)

Gander, Terry and Chamberlain, Peter. *Weapons of the Third Reich: An Encyclopedic Survey of all Small Arms, Artillery, and Special Weapons of the German Land Forces 1939–1945* (Garden City, NY: Doubleday, 1979)

Grossman, Vasily. *A Writer at War: Vasily Grossman with the Red Army, 1941–1945* (New York: Pantheon, 2006)

Halleck, Elaine (ed.). *Living in Nazi Germany* (Farmington Hills, MI: Greenhaven Press, 2004)

Herzog, Rudolph. *Heil Hitler das Schwein ist Tot! Lachen unter Hitler – Komik und Humor im Dritten Reich* (Berlin: Eichborn, 2006)

Hillenbrand, Fritz K. M. *Underground Humour in Nazi Germany 1933–1945* (London: Routledge, 1995)

Hogg, Ivan V. (introduction). *The American Arsenal: The World War II Official Standard Ordnance Catalog of Small Arms, Tanks, Armored Cars, Artillery, Antiaircraft Guns, Ammunition, Grenades, Mines, Etcetera* (Mechanicsburg, PA: Stackpole Books, 1996)

Hooper, Walter R. *The First Sergeant's Handbook* (Philadelphia: Marine Barracks, Navy Yard, 1943)

Hurt, John L. and Pringle, Allen G. *Service Slang, a First Selection* (London: Faber and Faber, 1943)

Jones, Wilbur D., Jr. *Gyrene: The World War II United States Marine* (Shippensburg, PA: White Mare Books, 1998)

Kendall, Park. *Dictionary of Service Slang* (New York: M. S. Mill, 1948)

Kendall, Park and Viney, Johnny. *A Dictionary of Army and Navy Slang* (New York: M. S. Mill, 1944)

Küpper, Heinz. *Am A....der Welt: Landserdeutsch 1939–1945* (Hamburg: Claassen Verlag GmbH, 1970)

Laugesen, Amanda. *Diggerspeak: The Language of Australians at War* (South Melbourne: Oxford University Press, 2005)

Merridale, Catherine. *Ivan's War: Life and Death in the Red Army, 1939–1945* (New York: Metropolitan Books, 2006)

Partridge, Eric, Granville, Wilfred, and Robert, Francis G. *A Dictionary of Forces' Slang, 1939–1945* (London: Secker & Warburg, 1948)

Rottman, Gordon L. *World War II Pacific Island Guide: A Geo-Military Study* (Westport, CT: Greenwood Publishing, 2001)

Sanders, Clinton A. and Blackwell, Joseph W. *Words of the Fighting Forces: A Lexicon of Military Terms, Phrases, & Terms of Argot, Cant, Jargon, and Slang used by the Armed Forces of the United States of America* (unpublished manuscript, 1942)

Seward, Jack. *Outrageous Japanese Slang, Curses & Epithets* (Tokyo: Charles E. Tuttle Publishing, 1991)

Taylor, Anna M. *The Language of World War II: Abbreviations, Captions, Quotations, Slogans, Titles and other Terms and Phrases* (New York: H. W. Wilson, 1948)

Tessin, George. *Verbände and Truppen der deutschen Wehrmacht und Waffen-SS im Zweiten Weltkrieg 1939–1945* (Band 1, Osnabrück: Biblio Verlag, 1979)

Zandvoort, Reinhard W. *Wartime English: Materials for a Linguistic History of World War II* (Groningen: J. B. Wolters, 1948, 1974 reprint by Greenwood Press)